"Our fights are getting so fierce, the good times don't seem worth the arguments anymore."

"I've found the love of my life—I have to get out of my marriage because I can't end this affair and give up such a good thing."

"I've been smothered in this marriage too long—I need to go off on my own and prove myself."

"I don't respect or admire her anymore."

If you've been contemplating divorce, some of these statements might sound familiar. But before you act, read this book. There is . .

THE CASE AGAINST DIVORCE

by

Diane Medved, Ph.D.

WINNER OF THE 1990 CHRISTOPHER AWARD

Also by Diane Medved, Ph.D.:

CHILDREN: TO HAVE OR HAVE NOT?
FIRST COMES LOVE: DECIDING WHETHER OR
    NOT TO GET MARRIED

THE CASE AGAINST DIVORCE

Diane Medved, Ph.D.

IVY BOOKS • NEW YORK

Ivy Books
Published by Ballantine Books
Copyright © 1989 by Diane Medved, Ph.D.

Library of Congress Catalog Card Number: 88-45854

ISBN-0-8041-0633-9

This edition published by arrangement with Donald I. Fine, Inc.

Printed in Canada

First Ballantine Books Edition: July 1990

*For my husband Michael,
who reminds me daily
of the value of marriage.*

Acknowledgments

Many thanks are due for assistance in the creation of this book. My literary agents, Arthur and Richard Pine, were unflaggingly supportive, and it was Richard's expertise that brought this project to reality. My appreciation, too, to the Santa Monica public libraries, whose facilities are magnificent and staff helpful.

I would also like to acknowledge Rabbi Daniel and Rebbetzen Susan Lapin for their wisdom and encouragement, Pat Capon who through this project became a friend, Harry and Renate Medved, constant contacts through the process, and Charles Kaufman and Judd Magilnick, for their computer smarts and so much of their time applying it. Many thanks also to the staff of Donald I. Fine, Inc., and particularly to my wonderful editor Susan Schwartz, whose patience and skills are clearly evident here.

And finally, my most heartfelt love and thanks to my husband Michael, whose continued and bountiful boosts and suggestions kept me going, and to our daughter Sarah, who provided the most endearing and entertaining distractions from work possible.

Contents

CHAPTER 1

Not Just Another Choice

I have to start with a confession: This isn't the book I set out to write.

I planned to write something consistent with my previous professional experience—helping people with decision making. In ten years as a psychologist, I've run scores of workshops that specialized in weighing the pros and cons of major life choices. I've even published books on two of life's major turning points: whether or not to have a child and whether or not to get married. When I conceptualized this book on divorce, it was in that mold—a guide to help people decide if separation is appropriate.

I based this concept on some firmly held assumptions and beliefs. For example, I started this project believing that people who suffer over an extended period in unhappy marriages ought to get out. In my private practice, I'd seen plenty of struggling couples, and in every case, I anguished along with them when they described manipulation, lack of attention, or emotional dissatisfaction. I knew from their stories, as well as from my own experience, the heart-wrenching desperation that precedes separating and the liberation that leaving represents. I originally thought that staying together in turmoil was ultimately more traumatic than simply making the break.

I was convinced that recent no-fault divorce laws were a praiseworthy step toward simplifying a legally, psychologically, and emotionally punishing process. I thought that striking down taboos about divorce was another part of the ongoing enlightenment of the women's, civil rights, and human potential movements of the last twenty-five years. I had learned early in my graduate school training that crisis fosters growth, and therefore I assumed that the jolt of divorce almost always bring beneficial psychological change.

To my utter befuddlement, the extensive research I conducted for this book brought me to one inescapable and irrefutable conclusion: I had been wrong. The statistics and anecdotes I gathered forced me to scuttle my well-prepared plans. I had to face the fact that writing a "morally neutral" book showing divorce to be just another option—a life choice no better or worse than staying married—would be irreparably damaging to the audience I wanted to help.

The change came as I shifted my focus from still-married couples in conflict, who made up the bulk of my practice, to now-single individuals who had already received their decrees.

I asked questions—and got some predictable answers: Are you glad you divorced? Yes. Do you regret getting your divorce? No. I was pleased that the responses to these two questions confirmed my original thinking.

But then I plumbed beneath the surface: What kind of contact do you have with your ex-spouse? How has the divorce affected your children? What kinds of experiences have you had in the dating world since your divorce? How has your style of living changed?

"Oh, everything's fine, fine," the respondents at first insisted. Everyone was without a doubt stronger and more hearty than ever.

But my questions kept coming. And the truth was difficult to avoid. Often in a rush of tears, they described the suffering and anguish they had endured—nights of fantasies about the husband or wife who left them; days of guilt after abandoning a once-devoted mate. They talked about the nuts-and-bolts of daily life, of uprooting, of shifting to an apartment and splitting possessions, of balancing parental duties with now-pressing work demands. They spoke of changing relationships with their children, who moved from innocent babes to confidants to arbitrators and sometimes to scapegoats.

And they mourned a part of themselves never to be recaptured. The part they had once invested in a marital or family unit was now destroyed. Wearily, they told of the transformation of the optimism and enthusiasm they had devoted to the now-crushed marriage to bitterness, skepticism, and self-preservation. "Never again," echoed my respondents. "Never again will I combine my income with another's." "Never again will I trust my spouse away overnight." "Never again will I believe someone when he says 'I'll take care of you.' "

I didn't want to hear it. I wanted to hear that they got past their divorces and emerged better for it. And while the women and men I spoke to were more sure of themselves and capable of living independently, I also heard that they had gained this self-reliance out of painful necessity, not out of free choice.

For given a choice, they preferred to be married. Everyone said he or she wanted to find somebody new. Many women were panic-stricken, afraid that they would not find the "right" man before their childbearing years were lost. Others had become so jaded that they lamented the sobering truth that they were unlikely to find another mate at all. With their newfound strength, they all said they would survive; all said they were perfectly content with themselves and the lives they'd recently constructed. Still, there was regret. "Looking back now, do you think that you could have made it work with your first husband?" I asked.

"Well, he was crazy," they'd begin. "He was a slob. He was unromantic. He only thought of himself and his career. But knowing what I know now . . . yes, I probably could have made it work."

I was aghast. But the more I heard these or similar words, and the more I read from the library, the more I was forced to concede that the ruinous stories of my divorced clients and interviewees were true. Divorce was catastrophic—but not in the commonly acceptable terms of a simple year or two thrown away. I found that the mere contemplation of divorce—the acceptance of it as an imminent option (rather than dedication to working on a wounded marriage) is debilitating. The process of evaluating the injuries—of cajoling and pleading and threatening—is emotionally exhausting. The physical act of packing a bag and moving out is traumatic. And from there the trauma escalates.

Quite simply, I discovered in my research that the process and aftermath of divorce is so pervasively disastrous—to body, mind, and spirit—that in an overwhelming number of cases, the "cure" that it brings is surely worse than the marriage's "disease."

Of course, there are exceptions. There are times when divorce is clearly the only recourse. When physical or mental abuse exists. When emotional cruelty or neglect becomes intolerable. When one partner adamantly refuses to stay in the marriage or withdraws to the point where in reality you're alone.

I used to think that the range of situations when divorce is appropriate encompassed quite a bit more than that. But when I look at the balance of the bad and the good that divorced individuals endure, my only possible conclusion is that people could be spared enormous suffering if they scotched their permissive acceptance of divorce and viewed marriage as a serious, lifelong commitment, a bond not to be entered into—or wriggled out of—lightly.

The old wedding vows read "for better or for worse . . . until death us do part." They now commonly intone, "through good times and bad . . . as long as our love shall last." Until recently, I nodded at the "improvement"; now I soberly acknowledge the wisdom in the message of the past.

Too Late for Marleen

The grim stories of crippled couples whom I interviewed for this book got me thinking about the permanent distrust, anguish, and bitterness divorce brings. But the catalyst coalescing these thoughts was a simple workaday lunch with a friend I've known for about eight years. Marleen Gaines, a school district administrator, is a handsome woman of forty who wears sophisticated silks, renews season tickets to the symphony, and stays sharp on the decisions of the courts, cabinet, and city council. When a mutual friend originally introduced us, I instantly clicked into Marleen's quick wit, upbeat attitude, and direct, self-confident zest. But as we sat down to salads at a café near my office, her usual sunny veneer gave way to a depressing monotone of desolation.

Three years ago, Marleen startled her friends by suddenly walking out of her nine-year marriage. At the time she left him, her husband Bob, now forty-two, seemed unbearably boring, uneducated, and unmotivated to achieve. Marleen wanted more of a dynamo, a brilliant intellectual she could admire, successful in his career. She met lots of these stimulating men at the office, and casual flirtations suggested to her that once she was free to pursue them, she would have plenty of opportunities for a more satisfying marriage.

But after three years single, she has found only frustration—and the humiliating realization that at her age, she is considered witty and glib but not especially desirable. There were a couple of flings with married men and an unrequited crush on her self-absorbed boss, who encouraged her attention merely to further inflate his swollen ego. She fell in love with a coworker, who treasured her company so much he told her every excruciating detail of his romantic exploits and eventual engagement. Meanwhile, her three closest friends remarried one by one and had stylishly late-in-life babies.

Now alone in a rambling house in San Bernardino with only her three dogs for companionship, she yearns for the simple warmth of Bob's presence. Though he was a college dropout and works now as a supermarket manager, Bob had his virtues. Always gentle and good-natured, he doted on Marleen and provided consistent encouragement. He may not have been the go-getter she desired, but he had an intuitive intelligence and a good, steady income to maintain their comfortable lifestyle.

It took all this time for Marleen to realize her mistake. At first, Bob had begged her to return; rebuked, he rebounded into one, then another serious relationship. He now lives with a woman who's pushing for marriage, and he's grown quite fond of her two teenage sons. When they speak every few weeks, Bob confesses to Marleen that his current companion "can be a pain" and swears that Marleen is the only woman he's ever "really" loved. Now Marleen has asked for a reconciliation, but weak-willed Bob is too dominated in his new world to leave, and Marleen, realizing that "possession is nine-tenths of the law,'' has resigned herself to the fact that he's not coming back.

DIVORCES ARE FOREVER

Sitting in the restaurant trying to console my friend, I was struck by the frequency with which I've heard stories similar to hers—not only in my workshops and clinical psychology practice, but increasingly in everyday social chatter. It's a well-known U.S. Census Bureau statistic that half of all marriages fail; equally well-publicized is how both men and women suffer financially as a result. Sociologist Lenore Weitzman found that women's standard of living declines by a whopping 73 percent in the first year after divorce, and those who are mothers are further saddled with additional child care and logistics chores.

While everyone laments the immediate trauma of ''going through a divorce,'' more discomfiting is the alarming news of its lingering emotional and psychological effects. Research by the California Children of Divorce Project headed by Judith Wallerstein, for example, shows an especially dismal future for women forty and over—even ten years after the divorce. Half of the women studied at that distant point could be diagnosed as ''clinically depressed,'' and all were moderately or severely lonely, despite the fact that 50 percent of them had initiated the divorce themselves. Exacerbating their malaise might be alarming new statistics on their chances of finding another husband—chances *Newsweek* magazine (June 1986) claims are so low that these women face a greater likelihood of being struck by a terrorist!

Uncovering these facts during the preparation of this book only made me determined to probe reactions to divorce further. I jotted down some ideas and then developed an informal questionnaire that I distributed to an unscientific but diverse sample of two hundred people who had been separated or divorced. The results brought home undeniably that the effects of divorce last a lifetime. And they are in actuality far worse than we care to confront.

Everyone has some understanding of the pain of divorce. And yet, in these days of disposable marriage, at one time or another every married person contemplates separation. It may be in the heat of an argument, or during a fantasy about a more perfect mate. It may appear amid recurrent minor irritations, or it may come as the cumulative result of larger problems stored away for years. Everyone in the throes of a flirtation or affair considers the possibility of chucking the safe and boring for the exciting and glamorous. And people on the cusp of new success are tempted to leave reminders of the less glorious past and begin anew.

Clashing with this casual attitude toward divorce is America's reclaiming of traditional values. Religion has gained renewed respectability. Women who cried "career first" are now honoring their maternal instincts and realizing they may not be able to "have it all." Conservative politics have recently attracted many of yesterday's liberals. And college students, once esoterically majoring in philosophy and sociology, are taking the most direct routes to their MBAs.

Personal lives are more conservative as well, due to the sheer terror provoked by the specter of AIDS. People are practicing "safe sex" not only with frank conversation prior to intimacy and with the use of condoms, but through definite changes in outlook toward recreational sex. A 1987 bestseller, taken seriously enough to be the subject of a day's discussion on the Oprah Winfrey television talk show and a return appearance by the author, advocated sexual abstinence before marriage.[1] In addition, a representative national survey of twelve hundred college students undertaken by *Glamour* magazine revealed that "the AIDS epidemic is a serious damper on sexual activity; about half of all college students say the threat of AIDS had caused them to change their sexual habits."[2]

The AIDS scare and the broader shift toward conservative attitudes, however, seem distant to couples in the throes of conjugal combat. In the midst of a shouting match, a gloriously portrayed single life and freedom from the oppression of a particular spouse call much more loudly. Unfortunately, veterans of divorce like my friend Marleen, who yearn for families and secure, permanent relationships, now see that they have been sadly duped by those compelling myths, which suggest that divorce "can open up new horizons," that the dating scene is exciting, and that bright, attractive people will always find new partners with whom to share their lives.

It's finally time to renounce—openly and clearly—these self-serving platitudes about independence and fulfillment and look at the reality of divorce. We act too frequently as if every infirm marriage deserves to die, based simply upon the emotional report of one distressed partner. Rather than viewing a separation first with alarm, we're full of sympathy for a divorcing friend, and we offer understanding of the temporary insanity involved in severing old ties.

Still influenced by the "do your own thing" era, we don't act constructively. We don't take the husband (or wife) by the shoulders and shake him. We don't shout in his ear that he might be making a disastrous mistake. Even if we care immensely about him, we feel it's too intrusively "judgmental" to do more than step back and say, "Okay, if that's what you want," and close our eyes to the consequences. My research suggests that this is more cruelty than friendship.

EVEN WINNERS PAY THE PRICE

Some people who know me well ask how I could take this position, having been divorced and then happily remarried myself. It is partially because I have faced divorce that I can speak with some authority. It is true that I am one of the very lucky few who entered the chancy world of potential happiness or permanent pain and was ultimately given a break. But there are so many others— just as bright, just as desirable or more so—who bitterly ask why their "best years" must be spent alone. Even though I found a satisfying relationship, I am still paying the price of my divorce.

It is difficult for me to discuss something as personal as my own divorce, partially because I now invest so much in the new life I have created. I also don't like writing about my divorce because I am embarrassed and ashamed, and those feelings are painful to express.

Though my ex-husband and I were constitutionally quite different, we were nevertheless also the same in many ways, or at least had grown that way over the years.

And because we shared our adolescence and formative adult period, we had a bond I found excruciating to discard. Unfortunately, like almost all of the divorced couples I have seen and researched, we cannot manage that ridiculous myth of being "just friends." So in becoming divorced, I severed an important extension of myself, negating a crucial and memorable chunk of my history and development. It is an enormous loss.

I am humiliated and mortified at failing in a relationship others at one time held exemplary. My divorce clashes with the self-image I work earnestly to cultivate: that I am triumphant in my endeavors, that the things I attempt are not only worthwhile but likely to succeed. By divorcing, I have proven myself inept—at least once—in perhaps the most crucial arena, one which by profession is my stock-in-trade—the ability to analyze choices and proceed wisely.

My divorce would have been bad enough were I able to keep my downfall a secret, like the dieter who sneaks a bag of cookies while driving on the anonymous freeway. But I am embarrassed further because of the public discredit and the possibility that former admirers now view me as diminished. Whether or not my associates really do see my character as smirched, or whether they are truly forgiving, is not as relevant as the fact that I *feel* I am now less worthy of their regard.

For those who do go on to build a second life, the future, built more on hope than confidence, may falter. Only about half of those I interviewed who remarried stayed with their second spouse or reported conjugal satisfaction; many found themselves reeling from their first marriages years later and admitted repeating the same mistakes.

The book *Crazy Time* by Abigail Trafford describes the weeks and months after separation, when typically people replay those crushing moments over and over in their minds. The one who is rejected remembers the years together in measured fragments, dissecting every retort, every misplaced movement, for signs of failure or symbols of flawed passion.[3]

The one who leaves in search of something better is so wracked by guilt and remorse that he can do nothing more than look ahead, shielding himself from the overwhelming self-loathing and embarrassment of looking at his past. Like Pharaoh, who refused the Jews' pleas for freedom even when confronted by the convincing pressure of the ten plagues, a spouse who negates his marriage must harden his heart against it. He must bury all the love that still exists for his partner, even if he realizes that it is love shaped by gratitude rather than attraction. The safe and cozy, welcoming home that the estranged partner once provided must be temporarily barred from consciousness. Years of striving together for the success of the other, for the enhancement of the unit, must be eliminated from mind.

No one ever emerges from a divorce unscathed—he or she is inevitably permanently harmed.

That the divorced end up even more unhappy is not their fault. They're told by innumerable subtle and direct messages that they ought to be "mad as hell and unwilling to take it anymore," to paraphrase the inciteful slogan of the movie *Network*. They're encouraged by magazines sold at checkout stands to dissect their relationships. They're led by business-seeking shrinks to believe they can't possibly be fulfilled unless they're undergoing turmoil and instigating change.

I've read more than fifty books off my local public library shelves that comfort and cheer on those involved in divorce. These volumes take you step-by-step through the court procedure and tell you what stages of distress your "normal" child will endure. These books ease you like silk into the singles game and tout your "new freedom" as if it, rather than marriage, is the ultimate means toward fulfillment.

I write this book as a counterbalance, to shake a few shoulders, with hopes that I might spare some children helplessness and some partners pain. I want to expose the forces that strive to hide the damage of divorce. Too many people think "If only I could be out of this marriage . . ." and conclude that sentence with their own private miracles. To repeat: It's not their fault; they're victims of propaganda. But the lure lets them down, for after they buy it they inevitably remain the same people, with the same problem-solving skills, values, and styles of relating to another. And so they can't help but choose and shape new relationships into duplications of their spoiled romance. How can they be expected to see that divorce is, with very few exceptions, the wrong way to improve their lives?

And so this book is for everyone who is now focusing on some infuriating characteristic of their mate and thinking, "I can't take this much longer." It is for those who have already packed and moved out, either physically or emotionally, who look ahead and therefore can't see that their brightest path lies behind them. It is for those who have been hurt, whose wounds are so painful that they simply want to run away, and for others who see the signs and want to prevent a breakup before the repairs become too overwhelming.

Perhaps you or someone you know has uttered something similar to one or more of these lines:

"Our fights are getting so fierce, the good times don't seem worth the arguments anymore."

"Sure I love him. But I know I could do better."

"I've found the love of my life—I have to get out of my marriage because I just can't end this affair and give up such a good thing."

"I've been smothered in this marriage too long—I need to go off on my own and prove myself."

"I don't respect or admire her anymore."

"He's been bugging me for a long time. I've just stuck it out for the sake of the children."

When any of these statements are used long after the fact—years beyond a final decree—there's nothing to be done. But in many other cases, it may not be too late. I've found that none of these sentiments automatically signals an irreparable tear in the basic fiber of a marriage. If you hear someone for whom you have any feeling at all hinting at separation, instead of tacitly endorsing the move, instantly protest. Nearly every marriage has something worth preserving, something that can be restored. Revitalizing a relationship brings triumph and ongoing reward; and as you'll see, avoiding divorce spares those concerned from the greatest trauma of their lives.

The Case Against Divorce

Of course, nobody *wants* to get divorced. Or does he? Joseph Epstein, in *Divorced in America*, recognizes the respectability of divorce: "In some circles, not to have gone through a divorce seems more exceptional than having gone through one; here living out one's days within the confines of a single marriage might even be thought to show an insufficiency of imagination, evidence that one is possibly a bit callow emotionally."[4]

God forbid we appear emotionally callow! How dare we assume that those in the same dreary marriage they claim to have treasured for years could have gotten a lot out of it! The unspoken popular wisdom declares that only by undergoing this rite of psychological passage can anyone mature. I've heard the tales of postdivorce development: people who finally find themselves; who finally learn to be self-sufficient; who finally achieve independence. It is true that after divorce women especially, and men to some extent, report emotional growth. But they won't admit that they might have blossomed even more had they gathered the gumption to stick with and heal the marriage.

Of course, it's useless to speculate about what might have been accomplished in any particular relationship. But some things we *do* know—and these comprise the major arguments in the case against divorce:

1. *Divorce hurts you.* Divorce brings out selfishness, hostility, and vindictiveness. It ruins your idealism about marriage. It leaves emotional scars from which you can never be free. It costs a bunch of money—and significantly reduces your standard of living.

2. *Divorce hurts those around you.* It devastates your children for at least two years and probably for life. It hurts your family by splitting it in two, both family and friends are compelled to take sides. It forces you to be hardened against people you once loved. It rips the fabric of our society, each divorce providing another example of marriage devalued.

3. *The single life isn't what it's cracked up to be.* Ask anyone—the "swinging singles" life is full of frustra-

tion, rejection, and disappointment. The Mr. or Ms. Right you assume waits for you may be only a futile fantasy. Even a successful affair that bridges you from one marriage to another often becomes merely a second failure.

4. *Staying married is better for you.* You don't have to disrupt your life for two to seven years; instead, solving marital problems provides a sense of teamwork and stands as a concrete accomplishment that enhances problem-solving skills in the larger world. Marriage is statistically proven to be the best status for your health, divorce the worst. Marriage gives you something to show for your time on earth—children (usually) and a bond built on continuity and history.

I don't expect that everyone will agree with what I've found. It's largely a matter of values and also one of semantics. For example, I write that a family is worth preserving, and therefore it is worth compromising your goals or habits to save your marriage. Others holding different values might say that no marriage is worth burying your "true self" by dashing the goals you truly desire or stifling your personal inclinations. Obviously, it's not so easy to make a marriage work. But few achievements are as major or lasting.

NOTES

1. Pearsall, Paul. *Super Marital Sex.* New York: Doubleday, 1987.
2. "How College Women and Men Feel Today About Sex, AIDS, Condoms, Marriage, Kids," *Glamour*, August 1987, pp. 261–263.
3. Trafford, Abigail. *Crazy Time: Surviving Divorce.* Harper and Row, 1972.
4. Epstein, Joseph. *Divorced in America*, New York: E. P. Dutton, 1974, p. 18.

Section I

THE DIVORCE EXPLOSION

When your marriage is in trouble, it's almost as if the rest of the world does not exist. Which is good, because you certainly don't want them to know what you're going through.

Your husband snaps at you in the morning, which leads to a conflagration before breakfast that colors your every decision and desire during the day. *That bastard. He thinks he owns me.* You're typing a letter; you hit the wrong key. You dial the phone and scream at an interminable answering machine message. *He did it to me before; he knows how I feel. He only thinks of himself.* Your anger builds to rage and when you get together once more it is with the ammunition of the day's one-sided debate.

The problem is her (or him); it's no one else and no one else's business. It's this incident or that, or a collection of incidents and second chances that become an insurmountable barrier to calm discussion. Perhaps it's the words that she said to the therapist, the wounding misgivings and analysis of your flaws that you never knew bothered her. They entangle you, surround you until the rest of humanity is merely a gray, humming backdrop for the crimson and vermilion in your relationship.

That's how it feels. But how you respond to your mate is really a combination of your personality and your conditioning. Even if you were socialized to believe that men

15

(like you) should be chivalrous gentlemen and women (like you) should be submissive helpmeets, or simply that marriage is a till-you-die proposition, *you are not immune to the ubiquitous destructive pressures in your environment.*

You see a film, and even in your sophistication you are subject to its power. You can't avoid it—the plot and the interaction are rigged to draw sympathy to the main character (the philandering husband?) and antipathy to the villain (the shrewish wife?). You may disagree philosophically and discourse intellectually about the erroneous values portrayed, but its message permeates your consciousness.

That other people find the message valid—perhaps despite your own vehement opposition—does the damage. You personally may not condone what you see, but the mere knowledge that others do, reinforced in myriad other ways throughout our culture, rips your own resolve and certainty. *I am right*, you firmly assert. But after a while, after the relentless hammering of a "divorce is acceptable" message, you unconsciously amend that to say: *I am right. But maybe, for them, their way is right too.* Once you've desensitized, it's not long before you're acknowledging to others, "I didn't think it could happen to me."

The following chapters highlight the factors that have made divorce not only socially permissible in our culture but honorable—and even desirable. They include messages carried over the media from both clandestine and straightforward sources, in the name of both reasonable-sounding and controversial causes. They share in common the dangerous underlying message that marriage can be discarded to a beneficial end.

CHAPTER 2

Sliding Standards: The Devaluation of Marriage

Facing a crumbling marriage is perhaps the most wrenching of human experiences. You doubt your sanity and wonder if it's you or the person you once loved, once thought you knew better than anyone on earth, who has gone bananas. The pain alone drives you crazy; it sneaks up at the most bizarre moments.

And the determination settles in with it. You're going to try to pick up the pieces, to give him or her another chance, to see your own potential for the first time. You alternate between hope and despair, and no matter what anyone else says, no matter that they've gone through it too, they cannot understand.

When I told a successful independent producer about the subject of my book recently, she immediately became combative. "I wouldn't want to read it," she quickly snapped. She had just spent a year hashing through the problems in her disappointing marriage, culminating in her separation only a month before.

But a week after I talked to her, she phoned me and asked to see my work. Hoping for some constructive comments, I offered her the manuscript. The next day, she called back angrily.

"How can you suggest that even one person who gets divorced would be better off staying with her spouse?" She charged. "You don't know what I've been going through. We've been to counselors. We've spent nights fighting and crying. He promises and then doesn't follow through. I'm at the end of my rope. I need compassion, not to be told that I'm making a mistake."

If divorce is that horrible, why do so many people go through with it? And if every divorcing person cries out for compassion, why doesn't the rest of the world—especially anyone considering this step—hear them? Instead of being frightened off by the tales of emotional wreckage, near-record-high numbers of people are choosing to put their names on the courts' dockets.

Despite its emotional casualties, over the decades the divorce rate has risen unmistakably. The National Center for Health Statistics, U.S. Department of Health and Human Services, reports that in 1940 the rate was 2.5 per 1,000 population; by 1970 it rose to more than 4 per 1000. By 1975 the rate had jumped to almost 5; just five years after that it peaked at 6, leveling off since that 1980 high.

Okay, so we know that divorce is hell. Divorcing people are everywhere lamenting their plight. We hear them on every call-in psychology radio show. We see them on "Oprah" and "Donahue" during the week. Beauty-parlor magazines and checkout-stand tabloids alike are rife with stories of latchkey kids, custody kidnappings, roundups of delinquent dads, and single moms and their offspring populating shelters for the homeless and battered. The horrifying news of divorce's consequences is out there. But the divorce rate is healthy.

So we must ask: What is it fueling this divorce delirium? Have those who lived through the "Me Decade" become less decent to live with—more selfish and grumpy and unwilling to compromise? Have expectations about marriage become so impossibly high that fewer can fulfill them? Or is it that divorce has simply lost its stigma and become easier to obtain—if not fashionable!—and therefore beckons to a larger number of disgruntled spouses?

I suspect it's a combination of all these factors. But if you examine the commonality of these developments, you'll notice that they all represent a drastic *change in values* toward mores almost diametrically opposed to those honored throughout the preceding centuries. The skyrocketing divorce rate happens to coincide with sliding standards of behavior in etiquette, courtesy, and sexual conduct and the relaxation of our view of the marital vows. In the seventies, many were brazen enough to discard time-tested values as outmoded; now, it appears, we are seeing everywhere the sad consequences of the "improvements" that resulted.

Let me contrast four basic values held through the mid-1960s with those implicitly accepted today. You'll immediately see how our present mind-set undermines marriage and fosters divorce.

"MARRIAGE IS FOR KEEPS" VERSUS "MARRIAGE UNTIL PASSION FADES"

Granted, you won't hear anyone announcing, "My marriage is disposable." Certainly every engagement ring carries with it the hope of "forever." And yet, everyone now is conscious of and often grateful for the newly taken-for-granted option to leave. Look at all the couples who openly plan for divorce by actually paying a lawyer to draw up a prenuptial agreement. They pledge to stay together for life but insist on acting "prudently" to protect their assets. They look around—to friends, role models, their own experience—and acknowledge silently that if life gets impossible, there's always an out. I'd even guess that some people wouldn't get married unless they knew that if they wanted to they could leave.

But what this attitude does is create a vicious cycle: The more people accept the escape hatch, the more people escape. And as the hole widens, the easier it becomes for others to follow. It started with well-intentioned social pressure for all sorts of equality: everybody equal, every reason for leaving equally fine. The world decided it was nicer to be nonjudgmental—so why should a man support an ex-wife, and not the reverse? And there would be no deciding which grounds for divorce were worthy and which weren't—we needed neat-and-clean "no-fault" proceedings. Smoothed consciences, a zippy divorce, mediation—make love, not war, even if you hate each other. The natural result: couples speed through greased legal channels that process them so fast they have no time to cool off and think the move through logically.

Sociologist Lenore Weitzman of Harvard University, author of *The Divorce Revolution*, has studied the effects of liberalized divorce laws, especially in the pioneering state of California, more extensively than anyone. Her book details these outcomes, and she concludes that efforts to be more "humane," "nonsexist," and "fair" in reality have been disastrous for women and have caused the downfall of otherwise savable marriages.[1] In an interview she told me that under the old system where plaintiffs had to prove infidelity or other grounds for their divorce actions, "The charades and false testimony were bad. We're better off rid of them. But the new ethic that you can leave so easily undermines the value and sanctity of marriage."

Dr. Weitzman sees these changes as part of a longer-term trend described by historian Lawrence Stone in *The Family, Sex and Marriage in England, 1500–1800*.[2] Stone notes that in the past, people were linked much more closely to their families and their lineage. As decades went by, the "nuclear family" became disengaged from the larger kinship network. And now, perhaps two hundred years later, the "progression" finds marital partners becoming disengaged from each other.

HOW RELIGION STRENGTHENED MARRIAGE

Why are families falling apart? Joseph Epstein, in *Divorced in America* says that divorce trends mirror a general decline in the credibility of religion. Originally, he suggests, belief in God and adherence to His will kept the family together. When piousness lost its power, the *community's* will was the glue, binding through social sanctions. Now that the sense of community has crumbled, there's really nothing to prevent the centrifugal forces of whirlwind lives from flinging couples apart.[3]

Epstein's argument about religion's positive influence in maintaining marriages makes intuitive sense. When there's no one judging you, when your values no longer came from an unchallengeable and ultimate source, only you define right and wrong. According to most religions, God said marriage was to be permanent. When you aren't sure about God or don't believe in Him, then you do what you want. People then become the source of values, and who's to say that one person's sincere belief is any better than another's?

This is not to say that nonreligious people behave less

morally than the devout. All people hold values of right
and wrong, gleaned, they usually say when pressed, from
early socialization or an inward feeing about universal
truth. But because these values are not clearly presented
by what many people consider to be an unbreachable
source, they can be made to accommodate rationalizations for behavior, conflicting elements, and immediate,
on-the-spot contingencies. Usually, the secular ethic
holds that personal lives and behavior should be regu-
lated by each individual—any kind of restrictions should
be imposed only when actions infringe on the health or
liberties of others.

The impact of this humanistic scheme on people who
support it is to legitimize their desires to separate—after
all, it's nobody's business to judge whether your reasons
to split are good or whether you should stay together.
Forget the wedding license! Who asked the state to butt
in on your commitment to the one you love anyway? Forget marriage counseling—your feelings cannot be disputed! You need to express how you feel! Whatever you
want to do with your life has to be respected. And so
you're empowered to leave.

But who would deny themselves the possibility of divorce? Freedom to enter and leave relationships is appealing intellectually, as the experiments of the sixties
and seventies proved. Of course, the emotional comfort
and workability of cohabitation had its drawbacks, and
then as now most people support marriage based on the
satisfactions they've personally experienced in a happy
union. But when the marriage hits rough spots, or when
the psychological or emotional evolution of both partners
is not perfectly timed to coincide, people decide far too
frequently that the whole thing has died. I hear so many
of my clients intone, "I can't handle it anymore!" Instead of dissecting the relationship to see which parts of
it need improvement, they hastily junk the entire endeavor, including the values they *do* share, the history they've
carefully assembled, and any potential for the future.

One of the most critical facts I try to impress on couples who come to me for premarital counseling is that
passion fades. No matter what you've got going for you
now—even if you're convinced it's rock-solid and destined to last a lifetime—it will not exist three, ten, or

twenty years from now. The sizzle fades, which to many means that love poops out, compared to what you first had or to what the media try to tell you love is—fireworks, sexual frenzy, heated exploration. When that happens, I've seen far too many couples decide that what they *do* have is lousy. Their expectations are twisted, and so they throw away something that is decidedly precious. They don't stick around to investigate the evolution of their love, or to notice that change and redefinition of relationships is *growth* rather than merely loss of novelty.

"WORK TO BUILD A FUTURE" VERSUS "LIVE FOR THE 'HERE AND NOW' "

Deferring gratification is always difficult, but at least when several generations lived together, it was easier to consider the payoffs. You saw what it was like at each station of the life cycle, and you were forced to remember that what you did had consequences down the line—because you would still be there with the family later to see them.

But the average person lives at a single address only about four and a half years at a time nowadays, and usually it's far from the homestead. Kids count the days until they're eighteen, when they zip away to college, establish their separate identities, and cast off the rules and restrictions by which they were forced to live. In our "instant" society, we tend to see only the short-term benefits and drawbacks of our actions because long-term results are obscured by uncertainty and instability. Or perhaps we just structure our lives that way.

It's true that vestiges of the value of deferred gratification remain (e.g., prosperity-oriented college students stick it out through advanced degrees in order to earn whatever certificate is the passport to a high-prestige, lucrative profession), but for the most part people are less willing to tolerate discomfort or inconvenience for the sake of distant goals.

The new logic has served to cripple the institution of marriage. Why stick around hashing through a bitter argument with your spouse when you can tromp out the front door and feel better right now? Why worry about the kids' response to your discord when *at this moment* your partner's insulting you by having an affair? Why try to change your workaholic mate through counseling when *this second* you're suffering from being left alone? People in pain just want out. They'll do anything for immediate relief. That's when they're most ripe to come to a psychologist. That's when they're willing to take risks, like leaving their marriages, to make the hurt go away.

Those who are rooted in the "here and now," a phrase popularized by the human potential movement of the sixties and seventies, betray a pitiful lack of confidence in the future, an insecurity that later on they'll be able to have what's available right now. So they feel compelled not to miss out, driven to enjoy whatever they can this minute. I've seen this mentality acted out by patients struggling with overeating: they see food and urgently devour it, assuming that a double-chocolate fudge doughnut will never be within their reach again.

If you've considered leaving your mate, you may be a careful person. You may have been one of those well-schooled achievers who not only succeeded through college but worked your way up in your profession. Many people who are savvy about their portfolios, able to look at the long-term when it comes to work or money, have a far more difficult time when they try to apply this to their relationships. Few people are taught methodically how to react to or control their feelings, as they are taught how to program a computer or analyze the stock market. And so when their spouse acts childishly, or they feel walled in by anger and frustration, they simply do not know how to cope.

Let's say it happens to you. But what does this say about your self-esteem, your optimism, your ability to control or make a go of the life you've given? Obviously, a focus mainly on the present implies crumpled self-esteem and a feeling of little control. You cannot take a vow "for better or worse" because you are unsure that you'll be here tomorrow.

Now, *everyone* suffers from a lack of self-esteem; it is everyone's life task to grapple with this to no perfect resolution. However, lack of self-esteem differs among people in degree and area of self-consciousness. It is amazing to me how many people feel unsure that they deserve their partner's love—which is a major motivation to ending their marriages prematurely. They find it far more difficult to demand satisfaction and to work through problems than to storm out. After all, because they feel they've somehow captured their partner's love through false pretenses, it's simply more emotionally comfortable to accept and respond to present unpleasantness, which *is* deserved, than to look beyond immediate quarrels, attractions to others, and periodic slumps to prove to their partner that they are not only worth loving but worth changing for.

"DIVORCE IS A SHAMEFUL FAILURE" VERSUS "DIVORCE IS NO BIG DEAL"

Until "no-fault" divorce came along, divorcing people were forced to confront the fact that they'd failed. They had to tell their lawyers and make public statements under oath that so-and-so had been unfaithful (intimating that you must be an inadequate lover) or abusive (you must've deserved it, or perhaps you were simply masochistic) or had some terrible character flaw (that you couldn't handle); and part of the punishment was airing one's failures and misjudgments for all to hear.

The fact that the judicial system had to be involved at all simply magnified the public humiliation. But thanks to recent reforms, we've gained a different attitude toward the judiciary. Every day people approach the bench to redress the mundane as well as the malevolent. It's no longer assumed that someone must be a "bad guy" or a "good guy" to be in court—anybody can and does sue anybody else, for the most petty affronts. Law firms like Jacoby and Meyers in California have set up storefront offices to glide customers onto the newly greased wheels of justice. Do-it-yourself books proliferate on how to file your own divorce. It's a snap, they insist, especially if you've been married less than five years and have no children or disputed assets. You don't even have to show up in court.

Divorce is also no longer a failure on a social level. When the Hallmark Card company thinks they can make money with the debut of a new line, you know its message must have mass appeal. A couple of years ago, they marketed a series called "Hallmark Lite . . . a third less

serious than regular greeting cards," which features one
offering with the stellar prose: "You're de-lightful . . .
You're dee-lovely . . . You're dee-vorced!" Frankly, I'm
dee-sgusted, and apparently I'm not the only one. Barbara Grizzuti Harrison, editor of *Mademoiselle* magazine, decried these "trendy" cards in the August 1986
issue, noting that legitimizing everything from anti-
Semitism to herpes via these *nouveau kitsch* exchanges
proves that "vulgarity has taken a brand-new turn."[4]
Suddenly rudeness, selfishness, promiscuity, disloyalty,
and racism are laughing matters. And in the long run,
this really does matter, because it diminishes the gravity
of being polite, altruistic, monogamous, loyal, and fair.

"Affairs Are Wrong and Should Be Concealed" versus "Affairs Are Often Okay, and Honesty Is the Best Way to Deal with Them"

Never underestimate the impact of Nena and George
O'Neill's book *Open Marriage* on the public view of connubial sexual exclusivity.[5] The 1960s and 1970s were a
time of self-centeredness for many of those born during
the post-World War II baby boom, and what better expression of self-absorption than to have your cake and eat
it too—in other words, to have the benefits of marriage
as well as the benefits of being single? Those of us in
that influential generation armed ourselves with padded
"encounter bats" when the frustration of such arrangements got to be too much. Under the noble banner of
honesty and forthrightness and the glorification of direct
communication—no matter how it hurt anyone else—we
proudly proclaimed our dalliances in magnificent detail.

In such a milieu, to appear shocked or hurt when your
partner began a self-congratulatory diatribe of his sexual
activities was to admit being "unhip," "uptight," and
hopelessly outmoded. Those were the days, you'll recall,
of the film *Logan's Run* (1967) in which everyone who
reached the not-to-be-trusted age of thirty was evaporated off the planet. Heaven forbid we would continue to
hold any of the values of our parents!

I don't suggest that we return to the sanctimonious
judgments of the 1950s, when people were unfairly crit-

icized and even ostracized because they were divorced. But there *were* some sound benefits to the old-fashioned virtues of a faithful marriage and stable family that are now regaining popularity. Unfortunately, for many this trend comes too late. While marriage is again respected, the *lack* of marriage via divorce is *not* at the same time *less* respected. Our new, revised values are unbalanced: It's great to have a nice marriage, but it's okay not to. The elevation of the status of divorce in our minds tells us it's okay to opt out; it's okay to run away rather than see a problem through. We generalize without thinking about it—our new attitude toward divorce is one more little nick in our sense of self-discipline, perseverance, and compassion.

Once "everybody does it," just about any behavior goes. For example, the mere publication of statistics on extramarital affairs justifies cheaters' activities. Certainly Shere Hite's disputed 1987 figures in *Women and Love: A Cultural Revolution in Progress*, which indicate that more than 70 percent of both men and women step out on their spouses—whether or not her numbers are true— do the trick.[6] The tallies seem high; they're shocking and eye-catching. They get satired in "Doonesbury" (December 1987): A busy Joanie Caucus, an attorney-mother character in Garry Trudeau's comic strip, is informed by her journalist husband of Hite's findings. Joanie's only question is, How can an overworked wife find the time for an affair? From all this a new mentality emerges: Monogamy is passé. Men are rats; women are retaliating in kind, and that's the norm nowadays—no big deal.

Wrong—it *is* a big deal. Open marriage and even reluctant acceptance of adultery has ultimately led to many divorces, especially those initiated by women. An August 1986 *Ladies Home Journal* report of 350,000 readers reveals that 83.4 percent of unfaithful wives divorced.[7] Philip Blumstein and Pepper Schwartz, in *American Couples*, note that "Husbands and wives who had had extramarital sex were more likely to break up whether it happened at the beginning of the marriage or after many years. In marriage, nonmonogamy is such a trespass that even those in established relationships do not shut their eyes to it."[8] So much for honesty.

Again, let me emphasize that we should learn from the

social advancements of the sixties and seventies. We certainly don't need the rigidly oppressive morality that branded high-schoolers "good" and "bad" girls and made "divorcée" synonymous with "horny" (the reasoning held that once a woman got used to having sex she would crave it so much that she'd be any man's pushover). But just because Masters and Johnson's research brought recognition of women's legitimate sexual needs and abilities does not mean that past caution about exploiting those abilities should be abandoned. With the birth control pill we may have more control over pregnancy, but that nonetheless does not blunt the problem of pregnancy as a consequence of casual sex.

In other words, the knowledge and experience gained during the sexual and social exploration of the sixties and seventies should have proven to us the sanity of many rules we at that time discarded. Unfortunately, not only are we ignoring many lessons, we are denying them.

NOTES

1. Weitzman, Lenore. *The Divorce Revolution*. New York: Free Press, 1985.

2. Stone, Lawrence. *The Family, Sex and Marriage in England, 1500–1800*. New York: Harper and Row, 1977.

3. Epstein, Joseph *Divorced in America*. New York: E.P. Dutton, 1974.

4. Harrison, Barbara Grizzuti. "Greeting Cards Don't Send Me." *Mademoiselle*, August, 1986, p. 116.

5. O'Neill, Nena and George. *Open Marriage*. New York: Evans, 1972.

6. Hite, Shere. *Women and Love: A Cultural Revolution in Progress*. New York: Knopf, 1987.

7. Enos, Clive, Ph.D., and Enos, Sondra Forsyth. "Twenty-Nine Secrets We Know About You." *Ladies Home Journal*, August, 1986, pp. 89–91.

8. Blumstein, Philip, and Schwartz, Pepper. *American Couples*. New York: William, Morrow & Co. Inc., p. 313.

CHAPTER 3

Feminism and Divorce

The nature of men's and women's relationships was forever changed by the feminist movement of the late 1960s and early 1970s. No longer were women boxed into rigid roles that stifled the use of their talents and inclinations. No longer could men assume that wives should or would behave submissively. No longer could doors be closed or condescension tolerated simply because the recipient of these actions happened to be female. A pioneer of recent feminism, Betty Friedan, in her book *The Second Stage* describes the "startling evidence that for women in general, the changes brought about by the women's movement have been liberating and life-opening beyond anyone's dreams. The results of two important mental health studies . . . show an unprecedented and totally unpredicted improvement in the psychological well-being of women, on a massive scale."[1]

The vigor of the time brought some women such confidence that they thumbed their noses at anything even remotely smacking of women's former roles. For example, over the past twenty years, in various contexts, I've encountered the following limiting "conclusions":

—Women who choose to dedicate themselves to their homes and families are missing out on the "real" world;

—The "real" nature of both men and women is to have

lots of romantic and sexual relationships throughout their lives;
—Women have been wrongly socialized into certain roles and attitudes—including inclinations to nurture, to build a "nest," and for sex with love;
—Divorce should be a straight split of assets; the parties should be treated equally without regard to sex;
—"A woman without a man is like a fish without a bicycle."

I remember well those heady days of discovery in the late sixties and early seventies. We thought we knew so much and stated what we "knew" so strongly. Of course, we're now grinning slyly as we admit that perhaps some of our platitudes didn't work out so well in practice. We thought that when inequities were resolved, we would all be unequivocally better off. Certainly there are still many inequities left to conquer. But meanwhile, we may have inadvertently thwarted our best interests pertaining to marriage and divorce.

MARRIAGE IS BONDAGE

One of the most basic premises on which sixties feminist ideology was based was the incarcerating nature of marriage for women. While certainly there were many cases where women were oppressed by unfounded role expectations, there were also many cases where perfectly happy women, when informed of this new "reality," were made to feel that their traditional marriages were essentially flawed and deleterious.

Suddenly they learned that, locked in this "constricting" and "smothering" institution, they had been denied the opportunity to find their true identities and therefore to become worthwhile and fulfilled people. They had been hoodwinked, they were warned, by oppressive socialization, and they owed it to themselves to escape.

"Marriage is bondage. *Therefore, divorce is liberation*," whispered the logic of the times. Otherwise content women listened and, flushed with the Superwomanitis of the era, decided they had to make a change.

Jenny Sanders was one of these women, twenty-four years into a marriage that began on a military base in 1945. "I'd known Harry for years and always resisted his proposals," the attractive sixty-five-year-old matron reported. "But one of the things that convinced me to marry him was his dependability—he said he'd take care of me, and in my romance and hopefulness, I believed him."

After their marriage, with money from an oil well Jenny inherited, supplemented by Harry's salary as a department head for the county public works department, they settled into a modern home in a fashionable suburb of Los Angeles. Their three children followed several years later, the youngest born in 1957. Once the kids entered school, Jenny spent her days shuttling them to classes, attending meetings, grocery shopping with the neighbor across the street, and enjoying relaxing afternoons reading in the sunny den. Harry prided himself on supporting the family, though as the oil well dried up Jenny was often forced to replace the steak dinners with spaghetti.

Gradually, just as her oldest daughter was graduating high school, the articles in her afternoon reading magazines began to talk about working: How to make nutritious meals in the tired hours after 5:00 P.M. How to find the right person to care for your child after school. Clothes to flatter an older worker at her first job interview. There were the testimonials: "I never knew I could do it, but I started my own business and now have five employees and a Mercedes!" Jenny began to get ideas.

The real impetus for her to enter the marketplace was the Sanders' property tax bill. As real estate escalated, their neighborhood had become pricier and pricier, and though they'd lived there twenty-five years, it seemed that expenses just kept climbing. Feeling sorry for Harry, who was advancing slowly in his career with the county, Jenny volunteered to bring in "just enough to cover the taxes."

At first Harry was incensed. "I promised I'd always take care of you and the kids. My wife will never have to work." But over the course of the next several months, as the day for delivery of the tax payment neared, Jenny was able to massage Harry's ego enough so that he relented.

Jenny's work experience after college and before her marriage was unimpressive. It had been secretarial, basically. She took shorthand, typed, had a pleasant voice and was an obedient worker. She'd always been genuinely shy, and it took all her courage to follow the instructions in the magazine to dress for her first interview. There she was, fifty-five but looking ten years younger, quaking in her pumps, explaining to Mr. Mervin how she could balance her part-time work for his real estate business with caring for her "almost-grown" family. The triumph of getting the job put her on a high she hadn't felt for years.

You know the end of the story. As Jenny's confidence grew, Harry's self-esteem diminished proportionately. He felt life moving out of his control; he felt like a failure for not fulfilling his financial promise. Jenny wasn't home when he phoned; she told him about people and events from which he felt estranged. He was proud of her—and yet Jenny was becoming someone he didn't know, someone with whom, after twenty-four years together, he did not know how to relate.

But the family became dependent on Jenny's paycheck, and Jenny became convinced that somehow earning money was more worthwhile than making meals and chauffeuring her children to after-school appointments. She didn't learn this from her feelings—which she had come to distrust—but from the others at the office, from the teller where she deposited her check, from the women's magazines she read on her lunch break. Jenny missed the sunny afternoons with her children, but she believed with increasing distress that times and demands had changed and she couldn't go back.

This attitude nearly ruined her marriage. When she was referred to me she had been living for eighteen months at the apartment of her elderly and infirm mother, ostensibly "nursing" her in her time off but at the same time estranging herself from Harry. She was still sending him her paychecks to cover the tax payments; she still felt a familial allegiance. Divorce seemed so radical, almost unthinkable; and yet she had no real marriage anymore and felt guilty for not providing Harry any companionship or services. She didn't know what marriage was supposed to be anymore; certainly she could never recapture the comfort that had marked the years before she "regained her career."

Happily, when Jenny understood that her lack of self-esteem had caused her to betray her true values—those that were no longer "in" but which had served her well for so many years—she was slowly able to reclaim her own goals and priorities. She loved Harry, loved her family, and indeed, loved creating a home. She learned to stand up for herself, not against Harry but against the pressures of a society that overlooked the contribution she was already making. She could view her part-time work as a necessary financial supplement rather than a "career," and she no longer felt she had tangled her proper priorities.

"Marriage is bondage. *Therefore divorce is liberation.*" There is something appealing about the notion of standing on one's own feet, pursuing a career selected without a husband's influence. After an exhilarating few months, and undoubtedly some psychological growth, comes the letdown—the realization that loneliness, or at least *alone*-ness, stretches endlessly ahead.

In my practice I have seen strong evidence of a phenomenon that seldom occurred in generations past: career women leaving their husbands, occasionally to pursue an affair, but more often because the man no longer measures up to a newly defined expectation of the ideal marriage. Lured by promises of identity-defining solitude, continued emotional development, and faith in the strength of nonmarital "networks," scores of women I've counseled have found themselves feeling duped.

Most of these women are in their thirties and forties, people who felt compelled to latch onto new opportunities in the workforce. They are childless because they intentionally postponed having children and have become used to determining their own schedules and planning their own futures. Once ensconced in their careers, long hours of daily contact with achieving male colleagues have an inevitably magnetic effect.

Very few of these women whom I've counseled say their first marriages were unbearable; more often, they call them 'boring," "unfulfilling," or lacking in certain romantic or communicative rituals. They leave behind men who say they still love them; men who are willing to go to counselors. But these wives report that the sessions did not "work"; that their husbands spoke of changes that never materialized, that their men simply could not meet their evolved needs. Unfortunately, they often lament later that having *no* man meets their needs even less.

Complains Susan Crain Bakos in her book *This Wasn't Supposed to Happen*: "All of us, formerly marrieds and never marrieds, are finding careers have not and probably will not provide all the emotional fulfillment we once thought they would. And certainly they aren't paying enough. The press touts the accomplishments and salaries of the few; the many earn far less. We thought we didn't need marriage to support us, but it turns out most of us still do, especially if we are or plan to be mothers, which it turns out most of us still do."[2]

So much for the "liberation" of divorce.

WHAT EVERY WOMAN SHOULD KNOW
ABOUT DIVORCE

In reality, women now suffer far more than men do in the aftermath of divorce. Ironically, since we've revised divorce laws in order to be more fair, the consequences of divorce are less equitable than ever. Lenore Weitzman reveals in her definitive study of no-fault divorce laws, *The Divorce Revolution*, the hardships women can now expect:

—*Income plummets.* Women married less than ten years must subsist on 51 percent of their predivorce family incomes (while their husbands' incomes shoot up to 195 percent of what they were); wives married ten to seventeen years end up with 64 percent of their predivorce incomes (while their husbands' incomes mushroom to 222 percent of their earlier amounts).
—*Anxiety prevails.* 70 percent of women report being perpetually worried about "making ends meet" or "not being able to pay their bills."
—*Friendships stagnate.* Single mothers become "time isolators" because overwhelming home duties usurp their opportunities for contact with friends.

—*Lawyers intercede.* Without laws protecting their custody of their children, newly impoverished mothers must often give up chunks of what little earnings they have to hire lawyers.

—*Remuneration vanishes.* Women seldom receive alimony; those who get it receive far less than they used to, and for a shorter period of time.[3]

From these facts we see that well-meaning efforts to eradicate sexism in divorce proceedings have worked to women's disadvantage. The revolutionary ''conclusions'' of the women's movement I mentioned before unfortunately have served only to devalue marriage and foster divorce.

More specifically:

''Women who choose to dedicate themselves to their homes and families are missing out on the 'real' world'' has only made those who decide to stay with their children feel guilty;

''The real nature of both men and women is to have lots of romantic and sexual relationships throughout their lives'' has justified ''commitmentphobia'' for men and frustrated the women who want to be married and create stable homes;

''Women have merely been socialized . . . into wanting a home, children, and love with sex'' erodes the honor of building a home and a wholesome family life and tears down the values and wisdom of preceding generations;

''Divorce should be a blind split of assets, without regard to sex'' has led to the financial disaster Dr. Weitzman describes.

And ''a woman without a man is like a fish without a bicycle'' could well be the most easily ridiculed slogan of the century. Look at the staggering number of popular songs still declaring man's and woman's need for each other. Look at the shelves of pop psychology books commiserating with women who make ''foolish choices'' or ''love too much'' or otherwise have bad luck fulfilling their still-very-much-alive dreams of marriage and children.

WHAT WE SHOULD'VE CONCLUDED

What we feminists *did* conclude was that because we were just as good as men, we wanted to have what men had—what appeared to be "all the goodies" of influence, prestige, and wealth. We saw that men had all the power—as expressed in political and corporate leadership. They had all the options, as demonstrated by their easy access to every university, every private club, every high-paying career. They had the choices in their social behavior as well—the double standard saw to that. Why were unmarried older men considered desirable bachelors and unattached women of the same age considered withered spinsters, worthy of pity? We wanted the leadership, the access. We wanted the right to philander without any more social stigma than men had received. We wanted respect, not disdain, if we chose not to marry.

We wanted to be just like men.

This desire had its good and bad sides. While opening opportunity and access to power, leadership, wealth, and influence certainly benefits women and society at large, women wanted to do it on men's terms. We wanted to enter the male bastions but didn't aim to change them; we wanted to do what men did but didn't insist on preserving what is different and positive about being feminine. We wore the "dress for success" skirt-suits, severe and regimented. We tailored our aspirations and appointment calendars to resemble our male predecessors'.

And yet, feminists did capitalize on women's unique qualities in order to argue in favor of affirmative action and elevation of women to formerly male-dominated positions of power.

For example:

—The major arguments for electing a woman to the presidency focused on her innate differences from men: A woman's patience and desire to work through problems are so beneficial, the reasoning held, that they might even allow her to avert nuclear disaster. Her intuitive awareness would aid in "reading" others in negotiations. And her ability to key in on emotions would

open up others and let her bypass much jargon and hoopla to cut to the real issues.
—Women were touted as ideal bosses because they would better understand the stresses of the workplace, ultimately humanizing offices and boardrooms. They would see to fairness in employment policies because they had firsthand experience as an underdog and also with difficulties in juggling home and work responsibilities.
—Women would increase the profits of any company because their absenteeism rate overall was lower than that for men. They would present a better fare to the public because they had the capability to be not only businesslike, but also gentle and caring.

In short, the major selling points for women in leadership positions were the special attributes that made them different—and superior—to men.

WOMEN ARE NATURALS FOR MARRIAGE

The natural inclinations of women are supportive to marriage, stability, healthy families, and positive interpersonal relationships. And they are anathema to divorce. If both men and women accentuated "womanly" attitudes toward marriage and interaction, there would be far more harmony, far less discord, and, ultimately, far less divorce.

Let's look again at a few of the characteristics generally ascribed to women:

Nurturing.
More easily able to recognize and value emotions.
More communicative than men.
Inclined to "nest" and create a stable home environment.
Peacekeeping, preferring to mediate rather than instigate problems.
Adaptive and flexible (less invested in bossiness, asserting their power, or merciless execution of rules or policies).

Research is now validating these generalizations and revealing that they even had an innate, constitutional basis. Any parent who has watched young children play can verify that little girls, no matter how nonsexist their upbringing, are more gentle than little boys, and little boys more aggressive than little girls. There's little to explain why these children choose gender-traditional toys—even over the frustration of parents who have struggled to provide both trucks and dolls from the earliest age. And differences in mathematical versus verbal skills cannot be attributed to socialization alone.

After discussing the comprehensive evaluation of gender-difference studies of Eleanor Maccoby and Carol Jacklin summarized in *The Psychology of Sex Differences*,[4] Sara Bonnett Stein, in advising parents about the education of their children, concludes: "Boys really are boyish. And girls are girlish. Not only do girls lack well-defined boyish behaviors, but their chumminess and chattiness, the easy way they share their secrets and admit their fears, the careful way they do their work, and the closeness they keep to home and mother are stereotyped too, in keeping with sexist notions."[5]

The Encyclopedia of Psychology, a reference book summarizing research findings, also suggests innate gender-related characteristics in social as well as physical abilities: "Among personality differences, one of the best established is the greater aggression of the male. His difference is manifested early in life and is found consistently across cultural groups.

"There is considerable evidence that females exhibit a stronger social orientation and desire for social approval than do males . . ." conclude the authors.[6] In other words, women tend to care about others, and about what others think of them.

Obviously, these differences between men and women directly affect their conduct in marriage. *Typically "feminine" characteristics facilitate tranquil and happy marriages.*

Women know this. In research studies they describe themselves again according to *The Encyclopedia of Psychology*, as more "friendly, warm, trusting, talkative, cheerful, kind, loyal, helpful, praising, accepting, and generous," than men.[7] Women are the ones who keep the house up, even when they work outside the home as many hours as their mates; even when their executive-level jobs are just as demanding, according to a 1987 study by sociologist Donna Hidgkins Berardo in the *Journal of Marriage and the Family*.[8] Women are more involved in raising the children, again despite heavy outside commitments that may match their husbands'. The dedicatedly nontraditional fathers in Diane Ehrensaft's book *Together: Men and Women Sharing the Care of Their Children* still put in less hours of child care than their partners.[9]

Women, even in unions that strive to be egalitarian, seem to always be the ones to keep the social calendar, not only for themselves but for the couple and family as a unit. They're usually the ones to write the thank-you notes, plan and execute parties and dinners, and arrange for vacations. Childbearing and managing the family's time apart and together are perhaps the core activities that shape its cohesiveness and determine its unique identity.

THE TRULY FEMINIST APPROACH

It makes sense then that we ought to encourage men to master, at least in the connubial arena, a few of women's natural home-enhancing skills. Of course, recognizing and honoring women's characteristics have always been goals of the feminist movement. But we've undermined this aim with our simultaneous efforts to facilitate swift divorce and erase gender considerations in custody and alimony awards—so we need to repeat the message now. We've been so concerned with providing women new ways to leave marriages—presumably to further their independence and careers—that we've overlooked the effects of these changes on a more fundamentally fulfilling outlet.

A prowoman position preserves marriage. It protects an environment where women can express their inclinations. It states loudly that there's nothing inferior about the kind of patience that can soothe a frazzled child or spouse as well as avert nuclear disaster; that there's nothing wrong with nurturing or nest-building, even if it's boosting a family's morale rather than a company's; that personal—and societal—stability depends on the solidity of nuclear units where all the individuals involved employ "feminine" skills and talents. The truly feminist position is promarriage and antidivorce.

NOTES

1. Friedan, Betty. *The Second Stage*. New York: Summit Books, 1982, p. 52.
2. Bakos, Susan Crain. *This Wasn't Supposed to Happen*. New York: Continuum Publishing, 1985, p. 77.
3. Weitzman, Lenore. *The Divorce Revolution*. New York: Free Press, 1985.
4. Jacklin, Carol, and Maccoby, Eleanor. *The Psychology of Sex Differences*. Stanford: Stanford University Press, 1974.
5. Stein, Sara Bonnett. *Girls and Boys: The Limits of Nonsexist Childrearing*. New York: Scribners, 1983, p. 26.
6. Corsini, Raymond J., ed. *The Encyclopedia of Psychology*, Volume 3. New York: John Wiley & Sons, Inc., 1984.
7. Ibid., Vol. 1, pp. 32–33.
8. Berardo, Donna Hidgkins. "Women and Rape: A Follow-up Study of Rape Victims." *Journal of Marriage and the Family*, 1987.
9. Ehrensaft, Diane. *Together: Men and Women Sharing the Care of Their Children*. New York: Free Press, 1987.

CHAPTER 4

The Lure and the Lie of the Singles Life

What could be more healthy—and fun—than the kind of carefree existence sold as the "singles life" by advertisers? Understandably, entrepreneurs and corporations creating ways to sell their products aren't concerned with your emotional well-being—they're only thinking of the surest way to wrest those dollar bills out of your tightly clenched fist. They aspire to permeate your life with slogans that bid you to "buy this, trade up to that, don't be satisfied with what you've got when we can sell you what is new, different, romantic, exciting, titillating and self-esteem-enhancing. What we've got to offer is surely better than your old model—what you've grown comfortable with is bound to be embarrassingly obsolete."

Sometimes what they've got to sell is services—therapy, legal consultation, health clubs, plastic surgery. Professionals sell their power to give you what you cannot achieve on your own: "We can make you perfect; we can take you away from mundane and dismal reality and transform your life to fit your fantasy. You don't have to suffer, you don't have to hide—just step right up and we can make your dreams come true." It's because those fantasies are often at odds with marriage that singles life becomes glorified. Marriage means responsibility, stability, seriousness; these are inherently dull. Novelty, daring, and flippancy—these are the stuff of daydreams, and the only segment of the population free to pursue these selfish though gratifying ideals are the unencumbered.

While advertising is a major source of The Lure, popular romances and other novels, movies, and television shows also promulgate its contemptuously deceptive message. The Lure to be single is really composed of several impossible promises: of excitement; of adoration and desirability; of unlimited and passionate sex. The Lure asserts that you can "play the field" and "shop around" via a string of titillatingly memorable and meaningful relationships, sampling a delectable array of charming, devastatingly beautiful and successful people. The Lure entices you out of mediocrity into stardom; from boring complacency to the energizing uncertainty of constantly being "on the make" and ready for anything. It's easy to be caught.

Then there's The Lie. The Lie is a set of notions that glamorizes singles life, perpetrating falsehoods we wish could be true. These same advertisers, movie moguls, authors, and actors imply that meeting lovers is easy; that the control and independence of living unattached is like unfettered flight; that when you've tired of this heady whirlwind, you'll instantly and consummately meet the one perfect person for you; that the two of you will effortlessly glide off into the sunset for a perpetuity of adoring ecstasy. The Lie is not that being single is an endlessly idyllic lifestyle, but rather that it is the delightful prelude to inevitably meeting and pairing with your "happily ever after" match. The cruelest Lie says that as soon as the singles life becomes a grind, you can opt out and achieve the goal of your cruising—a happy, stable marriage.

The trouble is that magnetic as they may be, both the Lure and the Lie are devastatingly false. Singles life, as we shall see, can be acceptable and even enjoyable, but it is not what it has been hyped up to be. And after the urge to marry appears, few experienced single men or women find it so easy to meet and marry the person of their dreams. The problem may be exacerbated for singles who have been married before. Saddled with responsibilities to children in terms of time, concern, and money, as well as diminished resources for month-to-month expenses, divorced people may not seem quite as appealing to a never-married prospect. And the divorced themselves, reeling from past experiences, often set up barriers to their own successful recoupling.

But who's going to tell you that? Who's going to say to you that life is often unfair, that beautiful, brilliant, and successful as you may be, you may have a depressingly awful time finding even a suitable date? Who wants to let the air out of the party balloon and describe to you the awkward moments, obvious wrinkles, and trembling words that characterize many meetings in otherwise richly romantic locales? And what about the panic of the single woman in her late thirties who's so far done everything "right"? Vivacious, talented, achieving, and gorgeous, she harbors a desperate fear that she'll never have the husband and family she's envisioned since she was a little girl.

We'd all rather hear the story of the ones who find their soul mates, the heart-rending "happy endings" that fuel our fantasies. Without them, it's difficult to go on. Nobody wants to be morose; nobody wants to emulate the pessimist. Life is much more worthwhile viewing the proverbial cup as half-full than half-empty. And so it should be with your marriage—but the media do their best to veer you away.

LURES OUT OF MARRIAGE: THE "GREENER GRASS" SYNDROME

Advertisers and movie-makers know what I've learned in my psychological studies and clinical practice—everybody has some degree of low self-esteem. So they play on this universal need for reassurance and acceptance and feed on everyone's inevitable insecurity about making the right life choices. They can sell you anything that doesn't require real achievement—lavish sexual encounters, status by association with glamorous others, charisma to attract desirables to your side. They're banking that at least a corner of everyone's psyche has bought into the "single is better" lie. After all, the sex, shoulder-rubbing, and charisma they flaunt are most valuable to *singles*; they mean much less—and are therefore poor sales tools—to the devotedly monogamous.

LURE #1: YOU'LL HAVE MORE AND/OR BETTER SEX

The 1986 movie *9½ Weeks* is a prime example of how being "available" allows you to jump into intense and creative sexual entanglements. The film is calculated to arouse you with artsy, sensual electricity between its main characters, played by Kim Basinger and Mickey Rourke. As you watch them, you can feel the heavy chemical clutch as they first brush against each other in a crowded food boutique, their pregnant eye contact so straightforward and determined. Their almost wordless trysts are lit from strange angles, fashioned in muted colors, and filled with confident unbuttoning, sliding fabrics, and slow moves in satin sheets. Scenes of hot pursuit, delicious teasing, creative touches and tastes stroll across the screen and through your mind. The actors pull you effortlessly behind their bedroom doors so that you have the voyeuristic benefit of their mystery, delusion, and perversion. As if it could happen to you.

This is but one stunning example of a whole genre of steamy sex-is-easy films. In *Bull Durham* (1988) Susan Sarandon (at least it's the woman, for a change) took her pick of the town's baseball minor league studs to bed each season. *Three Men and a Baby* (1987) glorified parenthood but never even gave a hint that the three swinging bachelor leads should abandon their freewheeling social lives and settle down. In *A New Life* (1988), Alan Alda and Ann Margaret ended up postdivorce with gorgeous Veronica Hamel and hunky John Shey respectively, while pal Hal Linden continued acquiring a parade of stunning escorts.

This genre, by showing us footloose singles stumbling into passionate liaisons with luscious partners, implies that sex connections may be found everywhere—and often when you least expect it—in offices, elevators, and certainly where everyone sweats. Eager and willing partners wink behind the steering wheels of their scarlet convertibles on the freeway. It's only one's reticence that prevents these roadside invitations from culminating in bedroom adventures.

Settings for films may vary, but the plots all thrive on meaningful eye contact, wordless first caresses, and the "zipless" encounter that Erica Jong described so well in

Fear of Flying.[1] In this breathless world there is no such thing as cellulite; nobody has holey underwear or herpes. No hormone-driven couples have even the momentary trepidation about that first wet kiss, or hesitate even briefly over whether to defer the inevitable gratification of a first-date flesh feast. The result is Message Number One: "Singles get more sex than married people."

The sex that lust-crazed movie heroes enjoy is far better than any we mortals ever had in our highly experienced lives. Sometimes movie-makers literally spell it out for you, as in the climactic scene in the 1984 film *Bolero* starring Bo Derek. Playing a virgin seeking relief from her unspoiled condition, she finds a willing candidate and they begin to writhe and roll. Finally, at the zenith of their passion, billows of dry-ice smoke waft from the two entwined bodies, and a purple neon sign flashes unrelentingly: "Ecstasy, Ecstasy, Ecstasy!"

No matter which flick you choose, when the couples jumble on those unpatterned sheets and the camera angles in a little bit of bare breast, the passion never flags. It's always so great, so sincere, so perfect—which is obvious to us from their grunts and sighs—that the pair can't wait to flex their sexual muscles again and again. In many of these films, it appears that the most important criterion for a relationship is abundant, perfect sex. Then, if those chemistry-inspired gazes lead to actual conversation, and the pair find they have more to share than simply their carcasses, fine. At least the preliminary hurdle has been humped. And when the relationship goes awry, bad sex is never to blame—chemistry can never fail, you see; the problem is never the body, always the mind. Message Number Two: "Singles have sexier sex than married people."

Though publicity about AIDS has saturated every household, the sexual behavior of heterosexuals seems not to have changed. The sexual activity of women aged eighteen to forty-four *increased* 8 percent in the five years between 1982 and 1987, said a 1988 report by the Alan Guttmacher Institute. And the study showed that a whopping 45 percent of girls aged fifteen, sixteen, and seventeen are also sexually active. The researchers concluded: "These findings run counter to the assumption many have made that emphasis on urging teenagers to say no . . . and concern about AIDS have caused large proportions of heterosexuals to abstain from nonmarital sexual intercourse.''[2]

Perhaps the most aggressive educational attack on the AIDS problem has been the push toward ''safe sex'' and condom use. A survey by a New York research firm in 1988 showed that nonmonogamous single men and women—48 and 38 percent respectively—used condoms with their most recent sexual partner; 54 percent of the men and 67 of the women said they would insist on condom use with a new sexual partner.[3] The Alan Guttmacher study, however, showed unmarried women to use condoms only 16 percent of the time. But no matter, public awareness of the link between disease and prophylactics is enough to bring the subject artistic recognition: Tom Hanks, in the 1987 film *Dragnet*, prepares on screen for a tryst by packing an entire box of condoms.

In 1982, Jacqueline Simenauer and David Carroll published the results of their national survey of three thousand unmarried people, *Singles: The New Americans*.[4] Their findings can be generalized to all 50 million American singles—a useful tool for examining the reality of singles life. If anything, the study's outcomes may err toward optimism, since respondents tend to show themselves as favorably as they can. Simenauer and Carroll also administered a special questionnaire to a subset of their original sample: 367 people in their first year after divorce. This smaller sample revealed the truth behind that glittering door of unrestricted sexual fulfillment.

Asked to compare the frequency of their sexual activity before and after marriage, it *appears* as if the movies are right: 54 percent of both men and women report an increase. (Remember that these were all troubled marriages that ended in divorce, so an increase could be because the divorced couple was sexually estranged to start with.) But a closer look reveals that at the same time, that giddy first year unbounded by marriage's limitations brings a myriad of not just sexual frustrations, but actual sexual problems. For example, 20 percent of the men, and an amazing 45 percent of the women report dysfunctional lack of sexual desire in their first year on the ''swinging'' singles scene. Eleven percent of the men reported impotence. Thirteen percent of the men and 20 percent of the women said they were now unable to achieve orgasm; 8 percent of the men said theirs came prematurely.

When Simenauer and Carroll asked their larger sample, representative of the wider population of American singles, to rate the media's portrayal of their lifestyle as either accurate or distorted, the respondents choroused that distortion is not only rampant but also produces some damaging myths. "The first of these is that being single is tantamount to an endless sexual party," conclude the authors.[5] They go on to quote a psychology professor from American University in Washington, who says these false impressions are "particularly harmful to people in the middle years of marriages. It creates pressures to break out and divorce."[6]

Bradley Dorfman, a junior high school teacher in Cleveland, Ohio, recalled for me his reaction to the singles sex scene in the three years since his divorce. He'd been married thirteen years to his high school sweetheart, was supportive through her Ph.D. in biology and subsequent climb through academia, and then six years later was shocked when she announced that she wanted someone more aggressive in his career. The separation and divorce happened so fast he barely grasped the drastic changes that seemed to happen around him—a new apartment, an assignment at a different school, and loss of the major security of his life, intimacy with the one person he thought he'd really known.

Bradley, soft-spoken and generally optimistic, tried to make the best of things. He was depressed, disoriented, and deeply hurt for a while, of course. But then friends encouraged him to date, and always eager to do the right thing, he started asking out the many women in his world: fellow teachers, friends of friends, residents of his predominantly single neighborhood. All the ladies seemed to find him irresistible; he'd been faithful to his wife and now realized how little he'd experienced sexually. Most of the women Bradley saw weren't all that interesting—he couldn't help but compare them to his ex-wife, whom he'd always cherished. But he did like the way they came on to him; the way they seemed so charmed and interested and genuinely impressed by what he was doing. He had dates almost every night of the week—and it seemed that the women were even more eager to jump into bed than he was.

Jody, who lived in the building across the street, was especially sweet and sympathetic. She was blonde and about the same size as Bradley's ex-wife; she was only 26—ten years younger—and seemed awestruck by Bradley's knowledge of film, world events, and popular music dating all the way back to the early sixties. She left adoring phone messages and pans of lasagne on his doorstep. She offered to sew on Bradley's loose shirt buttons.

Being a romantic, Bradley fell in love. Jody looked up to him and made him feel like a man. Jody loved being taken care of, in contrast to Bradley's self-sufficient ex-wife. It was only two months after their relationship became intense that Bradley moved in with her; six weeks later they were talking about marriage. The sex was fantastic—creative, frequent, exciting. They went to Higbee's to register for their wedding china.

It was then that Bradley began to get disillusioned. He saw how Jody whined when the sales clerk couldn't order her first-choice pattern. He saw how greedily she wanted every expensive but useless gadget in the store. He realized how dependent she had become. As the weeks went on, friends called, saying they were worried about Bradley. His closest chums since high school confided that they thought Jody was rather "simple" and that he could do better. Increasingly, Bradley tired of explaining things to Jody; her gratitude and admiration weren't enough compensation. Still, he had become dependent too—on her physical presence, intimacy, and sex.

When Bradley finally summoned the courage to leave Jody, the wedding date was only two months away—thankfully, the invitations had not yet been mailed. Jody was venomous in her anger, sending Bradley hate letters in terms as intense as the adoring words she'd lavished before. Bradley learned the hard way what it meant to be "on the rebound," and he confesses that it was the high he got from the shallow singles sexual world that ultimately led him to so much grief.

Lure #2: You'll Associate with Exciting and Beautiful People

Husbands and wives tend to think that "if only" they were single, they'd have the glamorous, sexy existence that the media insist is possible. Men fantasize that they'll then be able to flirt with the sensual waitress at the ritzy bar, or that they'll meet a gorgeous actress who also knows all the Beethoven sonatas. Women are sure they'll find long-term happiness with a dynamic lawyer or entrepreneur who not only is a star in his field but sends her long-stemmed red roses every Friday. This is the clearest manifestation of the "grass is always greener" syndrome: comfortable in your predictable routine, you crave the spicy, titillating novelty of the ideal.

Single people maintain few of these delusions. They don't expect that Robert Redford will suddenly demand them just because they're available. They don't anticipate that everyone they flirt or go to bed with will be exciting; indeed, experience shows them that most of the dates they have will be duds. In the words of one of Simenauer and Carroll's respondents: "It's certainly not the steady fun and thrills which what I call the 'Good News People' are always talking about in their hype."[7]

So let's take a look at a few examples of this misleading hype. It's a lure out of marriage that's become so familiar that we glance at advertisements, television, and movies expressing the message with a yawn. *People* magazine, for example, builds its considerable circulation on the movements of the on-the-make rich and famous and their visible, and therefore exemplary, escapades. There's disco dancing at exclusive clubs where beauty and glitter are required for admission. There are excruciatingly detailed accounts of who is dating whom, and who's been left out of the latest round of musical beds.

Soap operas on television—including nouveau-respectable nighttime versions like "Dallas" and "Dynasty"—show married people behaving like singles, and singles behaving like they'd never heard the words *morals* or *values*. Their lives are naughty and exciting, never lulled by even a few months of nonsalacious R and R. And somehow none of the characters in any of these sagas looks homely or even average—in fact, most of the actresses signed for these roles are at the same time receiving handsome annuities for endorsing health spas, which often suggest in their advertisements that if you join you'll hobnob with the likes of these shapely celebs.

Print ads lure patrons in, and you out of your marriage, by implying that mainly the successful and/or perfectly formed attend or purchase their offerings. Their come-on: "You too can be just like our stars and own/use our product/service!" On one magazine page, the statuesque model exiting a limosine with her Adonis date is eyed admiringly by two heartthrob hunks, coincidentally standing nearby to catch an enthralling glimpse. Only the lighting, brighter on her shins and her indelicate, thigh-revealing stance as she steps out of the sleek black car, expose this as a panty-hose ad. Ladies, don't you want that kind of masculine adoration? Fellows, don't you wish your lady had those legs?

Liquor manufacturers also play on the implied excitement of singles interaction, possibly because they rely for sales on consumption at bars where the clientele are themselves cruising. A slick cognac ad shows a dressed-up couple—he in a tux, she in lace and dangling earrings, holding snifters of amber liquid, giving us unmistakably come-hither expressions. This pair seems wealthy—after all, no tux-and-gown occasion is cheap—and with their potent imbibements in hand, they promise imminent adventure.

The stuff of fantasy, maybe. But anyone who has been single awhile knows that this image of imminent excitement is a crock. Leggy and intelligent blondes with perfect characters are not lurking in your shadow. That irresistible hunk you see at the wheel of the convertible is bound to have some fatal flaw. When you're single, as when you're married, you associate with a reliable band of tried-and-true friends with occasional peripherals and possibilities that drop in and out of your life. But that truth doesn't sell liquor or cigarettes or movie scripts—it's much more effective to offer the promise of abundant new associates, all more beautiful, more vibrant, and more exotic. The hype is almost good enough to convince you that it's real.

LURE #3: YOU'LL BE POPULAR AND ADORED

While it's certainly wonderful to earn status by association with beautiful and powerful people, it's even better to confirm your desirability directly, with the expressed adoration of the multitudes of starlets and business magnates with whom you'll supposedly rub shoulders. Sooner or later, this hook will entice you, because everybody grapples with weak self-esteem. If you're in an established marriage with problems, kinks, or flare-ups, you'll eventually come to wonder if it's circumstance or you that's messed up. Your wife yells at you, calls you irresponsible, unresponsive, sloppy, or stupid. At first you defend yourself, maybe even protest. But that chink in your veneer is created; privately you think, "Maybe she's right. Maybe I am no good." You become vulnerable. You need a lift.

Either you have an affair—which at least two-thirds of married men and a fourth of married women do—or, if the heat is too intense, you opt out. Separated, you can go for your ego gratification unimpeded. And you get lots of sympathy from all who hear of your plight. "My wife doesn't understand me" is the classic line. "Sure, sure," we mutter, aware that this is but a veiled request for comfort. Next, we are expected to respond, "You poor guy, let me make you feel better." The fact that by mere social convention you are accorded warmth and caring is in itself a motivation to fan small marital distress into comfort-engendering conflagration.

There are times when you simply need some soothing, when you get sick and tired of hearing your husband nag; when you've waited beyond endurance for some kind of common courtesy, or just a sign that you're valuable as more than a cook or an income supplement. You think of your unattached friends—there's Sally who forever has three men hanging on her every word. When you phone her you're always getting interrupted by her "call waiting" and then she comes back to breathily inform you that Jason or Dan absolutely must speak to her this minute. Or you remember Lance, who lives like Richard Gere did in the movie *American Gigolo*, escorting attractive ladies to exclusive affairs simply because he's incredibly handsome.

But we're realistic: maybe we don't have the looks of Richard Gere. It doesn't matter—there are lots of older, paunchy guys tooling around town whose nubile young girlfriends snuggle up to them adoringly. We remember the famous ones: Groucho Marks and Erin Flemming; Jacqueline Kennedy and Aristotle Onassis; Hugh Hefner and Barbie Benton, Sondra Theodore, Carrie Leigh, and now Kimberly Conrad each more perfect and youthful than the next. Peter Bogdanovich didn't do poorly nabbing Dorothy Stratten. John Derek was able to score with Bo. If all these guys can do it, without our charm, without our sincerity or sweetness or whatever other advantage we've got—then surely there's some lovely creature out there just dying to make us coffee, wear filmy lingerie, and cater to our every whim. Surely there's at least one.

But while the "you're-the-greatest" lure pulls many men out of marriage, it looms even larger for love-starved wives. As an Ann Landers poll in 1983 showed, women crave touching, caressing, and signs of affection more than they crave coital sex. Men, on the other hand, often consider the kissy-huggy stuff superfluous to the Main Event.[8]

Being desired is probably a woman's dearest—and perhaps most erotic—wish. Simenauer and Carroll note that "Women's sexual fantasies are usually less lurid than men's. Love is more often a part of the fantasy for women than for men."[9] Even Nancy Friday's explicit recountings of specifically sexual fantasies in *My Secret Garden* and *Forbidden Flowers* include lengthy set-ups for the actual nitty-gritty.[10] Along with other things, women want men to find them attractive, to crave them, to pursue them. They like to imagine a person and a setting— whether it's a stranger or a friend, familiar turf or exotic locales.

The need for attention and love becomes especially acute as marriage progresses. During the courting phase, women receive adoration—and then succumb to their suitors' proposals. The "honeymoon period" is so called because that first secluded week or two of blissful passion quickly settles into a humdrum, mundane relationship. In the best of circumstances, the honeymoon ends gradually, usurped by other responsibilities and entropy, but it is replaced by a far more significant love.

The problem is that the wife's need for reassurance and attention doesn't diminish—she assumes that her husband will always be as sweet and attentive as he was in their early relationship. Meanwhile, he's no longer concerned with pursuit; he just needs the stability of a spouse to listen, to have sex, to be a companion. She's now a wife, not a girlfriend who needs to be wooed. Men and women's needs and expectations don't always mesh, and so they become susceptible to The Lure.

That was the problem for Arlene and Craig Borden. In their mid-twenties, they'd only been married a year when they came to me for counseling. Craig was an affable fellow in public health graduate school, working full time assisting a professor to bring in some money to pay for their one-bedroom apartment in West Covina, half an hour outside Los Angeles. He was a strapping, brown-haired athlete who wore plaid shirts and a hopeful grin even when he should have been angry or depressed. He'd met Arlene through mutual friends at a party one night after he'd had a couple of beers and was feeling pretty good—he had asked her to dance, and on the slow number lost his usual shyness enough to slip his hand under the back of her blouse. He was shocked at the enthusiasm with which she responded.

Arlene was a receptionist-bookkeeper in an oral surgeon's office, the doctor's right hand, efficient, cheerful, bright—and beautiful. Her jet-black hair cascaded around her shoulders. Her laugh was infectious, her voice melodic, and her speech articulate. She enjoyed life—men, food, music, even work, where she teased the doctor suggestively and earned the response of all the patients who phoned or walked through the door. Even sitting in my office she was eminently likable. She knew what she wanted, and if she couldn't get it, well . . . she'd have to get it, that's all.

It wasn't sex she wanted, either. In the last six months she'd lost all interest in sex and found Craig a turn-off. Oh, in the beginning it was fantastic. Lusty midnights in the back seat of Craig's six-year-old Pontiac. An escapade under a blanket at the public beach, when a sudden policeman's flashlight beamed on them just at orgasm.

Mornings at her mother's house, in front of the television turned up loud in case she should decide to come home for an early lunch. "We couldn't get enough of each other," Arlene fondly remembers. When she speaks, she doesn't look at Craig.

Craig wanted to please her but felt stymied. He had to be away from home a lot, between the job and school, and at home he had to study. But he really loved Arlene, really would be willing to do anything. Arlene said she wanted more attention: Okay, he'd spend fifteen minutes a night recapitulating the events of his day. He'd leave her love notes and bring her dandelion bouquets. He'd try to be more outgoing at barbecues with her family. He'd try to act more mature around his group of high school buddies who used to come over Saturdays for a few beers in front of the tube. He'd try to be someone he was not.

But Arlene craved adult passion, sincerity, and romance, not the feeble attempts of a boy-man hoping to please a superior. And she knew she was clearly superior to the youth she'd mistakenly chosen for a husband. Real excitement, she explained to me one time in a private session, was initiated by a man of achievement, stature, and physical magnetism. He'd send her flowers—Craig never even thought to do it once. He'd take her to nice restaurants—Craig couldn't afford a hamburger from Jack-in-the-Box, but it wouldn't occur to him to take her there, or anywhere, anyway. The fantasy man would compliment her hair, her lips, her sensuous curves. Craig was most fluent with his computer printouts. Mr. Right wouldn't have to do romance homework assigned by a psychologist—he would want her so much that he couldn't wait to invent new ways to say "I love you."

Arlene knew such dream lovers existed. She read about them in the Silhouette novels she devoured on her breaks at work. She had friends who'd found attentive guys—and she'd dated lots of them before she so ill-fatedly married Craig. "I guess I mistook good sex for passion," she sighed. I worked with Craig and Arlene for almost a year; two years afterward, I was not surprised to hear that they'd divorced and that Arlene was living with a young and zealous corporate vice president. In her mad scramble for adoration, Arlene saw only what Craig lacked, and soon latched on to The Lure.

While The Lure pulls you out of your existing marriage with promises of a more rewarding life unattached, it is only half of the total falsehood about being single. If you're married and thinking of leaving, read on for more evidence that being single is not what it's cracked up to be.

NOTES

1. Jong, Erica. *Fear of Flying*. New York: Holt, Rinehart and Winston, Inc., 1973.
2. Parachini, Allan, "Women, Sex: AIDS Having Little Impact" *Los Angeles Times*, July 26, 1988.
3. "The Trojan Fior Women Survey on Sexual Etiquette," Research & Forecasts Inc., October, 1988.
4. Carroll, David, and Simenauer, Jacqueline. *Singles: The New Americans*. New York: Simon and Schuster, 1982.
5. Ibid., p. 345.
6. Ibid., p. 344.
7. Ibid., p. 343.
8. Landers, Ann. "Ann Landers Learns That Most Women Would Rather be Hugged Than You Know What." *People Magazine*. January 21, 1985, p. 81.
9. Carroll and Simenauer, p. 190.
10. Friday, Nancy. *My Secret Garden*. New York: Trident, 1973.
11. Friday, Nancy. *Forbidden Flowers*. New York: Pocket, 1975.

CHAPTER 5

Three Lies About Being Single That Destroy Marriage

Lies and Lures are related—both glorify the singles life and play on peoples' unrealistic but potent desires for freedom, fame, wealth, and perfect love. Lures differ from Lies in that they appeal more to those unable to experience their falseness—i.e., Lures are the hopes and fantasies of married people. Lies, on the other hand, fuel the hopes of both married and single people—they mollify and justify continuing on alone and provide the stuff of fairy tales where everyone eventually falls in love and lives "happily ever after."

LIE #1: BEING SINGLE IS BETTER THAN BEING MARRIED

Off the top of your head, try to make two lists, one list tallying the characteristics of marriage and another describing the singles life. Then decide which of the two states is more attractive. Here's a sample:

Characteristics of Being Single	Characteristics of Being Married
Independence	Interdependence
Make own appointment schedule	Coordinate appointment schedules
Sexual freedom	Sexual limitations

Characteristics of Being Single	Characteristics of Being Married
Make own career plans	Coordinate plans with spouse
Financially independent	May be responsible for others, dependent, or, less likely, independent
Companionship as arranged	Predictable companionship
Nonparenthood	Joys and hardships of parenthood
Give and receive love (or not) with one or more people	Exchange love with one person

The truth is that married people tend to take on obligations and responsibilities. They tend to be more oriented to a secure, long-term future than singles. Their lives are more predictable and stable. Because married people must at least consider and often look after the welfare of others, they make ''sensible'' and ''reasonable'' choices and eschew the risky. About 95 percent of the population aspires to be married and thinks this is a pretty good way to live.

But it's not exciting. It's not thrilling. It's not wildly and romantically impractical. A stable life is not conducive to throwing caution to the winds, packing your bags, and flying to Rio de Janeiro for Mardi Gras; so, forbidden fruit being what it is, this kind of spontaneity and mobility then becomes enticing. Even Walter Mitty *dreamed* of swashbuckling, heroic escapades, and there's a corner each of us that longs for excitement too.

Theoretically, single people can morally and without serious guilt create or fall into these kinds of situations relatively easily; married people can't. *Plus*, in our permissive milieu, single people can reap most of the benefits of marriage and still have an out. They can live with someone and enjoy predictable companionship. They can have a child or adopt out of wedlock and few would openly condemn them. They can have unlimited sex, as much stability as they choose, and as many possessions, including a house, as they can afford. All this and options too. Freedom's an attractive and salable commodity. No wonder I keep seeing license plate frames emblazoned with "Happiness Is Being Single."

Perhaps no two men epitomize the thrill of singleness more than the magnetic Tom Cruise and Brian Brown, playing two joyful bartenders in the film *Cocktail* (1988). What could be more alluring than night after night of showy performances, earning wide-eyed adoration and your pick of voluptuous admirers to escort home? What male wouldn't want to identify with these perfect men-on-the-make? You too can be the envy of the guys and the object of every woman's lust.

The image of the single's life as "swinging" is everywhere. Billboards, magazines, newspapers, novels—anything that could be called a medium, anything shoved in front of our eyes, is loaded with overt and simplified glorification of the sexual, free, and physically attractive aspects of individuality. Seldom do you see any reminders that being alone can get lonely; that the prospect of never having a family causes depression; that men and women get frantic when they think of aging alone.

Yet you *do* see visual reminders that married life can be hectic and grinding. Aspirin commercials show the harried mother, a two-year-old tugging at her skirt and an infant clinging to her shoulder, her kerchief askew, begging the camera for headache relief. A classic TV ad of the past showed a mother in a jogging suit, dashing from market to home to children's school, exclaiming breathlessly that in between all her errands she runs two miles a day! Cereal companies exhibit mothers serving their families an unappreciated and gulped breakfast moments before grabbing their lovingly packed lunches and lunging out the front door. Even the stereotypical Dad has his share of trouble. Faced with mounting bills for such necessities as "the kids' braces" he's tormented by worry and must consolidate his handfuls of statements into "one easy monthly payment." You never see curler-headed singles agonizing over how they'll foot the bill for their latest jaunt to Club Med, do you?

You don't see it because of the prevalence of The Lie. Simenauer and Carroll found, for example, that "a quarter of women who have never married say that being single is wonderful. Only 6 percent of women who have been divorced once say the same."[1] That means 75 percent of single women think their status *isn't* the greatest. Additionally: "Almost 40 percent of men who haven't married as yet say that being single is wonderful. However, after two or more divorces, only 7 percent of men feel the same." These data indicate that the never-married tend to rationalize and accept their status; those who have been wed—and therefore have a legitimate basis for comparison, *despite* the fact that their marriages ended badly, see marriage more favorably. Keep in mind too that most people do get married—and so the number of people preferring marriage far outnumbers the minority who don't. And those who *are* single, Simenauer and Carroll note, see their status as merely transitory, a pit-stop on the way to the altar: "Respondents who have previously been married especially view their single years as a pleasant if sometimes trying interim: a period of time in which they can pause, recollect, grow, enjoy, experience a wide range of romance, plan for the future—and move on."[2]

A national *Glamour* magazine survey of never-married young women in their twenties and thirties reveals that 90 percent "ultimately want to get married." They may be easing the pressure on themselves to marry young—fewer are "putting life on hold" in their twenties while awaiting marriage—but they sound traditionally eager to find a man. A section of the article called "And what about regrets?" consists of quotations from women aged twenty-one to forty-one—all remorseful that they're not titled "Mrs."[3]

A study by Drs. Carol C. Nadelson and Malkah T. Notman in a 1982 issue of the *American Journal of Psychiatry* found that the costs of isolation and loneliness far outweigh the benefits of autonomy and freedom that singles gain.[4] Sociologist Andrew Greeley looked at reports of marital happiness over the last fifteen years and concluded in *Psychology Today* that married women "are still better off on the average in terms of 'happiness' than their sisters who have not married or who are separated or divorced and not remarried."[5] He found that divorced women who have not remarried are less than half as likely to be "very happy" as their married counterparts. Marriage may bring its own stresses, the researchers found, but it also brings far greater satisfaction than the uncertain singles life.

Even Janice Harayda, author of *The Joy of Being Single*, seems to concede that being unmarried is second-best: "A single man or woman needs to be his or her own nurse, cook, housekeeper, social director, sex therapist, interior designer and career counselor—all jobs a married person can sometimes transfer to a spouse . . . Even at its best, being single is a far cry from the endless romp that the media have sometimes portrayed it to be. Life always requires tradeoffs . . ."[6]

And here's her pep talk: "The worst thing that can happen to you isn't that you'll never get married; it's that you won't do the things you want to do or become the person you want to be because you were always waiting for someone to give you the opportunity you already had."[7] While Harayda may not be saying that staying single is the ultimate lifestyle, her words bring small encouragement when what you've always dreamed of is intimacy, children, and a sense of family teamwork and closeness. No house deed, trip to Tahiti, or stellar career can substitute for *that*.

LIE #2: MEETING LOVERS IS EASY

While experiential wisdom denies this Lie, the media are still bent on touting the accessibility of romance and sex. Movies may be the worst offenders. For example, recall how simply the first erotic signals bypassed the salami in a crowded delicatessen in *9½ Weeks*. The eventual live-togethers of the film *About Last Night* sparked their amour in the classic singles bar. *Echo Park*'s star Susan Dey found a future roommate, Tom Hulce, on her doorstep delivering the pizza she'd ordered. The movie *The Personals* brought stacks of photos of potential lovers with the morning mail. The sex-obsessed heroine of *She's Gotta Have It* found her main squeeze while strolling down the street. And even if you're dripping with perspiration it's hard to avoid romance at the gym if you're *Perfect*. There's an old pop song called "Love Is All Around," and by golly, you'd have to be quarantined to avoid it in the movies.

Of course, meeting lovers for "a good time" is a bit

different than finding someone suitable to marry. The fact
that there may not even *be* that many qualified lifetime
matches becomes then yet another argument for taking
things more casually and grabbing closeness on a *carpe
diem* basis.

My good friend Angela Lerner—energetic, bright, attractive, and still unmarried at thirty-seven—rationalized
that she had the best that *all* men had to offer. "I'd be
bored with just one man," she used to say. "Dating several men gives me variety, interest, and newness all the
time. I've really got it all. I travel where and when I want
to, plan my own life, and always have two or three guys
to see. It's true that I'd never marry any of them, but they
each have something that I really like, and when I'm in
the mood for that particular side of someone, I know
where to go."

I remember when she had one beau she described as a
"hunk" who was gorgeous to look at, fun to be around,
creative and exciting in bed but as intellectual as the
dumbbells he so obsessively lifted. At the same time,
Angela was dating a political science professor who challenged her mind with history games and peppered his
conversations with literary allusions. When she wanted
adventure, Angela merely phoned up a third companion,
the one who liked to go hiking and bicycling, the one
who had all the maps to the national parks and loved
climbing some secluded trail at twilight. Angela made
love to all of them; sometimes it was passionate and
sometimes purely recreational. She simply decided that
she'd get what she could from the many men available to
her and not search for the one man who rolled every
desirable characteristic into a neat package.

It sounded so appealing: Never tied down. Always in
demand. New. Exciting. Different. I remember the time
when she was juggling so many guys that she didn't have
a night of the week to herself, and despite exhaustion she
said she was having the time of her life.

Now, there are two pieces of information that you
should know for perspective on Angela's glorious singles
experience. First off, before she adopted this cavalier attitude, Angela had been unhappy for a long time. After
turning down two proposals in her early twenties—one
from the heir to a fortune who seemed "too dull" and

another from a sweet, adoring fellow whose religiosity frightened her—Angela put her energy into earning a law degree and becoming a partner in a prestigious firm. Over the years, her flings disappointed or her true loves rejected her. With each hurt, she became increasingly depressed. Should she have accepted one of the earlier proposals? Had she become less desirable? Were her standards for a man possible? Finally she went to a shrink.

He made her feel better. He told her The Lie: There are lots of great guys out there if you've got the right attitude. Don't expect them to want commitment—men are afraid of it. Don't expect them to be the way you want them to be—because then you'll pass up lots of good times. Just take it easy, feel good about being single. So what if you never get married? In the meantime you'll have so many exciting vacations, so many wild weekends, so many choices. Angela believed him and put his suggestions into action. She dated the Football Team.

The second piece of information is something that happened recently. Angela met the man of her dreams. They were introduced at a conference she organized, and they quickly fell in love. They were engaged in six weeks later—wanting to wait a respectable amount of time, after all—and married three months after that. Her fiancé transplanted himself from one coast to the other for her. She gave up being a vegetarian so she could share the steaks he loved. They plan to have a family immediately. All her suppressed dreams have come true.

"But what about the fantastic singles life? All those men available to you whenever you wanted them? What about your insistence that staying with just one man is boring and stifles growth?" I asked at her engagement party.

"I got awfully tired," she confessed. "I got angry when the hunk told dumb jokes. I felt like punching out the mountain climber who was always so cheerful, upbeat, and full of energy. Didn't he ever need to rest? And the intellectual hardly ever touched me—it was 'wham, bam, thank you ma'am'—and I need a little caressing with my lovemaking. It's true that each of them had a uniquely satisfying angle, but who wants to spend the rest of your life grabbing for pieces of people? I finally found someone I liked *completely*. Just because there are lots of fish in the sea doesn't mean I have to spend my whole life fishing.''

One nibble from a catch she didn't want to throw back, and rod and reel were pitched overboard. Angela was fed The Lie, lived it, and clung to it when she needed to. But in truth she found its glory greatly exaggerated. For most people the Lie is just that—an impossibility. It's really *not* so easy to find decent lovers, unless you lower your standards like Angela did. Most people are unwilling to do that; they consider a sexually frenzied evening with a nerd to be a waste of time. They don't want to contemplate escapes from yet another blind date. They aren't looking to go out to dinner—they want a *relationship*.

The lengths to which people go in order to find an acceptable companion, one who might end up as their life's partner, are legendary. One recently burgeoning means to hook mates is the ''singles advertisements.'' They've so enamored lonely hearts that they've become big business—for newspapers, magazines, and even movie-makers, especially the producers of the film *The Personals*. Consultants can be hired who will write a flattering biography in three lines or less. Publications glean large portions of their operating budgets from readers' searching insertions. Post office boxes abound for the simple function of collecting return mail from hopeful respondents. Here are some honest-to-goodness samples from the back pages of the respectable *Los Angeles* magazine (August 1986):

''*Newsweek* claims single, educated women abundant. Italian Scorpio, athletic, 6'0'', 43, asks, Where? I adore women. Enjoy dining, dancing, traveling, sharing new experiences. Dinner, anyone?'' (Read on for more on the infamous *Newsweek* cover story.)

''Dear Mr. Wonderful—I have spent the last 33 years growing into the intelligent, independent, sensitive, attractive, shapely and altogether fantastic person who now greets me every morning all by myself. I hope you are done too, because I think it's time we finally met . . .''

''Millionaire—Made first million at 25, foreign, elegant, sophisticated, mature, slim, works out, large estate, travels to Europe, gourmet dining, seeks meaningful relationship with pretty, 18–30 woman . . .''

"I'm 29 and cute, love a man in a suit. Love spectator sports, I look good in shorts. So send me a letter, I'll get to know you better!"

Do "the personals" work? Sometimes. But their mere existence negates the Lie that acceptable lovers are easy to find. Why spend twenty-five dollars or more for the ultimate blind date? *This* unknown stranger wasn't even recommended by Aunt Sarah; *this* face-in-a-crowd could have sent a ten-year-old snapshot, one taken before he got bald with gray at the edges and added that "cute" bay window. It fact, *this* stab-in-the-dark could be risky, and who knows—even if you meet in a public place things could get ugly.

Or be ugly. Especially if and when he gets his clothes off. It seems far more prudent, reasonable, and reliable to plunk down the one hundred- to two thousand-dollar fee requested by video dating and computer matchmaking services. I know several people who have cast their lots with a five-minute tape that they hope will be viewed by hundreds of upwardly mobile professionals like themselves.

Almost all of these services make good on their claims to send you the names and/or faces of a given number of "select" men or women. You can look at their membership books, read the bios, go through their channels, and perhaps, after several misses, hit the one for you. It did happen to Liz and Allen, who were both shocked to discover the extent of their commonalities (they're now expecting their first child).

It *didn't* happen to Evan Foreman, a banker of forty who found most of the ladies he dated "pleasant" but not worthy of a second look. The rest didn't find *him* appealing. For Evan, it was two thousand dollars for the service and several hundred more for meals, some amusing evenings, companionship to concerts, and then boom, it fell flat. Oh, he could mosey on back to headquarters and see if they've filed any interesting videotapes lately. But after two years and five or six trips over there, he has a hunch about what to expect.

Some find-a-mate services are specialized, according to hobbies, educational level, or religion. A local ethnic newspaper offers no less than a dozen advertisements for such organizations: "Singles Exposure (ages 25–55) invites you to 'A Night for Romance!' "Mingle with Celebrity Look-Alikes!'" "Leslie's Singles Circuit (ages 25–55) Capture the Old World Charm at a Fabulous Rendezvous at the Tivoli!" "The Business and Professional Singles (ages 25–45) Mid-Week Dance Party—Deluxe munchies, no host bar. Chase the mid-week blues! Meet exciting people!" It strains credibility that every meet-your-match get-together should be worthy of so many exclamation marks.

Worthy of examination, however, are the many innovative means employed by respectable singles seeking romance. In East Providence, Rhode Island, for example, singles played ice-breaking games and sized one another up—in the aisle of a supermarket. "Shoppers entering the Star Market were each given a tag bearing the name of half of a famous couple and sent on their way to find the other half," reads a national press account. "Duplicate names were handed out, and Mary Mijal of Smithfield, whose tag read Lois Lane, met four Clark Kents before the night was over, apparently none a Superman. 'A lot of them were at, well, different ends of the age spectrum. Like twelve to seventy-two,' " she remarked. While love amidst the produce may seem bizarre, a grocery store near where I used to live was considered such a happy hunting ground that the best hours to catch a match were published in the local newspaper.

The muscular benefits of exercise have long been known, but only now is its matrimonial potential receiving attention. While riding on the Life Cycle one memorable day a couple of years ago, the supervisor of the gym where I was pedaling decided to amuse the row of ladies working up an admirable glow. She weaved among the stationary bicycles, holding up an issue of *Cosmopolitan* magazine (August 1986), which featured a listing of the best pick-up spots in several major cities.

"What do you think is the number one place in Los Angeles to meet guys?" she challenged us. The other five cyclists reeled off a list of trendy restaurants, Beverly Hills hot spots, posh screening rooms, and sophisticated singles bars. Only I came up with the correct answer: the very gym where we sat at that moment, sweating and grunting without pretension or makeup. Though we were in the women-only section, plenty of ready and willing males were bulging their biceps across the hall in the glass-walled coed weight room.

With all the publicity and even a couple of work-out movies on the screens, it's becoming old news that the most heavenly bodies shine with grease and goodness behind their Nautilus machines. What does surprise me, though, is the indoor tract tactic one aspiring wife nearing thirty uses to hook a hunk: "When I see a really good-looking guy coming up behind, I simply stick out my foot."

Putting your best food forward is always useful when attending one of the many "extension" classes now being offered on the subject of mate-location. An organization called "The Learning Annex," which has branches in several major cities, offers, during any one semester, the following course selections: "How to Identify, Love, and Marry Someone Stable," "How to Flirt," "Fifty Ways to Meet Your Lover," "How to Get Past the First Date," and "How to Make a Man (or Woman) Fall in Love with You." If The Lie were true, it seems that there'd be no need for such explicit and expensive aids to find a partner. By the way, these class listings are under the heading, "Meet Market." Back to the butcher's aisle.

LIE #3: PLAY TODAY: YOU CAN ALWAYS SETTLE DOWN LATER

The truth is that you *can't* just go *voilà* and find your lifetime mate whenever you feel like it. It's downright depressing looking for that elusive "click," especially when your aim is marriage and family rather than a "quickie" or a live-in liaison. The title of the book *All the Good Ones Are Married* by Marion Zola[8] sums it up by implying that the ones who're left out there for serious-minded ladies are dolts, nerds, and egotists, who are poverty-stricken or rebounding from recent divorce, with child support payments and unfinished emotional business. If, like my friend Angela Lerner, you're willing to look beyond these imperfections, then to hell with The Lie—you can find a man. But if you're particular in the least, you may "vahnt to be alone" rather than settle for less-than-acceptable for the rest of your life.

Newsweek magazine spawned a furor by making the results of a 1986 Yale and Harvard University study on single women's chances of finding a husband into cover story news. The June 1986 story describing the frustration of women over thirty who are hoping to wed contained these often-requoted statistics: "According to the (Yale-Harvard) report, white, college-educated women born in the mid-50s who are still single at thirty have only a 20 percent chance of marrying. By the age of 35 the odds drop to 5 percent. Forty-year-olds are more likely to be killed by a terrorist."[9]

The "terrorist" line put combative American women up-in-arms and inspired articles of protest in such well-read women's magazines as *Self* and *Glamour*. *Self*'s Rachel Wilder wrote a "a sensible look at the 'man shortage,' " called definitely "Who Will and Who Won't Get Married,"[10] Its aim was to comfort distressed unmarried women with the following arguments: (1) You greatly increase your marital chances if you *want* to get married; (2) Statistics can't be applied to individuals, and (3) You at least might find a man who's willing to live with you—so that even if you're not married, you won't be alone. What a relief.

Of course, William Novak wrote about the single women's dilemma years before the fateful *Newsweek* cover story. He lamented the demographic disadvantage that there are more women than men in marriageable age groups, the desire of men to choose younger women, and the number of gay men diminishing the pool of choices in *The Great American Man Shortage and Other Roadblocks to Romance*.[11] He chronicled how women's own demands *further* squelch their chances to find somebody suitable—they want an emotional man who's not a wimp; a superachiever who's not a workaholic. In other words, they want the impossible—a man who's got a ruthless personality regarding his career and a tender personality at home. Women are equally confused about the way they want to be treated, Novak adds. "They want equality when it benefits them, but they revert to the old rules when it doesn't."[12]

The best-seller *Smart Women, Foolish Choices*, by Drs. Connell Cowan and Melvyn Kinder,[13] tries to lay blame for women's mate-finding frustration on the way they've been trained to select a man. It tells marriage-minded ladies that yes, there's someone out there for you—but you've got to change your criteria and strategies for bagging him. These doctors confirm the prevalence of The Lie by acknowledging the vast numbers of women who are sorely disappointed that they cannot just settle down whenever they choose. But never fear, ladies, the authors soothe. Once you learn to recognize the "clams," "pseudo-liberated males," "perpetual adolescents," and "walking wounded" you have been erroneously choosing, you *will* overcome your unfortunate pasts to find the man of your dreams. Sadly, none of the single women I know who raved about this book when it first appeared have, through its instruction, been able to secure a mate.

At least Susan Crain Bakos (*This Wasn't Supposed to Happen*) is honest about The Lie. In direct language she admits that women want to be married; that the singles life is difficult, pressure-filled, and lonely. And she fears that too many of her unmarried peers are blithely ignoring reality and buying into the outdated and overly optimistic Lie that someday, somehow, they *will* find that ultimate connection: "I wish other women would put down the magazines now trumpeting Romance! Soft Clothes! Marriage! and Babies!—and examine the truths in the closets of their lives, which are hanging there exactly like dozens of miniskirts with two-inch hems.

"*Truth*: There aren't enough men to go around; and some of us will never marry or remarry no matter how many magazine articles we read on finding men at health clubs or through the classifieds.

"*Truth*: Some of us have waited too long to conceive; and we aren't going to have those babies.

"*Truth*: The overwhelming majority of us have to work now and will have to work for the rest of our lives, married or not."[14]

It's much easier to just swallow The Lie.

Tom Cruise demonstrates The Lie in the 1988 hit film *Cocktail*. After a fling with bartending stardom, he decides it's time to settle down—and turns around in the snap of a shaker to find the elegant and eligible Elisabeth Shue.

It would seem from all this that while women may have a tough time pairing with Mr. Right, men—including the Mr. Wrongs—have it made. With so many women itching to settle down and have families, all they have to do is blink and there will be several quite acceptable lasses eager to accept their proposals. But in my experience as a psychologist, that's simply not the case. Men who read *Newsweek* and still can't find a match feel even *worse* about the problems they're encountering.

In the last two months alone I've received half a dozen phone calls from eligible men in their thirties asking for advice on finding a "good woman." One thirty-five-year-old investor and pianist called long distance from Lincoln, Nebraska: "I know there's supposed to be so many women who want to get married," he apologized, "but no matter what I do I can't find them!" He claims he frequents a handful of church social and Bible groups, takes language and self-improvement classes, and looks earnestly at those in his workplace. He's a conservative from a long line of lawyers and judges—and he's also a virgin holding out for "that special relationship." I've never met him, but he sounded intelligent and sensitive—and I really couldn't figure out why he remained unattached. Except that The Lie is equally false for both genders.

Again, the truth is that you *can't* just find the right someone to marry when you feel like it. Art Carey, who, judging from his full-page book-jacket photo on the cover of *In Defense of Marriage*[15] would make any lady's heart go pitter-pat, had available to him a wide range of brilliant, beautiful, and sensitive women. During his single years, he sampled them all, always with a piqued interest and open mind that was inevitably disappointed. He found that appealing women, increasingly desperate for any "masculine" man, were eager to latch onto him—but he found most of them, in their newly cultivated liberation, domineering. He was eager to marry when he did find a compatible woman, and looking back, Carey concludes: "All I know for sure is that I'm glad I'm no longer swimming in that mirror-laden barracuda tank known as the singles' scene.''[16]

Susan Page summarizes the problem in the title of her 1988 book, *If I'm So Wonderful, Why Am I Still Single?*[17] She asserts that the inability to find a mate, even after desperately and actively searching for years, causes singles "the great emotional depression" that requires detailed strategies to overcome. Lurking in the path toward true commitment are dozens of lurid deceptions and snares, among them "pseudo intimacy," sneaky "masks" to honest emotions, and "the someday syndrome."

The marriage desperation bandwagon is getting crowded. Dr. Stephen Prince and Susan Prince, M.S.W., brazenly promise *No More Lonely Nights* (1988). They address the web of fears that keeps people away from marriage, and suggest that divorced people may be even more invested in staying single than those who have never married: "Although you once made your marriage a high priority, you ended up putting primary value on getting out of it. The postdivorce healing process lasted for at least two years, and today you find yourself well-established in your lifestyle as a single woman."[18] In other words, even when you *think* you're ready to take the plunge again, your past may skulk into your psyche to prevent it.

Just ask single people to talk frankly about the veracity of the Lies outlined here. Even though human beings are flexible and optimistic and tend to make the most out of whatever situation they find themselves in (and also tend to attribute this bright picture to their own choosing and doing), they also know when they're down. The shapely "instructress" at my gym whose car license frame reads "Happiness Is Being Single" probably *is* happy—but if she's like 95 percent of the American population, she still wants out of that status and into marriage. In other words, she doesn't believe The Lie even though she's driving around perpetrating it.

So what is the main effect of The Lie if even singles, whose image benefits most from its continuance, know it's false? *The Lie ruins marriages.* And combined with The Lure, it's a wonder anyone wants to stay married at all.

NOTES

1. Carroll, David, and Simenauer, Jacqueline. *Singles: The New Americans*. New York: Simon and Schuster, 1982.
2. Ibid., p. 328.
3. Stratan, Pamela Redman, "Forever Single." *Glamour*, September 1986, pp. 334–337, 394.
4. Nadelson, Carol C., and Notman, Malkah T. *American Journal of Psychiatry*, 1982.
5. Greeley, Andrew. "Marriage Wins . . ." *Psychology Today*, October 1986, p. 8.
6. Harayda, Janice. *The Joy of Being Single*. New York: Doubleday, 1986.
7. Ibid., p. 4, p.7.
8. Zola, Marion. *All the Good Ones Are Married*. New York: Times Books, 1981.
9. "Too Late for Prince Charming." *Newsweek*, June 1986, pp. 53–61.
10. Wilder, Rachel. "Who Will and Who Won't Get Married." *Self*, August 1986, pp. 76–80.
11. Novak, William. *The Great American Man Shortage and Other Roadblocks to Romance*. New York: Rawson Associates, 1983.
12. Novak, William. "What do Women Really Want?" *McCalls*, February 1985, p. 16.
13. Cowan, Connell, and Kinder, Melvyn. *Smart Women, Foolish Choices*. New York: Potter, 1985.
14. Bakos, Susan Crain. *This Wasn't Supposed to Happen*. New York: Continuum Publishing, 1985, p. 125.
15. Carey, Art. *In Defense of Marriage*. New York: Walker & Co., 1984.
16. Ibid., p. 48.
17. Page, Susan. *If I'm So Wonderful, Why Am I Still Single?* New York: Viking, 1988.
18. Prince, Stephen and Susan. *No More Lonely Nights*. New York: Putnam, 1988, p. 22.

CHAPTER 6

Friends Till the End

Even if you understand intellectually the Lies and Lures sinisterly drawing you toward divorce, you can wave them off as abstract and far removed. They arc interesting, provocative perhaps, but given your savvy, you find it easy to dismiss them as platitudes and slogans that don't apply to your daily life. Yes, you'll agree that their cumulative effect is to erode confidence in marriage, to beckon you to a seemingly more exciting plane, to desensitize you to divorce—but at the same time, you don't spend hours confronting these ideas or contemplating their effect. Their impact is subconscious, working subtly and slowly; it doesn't cause you urgent distress.

Some forces pushing to accept divorce, however, are closer to home. When a couple you've known since high school and whose marriage you've likened to the Rock of Gibraltar suddenly announce their separation. When you have a birthday, maybe your thirtieth, fortieth, or fiftieth and instead of joyfully reaching for a paper hat and roll-up noisemaker, you're struck sober by a sense that your friends are doing so much better than you are. When your spouse unexpectedly says she's been talking to her tennis pal, and, well, maybe the two of you ought to go see a counselor. These startling events leave indelible marks. And often, they begin a process that can push you into divorce.

Alice and Sam LeFever felt like the last married couple

in the world when their best friends since they were kids,
the ones they'd shared the Big Sur Folk Festival and the
1969 Anti-War Mobilization with, dropped their bomb-
shell news. It walloped them despite childhood experience with divorce. Sam's parents had split up when he
was in junior high, after years of his mother's nagging
and his father's retreating. His dad's affairs weren't even
so secret, and Sam could certainly understand why his
dad needed an escape—Sam's portly, coupon-obsessed
mother was unbearable with her incessant empty gab-
bing. Sam escaped his mother by hanging around with
Alice and her family, who were cool and tolerant and
who always looked the other way if they happened to see
Sam scurrying out of the bathroom at five o'clock in the
morning.

Before Sam, Alice had hung around for a couple of
years with a borderline crowd that was into marijuana,
boozing, and the fringes of show business. Her folks were
relieved when Sam, a good-natured, clever fellow, began
monopolizing her time, and ever since those days in high
school when he finally convinced Alice to give him a
chance, she's been dependent on him. Sam took care of
her, he bought her goodies, like dinners out and even a
new car, and she couldn't imagine finding someone so
devoted and tolerant of her quirks.

Their best friends, Christine and Alan Magill, steadies
in the same high school class, joined them every week
in the seventies for the Saturday night TV roundup—
"Mary Tyler Moore Show," "All in the Family," "Bob
Newhart," "The Jeffersons." The four struggled financially in their undergraduate years and developed their
little holiday rituals. They alternated Christmas morning
brunch, went to Disneyland every summer, planned ex-
travagant treasure hunts and surprise adventures to cele-
brate one another's birthdays. They were as close as any
friends could be, for sixteen years.

Until Christine told Alan she was moving out. At first
she said it was a temporary breather, which stretched
from weeks into months. Then she got her own apartment. Soon she was dating another fellow and had filed
for divorce. Enmeshed in building a new life, she rarely
spoke to Alice or Sam anymore.

Alice and Sam didn't know how to react. Sixteen years

of inseparability were puzzlingly shattered, and they could draw no understanding from the lame acceptance that Alan offered. "We thought that if any marriage was unbreakable, it was theirs," Alice told me. "When Christine and Alan broke up, it was as if the whole foundation of our own relationship was called into question. They'd gotten married even before we did—when they were nineteen and twenty-two—and we just thought that it was forever. They never fought, always continued to be so in love, so dedicated to each other, and then, without warning, the world fell apart." When their dearest friends divorced, Sam and Alice wondered if it could happen to them.

THE "WE-ALL-GO-THROUGH-IT SYNDROME" OR HOW FRIENDS ENCOURAGE DIVORCE

The motivations of friends as they react to your separation can be classified into two categories: helping you and helping themselves. Even while oozing the best intentions and the warmest wishes for your welfare, they may unconsciously and unknowingly push you out of your marriage and into divorce. No wonder a 1978 study by the department of psychology at the University of Colorado, Boulder, found that 87 percent of couples entering into a "trial separation" ultimately divorce, while only 13 percent reconcile. You can't help it—you're estranged from your spouse by the closest and most well-meaning forces in the world. And that makes you all the more helpless to recognize and combat their influence.

They only want to help.

Nobody who comes into contact with you during your separation will be openly hostile. The "fair weather friends" who think the split is your fault, who think you victimized someone unfortunate, or who project that you're now marred, different, or on the prowl—the ones who are traumatized by disaster anywhere in their environments (lest disaster strike them by association)—won't come around anymore. They won't return your phone calls. They'll scurry out of the room if you happen to meet at a party. They may even spread rumors and lies and perhaps act like betraying turncoats. But they'll do it all behind your back. Their actions hurt a lot, especially if you were convinced they were buddies of both of you or if you've known them a long time. You can basically write these people off.

It's the others who end up pushing you into divorce. And the most destructive may be those who on the surface appear to be the most supportive. They care for you; they want to listen. They think you're the greatest, that you deserve the best. What a rotten thing for you. It's just horrendous, and whatever happens, you know they'll be there with a towel-draped shoulder for you to cry on.

Eunice Brenner came to me as a client after four months of soothing from the members of her once-a-week breakfast group. All professionals, they'd gather every Wednesday at a certain downtown coffee shop at the ungodly hour of 6:00 A.M. to schmooze over espresso and danish. They'd been doing it for years, even before Eunice got her job as the public relations director for a large oil company, a job with prestige and power lunches, bow blouses and pastel linen suits. Before this job, five years ago, she'd tried to make a go of her own P.R. firm but struggled with a handful of clients and a fistful of bills for overhead. She finally gave up, and through it all "the girls," as she affectionately calls this "networking group" of seven, cheered her on.

They could do nothing but boost one another. Peggy made it through her M.B.A. solely on the caffeine and encouragement of the group; she lived alone and tended to think the blackest thoughts in the clock-ticking hours of the night. Elizabeth found child care for her toddlers and even some referrals for her decorating business through the group, but she mainly looked forward to it as an escape from the confines of her home responsibilities. Dory used the group to complain about the idiots she encountered in the field doing court reporting; tales of some of her personal injury depositions brought giggles to the still bleary-eyed. Eunice liked them all—everybody originally a long-time friend of someone else, they'd now spent seven years weaving their own close-knit camaraderie.

So she naturally sought out these women when she found out that Paul, her husband of eleven years, had been having months-at-a-time "involvements" throughout their marriage. Paul swore that his little flirtations never threatened their relationship; he was always solidly committed to it and would never leave her. All of his outside interests were just for ego enhancement and excitement—every lady knew he was married, and while he was titillated by the pursuit and their adoring responses, he always carefully avoided making promises to eventually divorce Eunice.

"I love you, I think you're the perfect wife," he repeated over and over as Eunice screamed and shrieked and cried and tried to hit him with all of her Jane Fonda Workout strength. "I want you, I want you, not them," was all he replied to her hysterical ravings, until she was too hoarse to continue and, slamming the door without grabbing so much as a toothbrush, raced her Datsun 280Z to Peggy's house.

It was 8:30 P.M. and Peggy was sipping a solitary sherry, listening to old Frank Sinatra records and staring out over the Valley lights twinkling into her apartment picture windows. She had the newspaper spread out over her lap, but as usual she found herself drifting, wondering why she was working so hard, why she couldn't find someone to give her life meaning, someone to give her a family. She was startled when Eunice knocked, called to her, and quickly let herself in with the key under the mat.

"Aww, poor baby," Peggy purred in her most calming voice. "Here, have some sherry with me and tell me all about it."

"That rat, that scumball!" Eunice barked angrily. "Here I am working my tail off, making him dinner, asking him about his meetings—his meetings where he gave these sluts flowers and set up clandestine trysts and stroked their hair—" Eunice dissolved into sobs and Peggy quickly put down her snifter and took her into her arms in comfort. The night blinked silently as Eunice unloaded every resentment, every suspicious evening, every choked-back sigh. That jerk. That bastard. That two-timing skunk! Peggy nodded and sympathized and supported. She was the perfect friend, telling Eunice how that idiot Paul didn't know what a good thing he was abusing, couldn't even appreciate the best woman that would ever walk into his life. He was a creep whose ego was attached to his groin, whose head was built on a greased pole. If he was worth anything he would've been down on his knees with gratitude for such a beautiful, loyal, and talented wife; but instead the slimebag lied and carried on and blew his chance for happiness.

Eunice was appreciative. She felt better. She was vindicated. She fell asleep on Peggy's sofa under her down comforter at 4:30 A.M. The next day was Wednesday.

When Peggy and Eunice, dressed in Peggy's suede skirt and blazer, told the group about the night before, everyone was concerned. Would Eunice be all right today? How about lunch? Elizabeth volunteered to pick her up after work. Peggy was already planning how to rearrange her closet to accommodate Eunice's wardrobe. Dory said she's stop by Eunice's house and pick up whatever she wanted. Everything was organized. They wouldn't let Paul get away with it.

Eunice sobbed through the first two weeks, then gradually started to calm down. She avoided listening to the messages Paul left on Peggy's answering machine. She instructed her secretary to simply note the times when he phoned her at work. Just thinking about him, about the eleven years they'd stayed together and her selfless dedication to pleasing him, tore her up. She spoke to Peggy twice a day. She called the other ''girls'' whenever she felt low. She alternated lunches with them. She put on a facade at the office and adequately disguised her smeared mascara. She felt like she was a zombie, except when she was around her friends. They listened unflaggingly. They understood. Every day, she said less and less. But she kept crying, it hurt so bad. The pain just penetrated her, without words or warning, and she relied on her friends' willingness to catch her in mid-fall.

About two months after she left Paul, after she'd stocked Peggy's refrigerator with her favorite yogurt and replenished the sherry, Eunice decided that she didn't want to mope around anymore. She still cried a lot, often uncontrollably. She cried at red lights. She cried when she was brushing her hair after a bath. She cried in her office, with the door closed. But her life had to go on. The girls told her that she was pretty and vivacious and deserved better than Paul. She decided she'd accept Dory's offer of a date with her cousin, who'd been through his own divorce five years before. He'd console her; he'd understand what it meant to have your heart ripped out—and maybe he'd take her to bed.

Dory's cousin was astoundingly good-looking. Eunice hadn't noticed for a long time that regular men—not just movie stars and TV soap opera leads—could be so lovely to look at. Ronnie had a scarf of blond hair, a chiseled nose, and a ga-ga physique. He knew it, of course, but he also knew how to make his date feel beautiful too. Eunice hadn't felt these sexual juices in years; she came alive when Ronnie touched her, felt her face flush when he kissed her tenderly, and let go of all emotion when he led her into his apartment, fixed her a Kahlua-and-cream, and casually unzipped her skirt. She was floating; she understood for the first time why Paul could not resist his flirtations. She felt desired and sensual, and she enjoyed herself with full lust and abandon. She'd been foolish to think there was just one man for her. She'd been foolish to let Paul tear her up. She knew she could make it on her own.

And the girls in the group agreed. Dory had heard from Ronnie how fantastic his evening with Eunice had been. She warned Eunice that Ronnie was a playboy, but so what, this was Eunice's time to play. She needed the upper, the reassurance that she was gorgeous. Why not sample what the world has to offer? Eunice got excited—at last she would be able to really live.

So she tested out her attractiveness. She flirted with guys in the coed workout room at the gym. She accepted invitations to parties. She smiled at men in the elevator of her high-rise office building. Her openness often paid off, and Eunice built her self-confidence along with her experience. She still thought about Paul occasionally, but now it was with more strength. She was finally showing him up. Two could play at his game. She fantasized about comparing notes with him and proving that she too was desired. And when she wanted to—if she ever wanted to again—she was sure she could find someone who would pledge his undying and faithful love; to hell with the man she could never trust again.

The first time she thought that she was going crazy happened when she was stepping out of the shower after work. She was dripping wet; her long auburn hair hung heavy as she wrapped it in a towel. As she opened the bathroom door, she caught the tail end of Peggy's message playing out through the answering machine; then she heard Paul's voice. "I know you probably won't listen to this one either, Eunice, but I have to leave it anyway. I still love you. I want you to come home. I need to know where you keep the spare garage key. I can't get out the lawnmower. I need you to sign some insurance papers. But mostly I want you back. I miss you. I don't want any other woman—I don't know what got into me to take you for granted. Come home honey—call me. Please."

When the dial tone sounded its interminable seven seconds, Eunice sat on the bed and cried longer and harder than ever before. Her wet hair saturated the pillow; her tears choked her throat and clogged her nose, but she didn't care, they wouldn't stop and she wanted to go to Paul so badly she felt physically torn in half. She was crazy, she was beserk—how could she love this dirtbag, how could she hate herself so much that she wanted to run into his arms and believe his every lying word? How could she think that after an eleven-year pattern of sneaking around and cheating he could ever change? Had he totally destroyed her pride?

No—her friends had simply manufactured a false sense of it for her. Their constant buoying had prevented her from sinking into her true feelings for even a moment. Their indulgence had become a barrier between her husband and herself. She had been pushed into moving out because Peggy was so willing to put her up, because Elizabeth and Dory were so eager to spare her the pain of ever having to face Paul. Eunice's friends were buffers who, out of kindness and caring, brainwashed her into thinking she could never give her marriage another chance. Once she decided to ignore their advice and talk to Paul about his affairs and her feelings, her occasional panics subsided and she realized that her marriage could continue. She suddenly had an option open to her that her friends had not let her consider. And it was the option she ultimately chose.

Marcia Hootman and Patt Perkins in *How to Forgive Your Ex-Husband (and Get On With Your Life)*[1] say friends can "nurture your resentment" by "listening interminably.'' They caution that only when you stop getting validation for self-pity can you move on—postdivorce, that means turning to other aspects of life; predivorce, that may easily mean reclaiming the foundations of your marriage.

One of the things that friends do in the name of support is run down your spouse. They come up with ugly descriptions that you'd never use in a million years. They think it's the appropriate time to tell you everything your mate ever did wrong, ranging from the slightest *faux pas* to the most embarrassing or insulting gaffe. They dredge up every old rumor and nasty story they can remember. They purge you of any vestige of good will by making you think you're a moron if you want to go back to this no-good. They think they're being kind, giving you a dose of reality that will make you forget him or her and lighten your misery. Instead, they compound it. And drive you to divorce.

When you're bitter and angry and eager to hear all the reasons why this separation is a good thing for you, these derisions of your spouse are uplifting. They bring justification for what happened, they prove that the relationship's lousy and therefore just not ''meant to be,'' taking the responsibility for problems and solutions out of your hands. No longer do you have an obligation to approach your partner; no more do you have to feel guilty for either leaving or accepting rejection. With all this validation from friends and relatives, you're sure that separation is the right thing. You're grateful to them for easing your burden.

That's because not facing up to the situation is the easy way out. And when you're hurting, the easy way looks awfully good. You don't want confrontation. You don't want teary scenes, weepy nostalgia, pleading, or yelling. Just resolution. The problem is that you're really only postponing the inevitable, hiding away for a while until your real emotions surface, until your history together catches up with you. You can't forget years of shared events. You can't just erase your courtship, the way it was when you first got together. You're still tied, no matter how much she fooled around or how dreadful his demanding ways. There's something left behind, and you'll have to return to it sooner or later. Even if you have to cross your friends' "picket line" to do it.

WELCOME TO THE CLUB

A prime motivation for your friends' interest in your welfare at this vulnerable time is their own needs. After all, it takes a lot of time, effort, and patience to sit through your expositions of who did what to whom way back when. Friends can certainly comfort you altruistically; but let's face it, many will at the same time be getting a psychological bonus for themselves. It's this personal need that determines how friends respond to your separation. Take a look at their individual circumstances.

A common motivation for their support is to legitimize their own marital status. *If they're divorced,* they say, "Hey, everybody does it, even stable and healthy people like me—so your breakup isn't a failure. It doesn't point to any kind of flaw in your relationship, in you or in your partner. Come join the ranks, there's plenty of us and the more of us there are, the less of the population is left to gawk and scorn us." The "safety in numbers" of high divorce rates—and especially large numbers of divorces among close friends and associates—lets this person rest assured that he won't stick out, won't be thought of as a freak.

If your sympathizer is *separated,* your own estrangement brings validation that his choice—or predicament—won't be endured alone. There's someone else suffering the pangs of regret, the humiliation, the isolation and loneliness. Maybe the two of you can get together. After all, this is Abigail Trafford's celebrated "crazy time,"[2] when your behavior may be so bizarre that you need someone to check up on you, someone to insure that you stay mainly sane. Who could be in a better position to understand, to listen—and then to reply that he's going through exactly the same thing, that his partner is equally audacious and despicable, that he misses his kids as fiercely, or is having just as hard a time dealing alone with them?

Being separated is a scary kind of limbo. You're almost untouchable to potential dates, who may refuse to get involved with someone who's too fragile, someone likely to be on the rebound. Longtime married acquaintances may be equally cautious, unsure of how to approach you or of whether you're really the villain or victim. Others who hear that you're freshly separated may step back to leave you a wide path, treat you condescendingly, or assume your incompetence, knowing the possible ramifications of that irrational "crazy time." Only someone else at the same precarious point in life can be your buddy, and with that temporary symbiosis you manage to stay separated from your spouse and survive.

Friends who are married who continue to see and support you suddenly have a new role: protector, guardian, "parent"—and superior. Your separation on the one hand may call into question the health of their relationship—thus frightening them—but this shock next produces a "circle the wagons" feeling about their marriage. They think it through. Then they come up with all the reasons why their marriage is flourishing while yours floundered. They have more even temperaments. They don't make ridiculous demands of each other. Their fights are of the psychologically constructive variety, where "fair" comments and responsible reconciliation clears the air rather than pollutes it.

You, obviously, didn't have these things going for you. It may have appeared all these years that you and your spouse could work out your differences, that you enjoyed each other, that you had a lot in common. Or maybe your marriage did show its foibles—a few knots in your relationship, a little fooling around on the side, some separate interests. Nobody thought too much about it because, hey, that's what modern couples endure; that's the norm nowadays. Now, however, they see how radically wrong your relationship was, while theirs is its polar opposite. After all, you've got to look at the end result. They're together; you're not. They're better; you're worse.

What can they do but summon sympathy for you, pity for you, you poor debilitated person who ultimately failed at this major endeavor? They offer compassion—"Can I do anything for you?" Condolence—"Oh, I'm so very sorry, you have no idea." Consolation—"Now you can start a new life! Why not come to dinner and meet Arnold's cousin Stephanie?" And they gloat about triumph in this competition (called "Surviving Marriage Through Thick and Thin") they've newly won.

It's this victory that puts you in a subordinate position. On the surface it may seem that freshly separated people would respond to this sense of competition with renewed motivation to return to the flagging marriage, just to regain lost status. Perhaps this mechanism works in a very few cases. But for the most part, once you've separated, the damage is done. Observers can forever say, "Sure, they're back together, but they separated last year." You've got a black mark on your record that can't be erased.

Couples who stay together through whatever stresses may, at least in their own minds, still feel superior. And still act paternally. How does that encourage your divorce? You join in with their game, their sense of competition. You think, "Maybe their marriage did survive, but I'll show them—I'll have a blast and find someone better and make them wonder why they're so proud of their relationship anyway."

Friends may be especially eager to disparage your crumbled relationship if there are cracks in their own marriages. One of the most pathetic situations is when one half of a couple you know well is cheating. Your separation reassures the philanderer that people just aren't angelic. Everyone's got problems. Everyone's marriage hovers on the brink of destruction. So why shouldn't he just join the crowd and make the best of a tough situation?

Anyone in an affair loves to see others break up. He (or she) sees you and says to himself: "Look how easy it is to kill a marriage. Joe and Ellen didn't make it— look at the agony they're going through. At least I'm not causing my partner pain. At least I'm keeping this thing going." Or alternately, he (or she) justifies his actions with "Joe here was miserable in his marriage like I was, but he's got it hard—what a basket case! I'm glad I've got the best of both worlds: a stable home, no smirch on my record, and all this excitement and passion on the side." No wonder he's eager to pat you on the back so sympathetically. No wonder he's so sure you've done the right thing.

One of the most subtly destructive influences you may

have going against your marriage is your social circle. Everyone *tsk-tsk*s when they hear that some couple in the group is splitting, and yet they don't realize the impact they have as a group on causing that to happen. Arthur A. Miller, in a chapter called "Reaction of Friends to Divorce" in *Divorce and After*,[3] says some crowds grant divorce a "positive significance," even when the individual members of the group think it's wrong. That's because the conscience of a group is looser than any given individual's—so you may behave in a way you wouldn't allow yourself if you didn't have that wider backdrop.

Even advice columnist Ann Landers warns that "divorce is contagious. When the word gets out that the Smiths (an ideal couple) have decided to go their separate ways, it gives the Joneses, the Johnsons, and the Millers the courage to announce that their marriages have also turned sour and they, too, are telling it to the judge." Writing in *Family Circle* magazine, she bemoans the change in values held by our society—and laments how such collective deterioration has been the banc of what was once our most revered institution.[4]

NOTES

1. Hootman, Marcia, and Perkins, Patt. *How to Forgive Your Ex-Husband (and Get On With Your Life)*. New York: Doubleday, 1983.

2. Trafford, Abigail. *Crazy Time: Surviving Divorce*. New York: Harper and Row, 1972.

3. Miller, Arthur A. "Reactions of Friends to Divorce." *Divorce and After*, edited by Paul Bohannan. New York: Doubleday, 1970, Ch. 3.

4. Landers, Ann. "What's Happening to Today's Marriages?" *Family Circle*, November 1982, p. 8, pp. 50–52, p. 180.

CHAPTER 7

The Crime of "Mid-Life Crisis"

One of the concepts most detrimental to contentment within a stable marriage is the recently popularized idea of the "mid-life crisis." It's okay to suddenly scrap years of cumulative caring, flip out, dump your career, and quest after lost youth because now it's got a handy-dandy label. "Oh yeah, Gary's just going through his mid-life crisis," friends may indulgently wink.

It's not your fault—you've just come to a common glitch in your world view. In large measure we can thank Gail Sheehy's book *Passages*,[1] which was followed in short order by a raft of other self-help tomes that legitimized this modern malaise. Laura J. Singer even titled her book *Stages: The Crises that Shape Your Marriage*, though the events she chronicles (aside from extramarital affairs) seem perfectly benign to me.[2] *Crisis* has indeed become a buzzword for normal though major change that we've just come to accept.

"Mid-life crisis," in case you haven't heard, is the point in your struggle to accomplish your envisioned goals when you realize that the effort is futile—you'll die without achieving everything anyway. (In the words of a newly popular lament: "Life is hard and then you die.") This crisis spurs you to radical change—since you've lost your idealism, you now know enough to live the life that feels best to you right now.

This happened to Deborah Lasman. She was only

thirty-two, on the young side according to the timetable, and thought she was in a happy marriage to Randy Lasman, an upper-level librarian for the city of Chicago. They'd gotten married young—she had been just a sophomore at Northwestern and he entering grad school. But they'd had a two-year courtship, and their twelve-year marriage had been relatively free of bumps. She was a struggling film-maker, trying to produce documentaries, and she had a couple of grants from foundations and several lucrative commissions from corporations to build up her credits. During busy days, she could leave their four-year-old son Michael with her mother, who lived just ten blocks away from their brick house in Lincolnwood. And she could do a lot of the editing at home.

It looked like Deborah was on her way up. There were vacations with Randy to Europe every couple of years, and she'd even started talking about having a second child. But her mind wandered occasionally when she sat at her word processor revising scripts for the hundredth time. "There's got to be more for me," she'd think. "This just can't be it." Randy was a doll—he adored Michael, he brought home his paychecks, he gave Deborah compliments as if they were newlyweds.

But Deborah became depressed: "There's got to be more." Partly it was frustration about her career—when would she ever become more than a second-rate-film flunky for companies hoping to impress stockholders? Partly it was her boredom and increasing irritation with Randy's lack of initiative and achievement. But mostly it was her father's heart attack.

When he died, she went to pieces. "Suddenly I realized how fragile life is," she recalls. "I thought my dad was the one person I could count on—that he'd be there forever. He was only sixty-eight, and he'd never had heart trouble before. In a nightmare of just three hours my whole perception of life evaporated."

Randy simply couldn't replace her dad. He cried and was a sweet husband. He comforted her. But Deborah saw him as the kid she went to school with, the one who bathed Michael but couldn't really be counted on to make arrangements, to plan the future. Deborah began to panic. She realized that at thirty-two, she didn't have time to start over. She didn't have time to accomplish what she wanted to. She didn't have security. She didn't have her father.

Friends attributed her depression and sullenness to the loss. Deborah's mother and two older sisters, also distraught, were too consumed by their own grief to help. Randy thought he ought to give Deborah some breathing space and didn't press. The bills weren't paid; Randy tried to figure out Deborah's accounting system without bugging her. Deadlines passed; one of Deborah's projects got canceled, but it didn't matter. Michael thought Mommy was a ghost, even though she spent evenings playing blocks with him in his room. "She's sick," he told Randy one night.

"She's just sad for a while," Randy responded.

Four months after her dad passed away, Deborah met Louis. She was still in a daze, floating through daily routines, trying to restore her tarnished reputation. As head of his own production company, Louis had picked up the project she'd bumbled and had some questions. He needed the information for his staff—his film company had won two Emmys and had just gotten funding for their second feature. Louis had accomplished what Deborah sought—success. He'd been divorced a year and didn't really want to steal Deborah from Randy, but there was just so much chemistry. They'd started talking business and ended up touching hands wordlessly across his desk.

With no promise for the future, Deborah decided to take Michael and move in with her mother. Ostensibly, she would take care of things there for a while, but she let Randy know she really needed a little time, a little space away from him. She considered relocating to California—Louis was heading west for his new film. The decision making was excruciating for Deborah—she cried and listened intently to the words of every song on the radio.

Deborah did move to California. She did get together with Louis, who quickly became attached to Michael. She didn't have to struggle—Louis' company attracted funds for her projects. On the surface, everything seemed to turn out fabulously. But her family and Randy were incredulous, devastated, and angry. They will never understand. And because of that, Deborah carries a burden of guilt and sadness. It's difficult for her to admit that what she gained was not worth the price.

"Mid-life crisis" is often merely a cover for quitting. Why do friends and family tolerate this kind of "forget my old life" childishness? Why are we so cavalier about shirking responsibilities and being accountable for choices? Why have we gotten so selfish that a sudden flash of mortality is enough to justify blasting apart the lives of everyone who counted on us—even if they wanted to help?

Here's another true story. Nathan Roth did very well in stocks and securities while living with his wife and four children in New York. He planned his life: a few years of struggle, wise investments and prosperity, then he'd move to Hawaii, where he could manage his money and live in paradise into old age. Harriet Roth only heard the part about the early years when she married him at age eighteen—how likely was it that two Brooklyn Heights kids, with family so tightly enmeshed in the city that they hardly ever ventured farther than Florida, would ever chuck it all and lie in the sun all day? Harriet knew better. So they got married and had the kids and did all right for themselves. Harriet found real estate to invest in. She managed the payments. They were a partnership.

But continually on and off, even when the oldest was in high school, Nathan never stopped talking about Hawaii. He became obsessed with it and reminded Harriet that this was always his dream. Nathan came back from an appointment with the accountant one day with a plan.

The family would move to Oahu. The money would be okay; he'd figured it all out. "Abandon this great apartment?" Harriet screamed. She'd decorated a gorgeous five-bedroom home in Manhattan's East Seventies. They'd come pretty far over the years. She had nice furniture, which she'd always taken pains to cover with plastic so the kids wouldn't ruin it. She had her collection of exotic paperweights. She had her friends and her family. No, Harriet definitely didn't want to move.

But Nathan prevailed, and Harried cried when the movers took away her things. Most of it she'd sold at Nathan's insistence. "We won't need quilted sofas in paradise," he teased. "We'll get new furniture." The family made the move and settled into a waterfront home in

Kailua, away from Honolulu on the western side of the island. Harriet missed the family, but the kids adjusted fairly well. Things became stable and then comfortable. They socialized with their neighbors and Nathan got involved with charity work. He was especially active with a drug rehabilitation program for teenagers—their second son had battled a drug problem while they were still in New York. Nathan became a figurehead in the organization. The kids in the program looked up to him. So did his family.

Right up until the day he disappeared. He just vanished. Harriet was frantic. She called the police, the hospitals, and everyone they knew. The kids searched for their dad. He simply didn't come home.

About a month later, Harriet got a call from an attorney saying he was representing Nathan. Nathan wanted a divorce. He'd had it with his responsibilities. He wanted to enjoy life, enjoy women, and escape. Here he was in paradise and he'd started to get into the same old grind, and he realized that he needed to get out. He didn't love Harriet anymore. Yes, it was a mid-life crisis, and that's all there was. He didn't want to talk to her: "Send all correspondence to my attorney," he'd instructed. Nathan didn't offer an address or phone number. The one time he called, hoping to avoid Harriet and talk to his daughter, Harriet grabbed the phone and tearfully begged to know why he left. "I want lots of young girls," he told her emotionlessly. "I want my youth. You cheated me out of my youth, and to be honest, I'm finding it." Then he hung up.

This story ends in despair. Nathan drained the family checking account, hoping to hide funds from Harriet. The daughter is the only one to get an occasional call from her dad, who communicates only on the condition that she remain neutral and not try to interfere in his life. The three sons are crushed; one resumed drugs, the other dropped out of his graduate program at college, and the third decided to join the military, abandoning his once-strong religious faith and all control of his future. Harriet is now trying to find financial backing for a small company she wants to start, making hand lotions from a "secret Hawaiian formula." Nathan's mid-life crisis ruined five lives.

What a rationalization for complete selfishness and cruelty. What a lame justification for creating complete chaos. The term "mid-life crisis" is not only overrated, it's exulted, and all this does is excuse a great deal of despicable behavior.

It's true that a sudden confrontation with mortality or failure or lack of achievement can lead to positive results. Dr. Daniel Levinson of Yale University posits that one of the four developmental ages in every man's life includes a "mid-life transition" characterized by this terrifying awareness of ultimate death.[3] This doesn't mean you have to abandon your marriage and strike out on your own. When a jolt of distress leads to renewed commitment and vigor toward laudable goals within the bounds of obligation and maturity, it's seldom a "crisis." Crisis implies destruction, calamity, and demise. The Cuban Missile Crisis nearly brought the end of the world. The "mid-life crisis" has a similar impact on marriages.

THE MYTH OF THE "FRESH START"

To minimize the impact of a sobering jolt, whether it's realization of mortality or consequential separation and divorce, everyone involved starts to euphemize what's going on. One of the most prevalent terms wounded people and observers use to disguise this trauma and disruption is "fresh start." What a glorious-sounding phrase. Fresh is clean, new, untarnished, undamaged, virginal. Fresh vegetables have been plucked from the field just that morning, glistening with dew. When we think of "fresh faces," we envision the well-scrubbed countenances of smiling children, eager to begin a boisterous school day. "Freshness" calls to mind taking an invigorating walk on a crisp morning, while the air stings delightfully on one's cheeks. What a lovely word, filled with hope and expectation.

It's redundant to combine *fresh* with *start*, because both words express beginning, birth, and genesis. It is everyone's dream to erase smudged history and be offered the proverbial "clean slate," to somehow obliterate mistakes as if nothing in the past counted or mattered—and in fact, did not exist. To "make a fresh start" justifies slipping out of a viable marriage. It legitimizes following selfish inclinations, abandoning once-cherished values, and hurting people who at one time meant the most to you. When someone leaves a marriage without exhausting its potential, it should be called "running away," "dodging responsibility," "slipping out the back, Jack." Abandonment of a partner who loves you shouldn't be softened with words like "fresh start."

Because no one really gets a "fresh start." No one leaves a relationship free of memories, of emotions, of guilt or rejection or hostility. No one can instantly shed years of shaping, of forged patterns of interaction. No one becomes a virgin again. Innocence cannot be restored. Later I'll specify the many ways that divorce leaves you different, and the way it can also leave you unchanged. But however you emerge from a marriage, you do so as a fully formed adult, someone with values and history and a world view that will determine your behavior. You take that with you to whatever your next endeavor becomes. The only thing you shed is your marital status and the connection to someone you vowed to cherish for the rest of your life.

Still, I can understand why people use the phrase "fresh start." Once they've been told that the marriage is over, once they hear the devastating words that a mate's love had died, once the books and records have been divided and the child support hashed out, and once the nights become eerily silent, there must be some term bringing consolation. A Fresh Start seems upbeat and optimistic.

"Here I am, sitting in front of my TV dinner in my empty apartment enjoying my Fresh Start," thinks a newly separated husband. He fumbles through his "black book," sweating with fear of rejection, unaccustomed to the vulnerability of the singles world. Even if he's had affairs, even if he's done this before, this time he's unattached. This time his flirting isn't "safe"—he's putting himself on the line and might be expected to enter a deep relationship and even get married again. Somebody could take his advances seriously. There's no home or wife or family to fall back on, no safety net, and the lack of these former ties are what comprise the Fresh Start.

Of course it's true that you do get another chance to form a relationship. You get an opportunity to grow and develop as an individual. But the terms "opportunity" and "chance" fail to recognize that now you're *forced* to do it alone. In a marriage, if you want to start a new career, if you want to take a risk, you may, if you want, do it independently—and have the support and backing of someone who cares. Or if you're married, you can instead choose to make major decisions together, if that's the way you prefer your relationship. The amount of closeness, intimacy, and overlap can be negotiated, but whatever you attempt, you have a context. As a single person, that backdrop, that "given," is taken away from you.

Yes, you can always cultivate a network of good friends, you can always turn to family, and you can always seek the support of therapy. But fundamentally, you are alone. After tumbling out of a secure context, this is innately distressing—at least at first, and often permanently. It is this distress, this anxiety and anguish, that people euphemize into a "learning experience," the source of great emotional and psychological growth. And I agree. Times of duress do force you to shape up, to evaluate and turn around what you don't like. But you don't *need* distress and pressure to make strides.

You have opportunity to change while you're in marriage, and you have opportunity to do so when you're single. The Fresh Start of divorce is in reality a myth that dupes you into thinking that leaving your marriage creates opportunity; what divorce really does is merely switch the setting for it—and it even complicates changes, since its urgency makes decisions less clear-headed and deliberate.

THE DIVORCE INDUSTRY

Most people find it disconcerting to admit that the very professionals supposedly dedicated to helping them achieve what they want actually usher them into an awesome system whose aim is not their happiness but simply expediting their divorce. While I'm sure all participants in the "divorce industry" believe they are acting ethically in the best interests of their clients and for expediency and the preservation of sanity and harmony, the activity of many of these lawyers, doctors, counselors, and self-styled "assistants" is keeping the wheels of divorce spinning. Once you contact an attorney, for example, he'll usually feed you into the moving legal machinery, where momentum tends to keep you processing through until you're finally spit out, divorce decree in hand.

Norman Sheresky and Marya Mannes in *Uncoupling, the Art of Coming Apart: A Guide to Sane Divorce* lament that the primary goal of professionals dealing with divorce is not reconciliation but completion of the divorce process. "Many unhappy marriages are not so hopelessly shot that with better understanding they cannot be made more workable, and perhaps enjoyable," they write. " 'Understanding' and 'timing' are the key words here, for the longer honest confrontations are postponed by unhappy husbands and wives, the more steadily the chances for accommodation erode."[4]

What's the first thing that individuals do when they move out? Call a lawyer. Suddenly they're vindictive; they don't want their ex-spouse to start pilfering from the joint checking account. They want to make sure they're protected. If they're angry enough, they want to show they mean business, and that usually means filing some "scary" legal papers. They think about custody. They think about losing their home, the family business, a percentage of their income earned via the graduate degree their mate put them through school to earn.

But attorneys are not marriage counselors, though most realize that they have to be to some extent. If they don't want to overstep their professional competence and prefer to stick to the legalities at hand, they won't try to influence you to stay in your marriage or go through with the divorce. They'll simply do what you ask. When you come in, lawyers are conscious of the two hundred dollars per hour or more you're paying for their time in your determination to get this show on the road; if you say you want a divorce, most lawyers will follow your instructions. After all, that's their job.

It's also their livelihood, and many have "policies" which, naturally enough, tend to maximize their profit—all according to standard procedures; all ethical and reasonable. But they scoot you through the system, sometimes forcing you to be more money-grubbing than you're inclined to be, sometimes urging you to be more ruthless in your accusations or modest in stating your acquisitions; and ultimately, this advice affects not only settlement figures and custody arrangements but the relationship you maintain with your spouse for the rest of your life.

Catherine Napolitane and Victoria Pelligrino, in *Living and Loving After Divorce*, baldly state "Facts About Lawyers" that ought to frighten anyone with the least amount of uncertainty about breaking up: "Divorce lawyers often push for divorce, to your detriment. Many lawyers will not be interested in helping you reconcile, if that is a possibility . . . The reason—they do not make money from a reconciliation . . . They want to wrap up your case as soon as possible so they can collect their fee." This information comes from authors who have experienced divorce themselves.[5]

If you happen to be rich, you're likely to seek and receive abundant assistance from the legal profession. After all, the more hours your counsel puts into your case, the higher your bill. And sometimes their fee is connected to the size of the award made, so they may maneuver tirelessly to gain the largest share of the communal pie.

Joseph Epstein also notes that the well-to-do often use their resources to circumvent restrictive laws: "Divorce is a process that favors the rich," he writes.[6] With the best representation you can, depending on your position, either receive substantial alimony or be excused from paying it. You can gain custody, or maneuver your assets so you don't have to split or lose them. Wealthy people often get what they want out of the dismantled marriage. "But they get soaked by lawyers doing it," Epstein concludes.[7]

And the person most likely to end up all wet is the husband. According to Robert Cassidy in *What Every Man Should Know About Divorce*, "The man usually gets stuck for all the legal fees, including the cost of his 'opponent's' lawyer, even in cases where neither party admits being wrong . . .

"As a result, women are encouraged to litigate matters that could be settled outside court," forcing even more of a irreconcilable, adversarial relationship between the spouses. Cassidy goes on to describe one man whose total attorney fees left him destitute and forced him "to go back to Brooklyn and live with Mama," a state he found "disgraceful."[8] You may think you're just getting out of a marriage, but you could be in for a whole new way of life.

Many people liken their divorce process to a nightmare or a feeling as if they're acting in a play, and so it is appropriate that divorce provides you not just with professional contacts but with a cast of characters. Your lawyer will take on his or her own role. Psychologist Kenneth Kressel, in *The Process of Divorce*, divides lawyers into two types: "counselors," whose main concern is cooperation for the sake of children involved, and "advocates," who are willing to battle head-on in order to gain their clients the best economic outcome possible.[9]

Then there are the other players, all with their separate scripts. Unfortunately, according to Kressel's findings, the various types of divorce professionals rarely orchestrate a unified theme—and each may provide you with his own shocking plot twists. Lawyers understandably focus on procedural and financial matters and try to minimize emotional interference; therapists tend to zero in on feelings, downplaying the importance of monetary concerns. These professionals end up giving conflicting advice or working at cross-purposes, complicating the plot. But they do share one ominous characteristic: both kinds of helpers encourage the same *denouement*—the tragedy of divorce.

Some of the most prominent personnel in the divorce industry remain disguised. For example, there's a radio psychiatrist in Los Angeles, where I live, who is known for his ability to cut through callers' rationalizations and euphemisms to expose underlying motives and fears. He really "lays it on the line" for the distressed people who phone begging for means to handle crises in their relationships. While they're in a state of confusion and anxiety, they want this doctor to tell them what to do; they appreciate that he's so direct and confrontive. So they're grateful when he says, as he often does, "If he's so inconsiderate of you, if she's so mean to you, if he's so verbally cruel to you, if she's so restrictive of you, if he's

so possessive of you . . . then get out!'' There's usually
a long pause.

"Well, I guess I should . . ." the caller tentatively
replies. Another long pause. Then, fearful of taking too
much air time and appearing ungrateful for the free insight, the caller acquiesces. "Thank you, Doctor,'' he
or she concludes resolutely, hanging up to phone the
"family attorney" and enter the inescapable system.

Now, I agree that if there's a serious, ongoing, damaging syndrome in a relationship, it should and must end.
And I agree that sometimes people need to step back—
maybe get away for a few days or even weeks—to see
things clearly. But when a radio psychiatrist, who only
knows the first name of the person he's counseling, who's
never met the other spouse, and who asks for no history
and receives no follow-up, gives firm "suggestions" to
leave a marriage, then you know that marriage bonds are
taken much too lightly. You know that it's too easy for
people with credentials to get away with things. You know
that many marriages are affected adversely—not only the
unions of those who hang up the telephone and head for
the legal aid society, but the relationships of perhaps
thousands of nameless listeners who grasp onto this psychiatrist's words and diagnose their own marriages as
terminal.

The power of the airwaves may give a single psychologist or counselor wide influence, but his impact may be
diluted by the fact that he's a disembodied voice anybody
can dial up for free. When couples pay for private therapy, they're much more likely to carry out their mentor's
recommendations. After all, by keeping an appointment
and writing out their check, they've not only made a
statement that they trust and have confidence in this care-
giver, but they're investing lots of cash to prove it. They'd
certainly look—and feel—foolish if they simply handed
over that check and then ignored everything they paid
for. Also, clients want to please their therapists, whom
they may unconsciously equate with parental authority
rather than simply a skilled, though fallible, source of
advice. It takes a lot of courage for a client to say, "I
think you're wrong about that,'' because he's basically
calling into question the therapist's ability. The whole
idea of going to a counselor is to find somebody whose

judgment is more sound than your own. Questioning the suggestions or conclusions of a therapist may be perceived as tantamount to saying that he's incompetent.

Unfortunately, the new attitudes about marriage, gender roles, and divorce that I've detailed previously here have become fairly standard among psychological professionals. In fact, many of the seminars and workshops over the past few years at the annual conferences of the American Psychological Association seem to imply several divorce-promoting themes, such as: "Being single or gay are just as desirable as being married (so there's no need to make marriage your goal or preserve the one you've got)"; "Don't put up with difficulties in your marriage—leave"; and "Independence and separate identities are good for you."

And why *shouldn't* counselors hold popular values—both the therapists and their clients are subject to social sways; the advice-givers are themselves part of general society. I would guess that psychologists are no less immune to bad marriages and other mind-based problems than the rest of the world. Indeed, many people seem to think that "you have to be crazy to be a shrink," or that therapists choose that profession because they have their own problems to solve.

Certainly movies have reinforced such stereotypes—remember Dudley Moore in *Lovesick*? Not only did he fall in love with a patient, but he regularly napped while one client silently watched the clock tick away his expensive hour.

In the Whoopie Goldberg film *Clara's Heart* (1988), a pompous pop psychologist played by Spalding Gray spies a comely young mother in one of his seminars, makes a play for her and, after winning her allegiance, convinces her to leave her husband for him. Furthermore, the mother's son is referred to the shrink's doltish colleague, played by screenwriter Mark Medoff, who is unable to see through the teenager's clearly fabricated stories. Obviously, such portrayals are ridiculous, but they do suggest that introspection and examination of emotions are often overly glorified and do not necessarily add to personal or marital health (yours *or* the counselor's, these films imply). You can overanalyze situations to the point where the normal seems pathological, to where satisfaction is picked apart into discontent.

Yes, I am saying that going to a shrink can exacerbate a small problem into a crisis, that rehashing specific words and actions can get you angry about something that previously just slid off your back. It's happened to all of us on our own, of course, when we've gone over an evening or incident in our minds. Just think of the potential hysteria when we have someone else to pique us into additional sources of ire. At the time, what Harry said was no big deal, you just took it in stride. But now that you think about it in connection with last week . . . and that other night . . . well, maybe that son-of-a-bitch *did* mean something nasty! It took a therapist to help you make the level pasture of your relationship into the Grand Tetons.

Then there are those psycho-healers who come on the scene after you've separated. Now that divorce is such a breeze, nobody's willing to live with marital discomfort for even a moment, and there are lots of quick decisions to call it quits. Many mental health professionals have decided to meet this growing need by actually specializing in facilitating personable parting. The separated couple comes to a therapist and says, "We don't love each other anymore. We're getting a divorce."

The counselor nods acknowledgment of this given and says, "Okay, so let's post-mortem the split so you can get past the trauma and so you won't make the same mistakes in your next marriage." The counselor *could* start out saying, "Let's see what went wrong so you can decide if divorce is really the best thing to do." But no, divorce is usually taken for granted; once a couple verbalizes that the marriage is over, too many therapists assume it's irrevocable, or that they really mean it, which they may not, or that it's not worth trying to see if the relationship can be repaired. I'm not lambasting everyone in my profession—indeed in many cases the efforts of counselors are the one factor that saves an otherwise crumbling marriage. I would certainly recommend that couples in trouble get assistance. But be careful whom you choose and what you say when you present your problem. A troublesome number of my colleagues tend to avoid "value judgments" at the expense of marriages and the long-term needs of the individuals involved.

NOTES

1. Sheehy, Gail. *Passages*. New York: E.P. Dutton, 1976.

2. Singer, Laura J. *Stages: The Crises that Shape Your Marriage*. New York: Grosset and Dunlap, 1980.

3. Levinson, Daniel. *The Season of a Man's Life*. New York: Knopf, 1978.

4. Mannes, Marya, and Sheresky, Norman. *Uncoupling, the Art of Coming Apart: A Guide to Sane Divorce*. New York: Viking Press, 1972, p. xi.

5. Napolitane, Catherine, and Pelligrino, Victoria. *Living and Loving After Divorce*. New York: Rawson Associates, 1977, p. 16.

6. Epstein, Joseph. *Divorced in America*. New York: E.P. Dutton, 1974, p. 114.

7. Ibid., p. 114.

8. Cassidy, Robert. *What Every Man Should Know About Divorce*. Washington, D.C.: New Republic Books, 1977.

9. Kressel, Kenneth. *The Process of Divorce*. New York: Basic Books, 1985.

EXIT LINES
AND EXCUSES

So you think you're ready for a divorce. You've had it; your love has died; it's over. Period. You send out icy vibrations: "Don't try resuscitating this corpse, because even if you did manage to resurrect the dead, the zombie-esque hulk wouldn't last long." No, there's no help for it, you want out.

Or maybe you're the one who heard those words. Who received the shocking or anticipated blow. He moved out. He's living with her. He wants a divorce. Speak to him through his lawyer.

You've asked yourself a thousand times: Why? What went wrong? What spoiled a relationship that in the beginning was all hope and sweetness and good intentions? You come up with reasons, convincing or not. You hurt, you cry—as you're leaving, or as you're being left. You're overcome with feelings and yet you grope for rationality, you cling to words.

And yet, the reasons most people give for separating and divorcing are poor or invalid. Sure, we've come to accept them; we've come to legitimize them and assume they've got some merit. But in many cases, they're just fancy excuses for fleeing to a more novel relationship, or for not facing up to the difficult problems you could overcome if you were willing to work at it. They're rationalizations for the cruel and nasty things you've done to your partner, they're retribution for the equally miserable things he or she may have done to you. But they don't mean you have to get a divorce.

Once, you had a spark. Once, you were in love. For a long time you plotted and shared your goals, your thoughts, your achievements. You forged a life together; you had a commitment. It's true that people change—they'd be dead if they didn't. Change is a fundamental part of living, and even those with the most regimented routines have peaks and valleys and new understandings and growing contentments. Just because people change is no reason to get a divorce either.

And neither are the usual common exit lines. Reasons are necessary—they're expected. Without reasons, you cannot escape, you cannot face others, you cannot face yourself. So you come up with something plausible, something others can accept, but the truth is that many times they're just facades for your own underlying needs, requirements that have nothing to do with your marriage. Please understand that I'm not suggesting that every reason is phony or that every marriage should be endured at all costs. Shortly I'll detail just which unions are inappropriate to continue. But in many cases, rational-sounding words are just masks for discomfort, cowardice, shame, or selfishness. Most of the reasons people give for their departure can be discredited. For example, which of the following ten major rationalizations for separation have you used, or do you fear hearing?

—"We're not well-matched."
—"I must pursue this opportunity for the love of my life."
—"I need my _____." (Fill in the blank: freedom, independence, sexual fulfillment, career, whatever.)
—"We can't seem to work out our differences—we're always arguing."
—"We've grown apart."
—"I can't live with your _____." (Fill in the blank: sloppiness, forgetfulness, hobby, habit, incessant talking, nagging, etc.)
—"I need love, passion, affection; I want to be appreciated."
—"If you think you can do that to me—good riddance!"

—"I can't make him want me."

"—She'll be happier without me."

These explanations can sound so logical, so sensible. You grow apart, and that's that; you just have no reason to go on. You feel stifled by your partner and you seek your "own space." You meet someone more beautiful, more lively, more exciting, and you can't be expected to pass up that kind of opportunity. Right? Wrong. In the following chapters, I'll tell you where each of these arguments fails.

First, however, we should define the cases where divorce *is* appropriate. I do not maintain that every divorce is wrong, and in some cases, divorce is imperative. We've just come to view divorce too casually, to ascribe to a large number of viable relationships the pallor of doom. Marriage is usually worth saving. But in some cases . . .

CHAPTER 8

Exceptional Situations: When You Should Divorce

At the same time that my research showed divorce to be a catastrophe too quickly embraced, it also reaffirmed the necessity for divorce in a limited number of sad situations. There are clearly cases when divorce is not only inevitable but the only sane way out of intolerable and dangerous circumstances; and there are other, less clear cases where it simply becomes foolish to keep headbanging against a very sharp and wounding wall. Not to acknowledge the reality of these situations is to doom people to dishonesty and atrophy in the best case, and physical harm or even death in the worst.

On the other hand, I should offer a caveat. Most divorced people reading this will probably think to themselves: "Of course, that was *my* situation. I just *had* to get out." Not surprisingly, they have good reasons why their failed marriages were really doomed from the start (only they just didn't know it). Hindsight allows them to see that they'd chosen the wrong person (though they just couldn't see it at the time). Or, as years intervened and things weren't exactly the same as they had been, they needed to part and move on to their present life—which, they unhesitatingly add, is better anyway.

I listen appreciatively and applaud the human spirit. I am not the one to judge the extent of others' pain, nor their prospects to heal their futures. Given our resilience, even in the midst of the painful, illogical, or bizarre, we cling to justifications, and sometimes rationalizations, for our behavior. In most cases, these explanations are, at least to some extent, accurate descriptions of what goes on. People do "grow apart," have affairs, deny affection, or ruin self-confidence. Articulating reasons for your divorce allows you to bounce back from depression and disorientation. Assigning blame is a legitimate way to protect your self-esteem. After the fact, you'll only feel more distress if you decide that it didn't have to happen or it really wasn't for the best.

But even those people who swore to me that their divorces were appropriate and beneficial agreed that nowadays people are too quick to let go, too focused on the moment's pain to see the whole of what they're throwing away. If only they'd slowed down; if only they'd talked it over with a counselor (with an open mind); if only they'd had something in writing to warn them of the perilous move they were making . . . they might have kept their families together and worked through the chaos.

I'm not saying that unless your particular situation is described below, you definitely should not divorce. Individual cases are idiosyncratic and personal; what is tolerable to one personality may make another crazy. Still, relatively few problems cannot be overcome given two people willing to work them out. Or even one willing to accede.

In fact, the times when divorce is necessary boil down to the following five categories of circumstances.

CHRONIC ADDICTION OR SUBSTANCE ABUSE

The Betty Ford Center is named after a woman whose family *understood* her addiction to prescription drugs and saw her through the crisis. From what I can tell, it seems that most of the celebrities who convalesce at this center are not abandoned by their loved ones, but rather strengthen their family bonds by completing a program of rehabilitation. In most cases, there is no question of divorce if a spouse is drug- (including alcohol-) dependent. Dependence in itself is certainly no reason for divorce. In fact, it may be a sign that the affected spouse cares desperately about the marriage—it is precisely because many people *value their marriages so much* and feel that they don't deserve a happy one, or believe they've botched it, that they become self-punishing, accepting all blame for their behavior and using that "failure" to further fuel their need for drugs.

Chronic substance addiction or abuse *is* cause for divorce, however, in the few cases where the addicted person:

—refuses to recognize that he or she has a problem (one way is by refusing to get counseling and/or treatment);

—acknowledges the problem but refuses to include the spouse in any efforts to change or receive treatment for the problem;

—repeatedly tries to reform or seek treatment for his disease, but always (over a period of years) slips back fairly quickly into dependency.

I interviewed Mona Kelly, a forty-three-year-old salesperson for a Providence, Rhode Island, corporation, a year after her separation from Morgan Kelly, six years her junior. Morgan was a struggling stockbroker who had enjoyed phenomenal success on one prediction made via a strategy he developed. He followed the progress of companies with certain characteristics and found one on the cusp of exploding. He tipped off all his customers, his family, friends—anyone he could buttonhole—and overnight their money multiplied thirty times. Suddenly he was the whiz kid of his already prestigious firm. He spoke on TV, he was approached by other companies, publishers asked him to write about his strategy, and computer programmers begged to market his program.

Since his college days at Brown University in Rhode Island, Morgan had smoked marijuana. He used it at first at "pot parties," and then whenever he needed to relax. When he met Mona ten years ago, he was using it about once a week; during their years together, it seemed he needed it more and more, until recently he was smoking it several times a day.

Whenever Mona wanted to have sex with him, Morgan had to smoke two or three joints to get "loosened up." Even then, he seemed strangely reserved, not at all like the wildly passionate youth who had driven her to Narragansett Beach one evening and, with the moonlit surf reflected in the windshield, thrown her down on the car hood. In those early days, they'd leap into bed in the afternoons when Morgan snuck home from his graduate courses; they'd languish in piles of leaves during weekend hikes in the mountains.

But when they moved to Los Angeles and Morgan left the academic world, he began to tighten. His mother, reeling from her own divorce from Morgan's father, moved nearby and unleashed her pent-up anger. Concurrently, under pressure to maintain an impeccable image for his new Beverly Hills stockbrokerage clients, Morgan bought thousand-dollar hand tailored suits and a BMW in which to scoot around town.

Morgan became competitive. He told Mona he had to concentrate on his work. He didn't mention it, but Mona knew he was using pot during the day. He grunted when she tried to talk to him about her feelings and her fears for his health. She tried to tell him that she needed his attention, his cooperation, to sort out their problems. In desperation, she dressed provocatively, pirouetted in front of him, and said she was going out for the evening, but Morgan's eyes remained trained on his home computer screen.

That was when he began smoking pot heavily every evening "to unwind." He had his little welcome-home rituals at 2:00 P.M. when he entered their two-bedroom apartment. He'd grab a beer, sit at his perfectly ordered desk, take out an antique Tiffany box, unroll his stash, and sit there, feet up, smoking and staring out the window, sometimes for as long as two hours. Mona dared not say a word to him during this contemplative time, and afterwards she felt as if the words she did say had to be carefully chosen.

Still, she respected Morgan and wanted their marriage to work. She wasn't intentionally looking for someone when Isaac Rossman, a drop-dead-gorgeous department store buyer, asked her for drinks after work one day. She became feverishly excited in a way she hadn't experienced in years. Still, she could never cheat on Morgan.

Instead, she confronted him with his withdrawal; she told him that she felt nervous about his unpredictable reactions, that she wanted the easy sexuality they'd once known, and some open communication. Morgan initially protested, but he relented when she insisted they see a marriage counselor. He swore that they didn't have any problems—"just the normal pressures of anybody trying to make it in this world."

In the counselor's office, Mona cried. She remembered the attention Morgan had lavished on her just two years before, when they still lived in Rhode Island. He didn't need the crutch of pot then; couldn't they just go back? What was this crazy need to be a financial success in the flashy but hectic world of Beverly Hills?

Morgan sat there, stone cold. He didn't even pass Mona the Kleenex to blot her tears. "She's just being emotional," he replied. "She knows I'm under a lot of pressure right now, and that soon it will all pay off. Can't she be patient?"

The counselor told Morgan that his wife was deeply unhappy—he needed to give earnest attention to his addiction as well as start talking to her. He asked Morgan to stop his damaging habit—or lose his marriage.

"Pot isn't addictive," Morgan countered. But sensing the seriousness of the situation, he momentarily softened. "I'll try to lay off," he pledged.

But he did nothing differently; in fact, he smoked even more marijuana than before, but now it was on the sly—Mona could smell it on his clothes and his breath. When she reminded him of his promise, he grunted, said, "Okay," and continued his smoking and his withdrawal.

"I needed somebody to talk to me, to respond to me. Somebody whose brains weren't fried, whose pupils weren't constantly dilated," Mona told me in our interview. "Morgan became a brick wall, he just tuned out the world. He said he wanted me, that he wanted our marriage, but he was simply too self-centered to change. We tried three different counselors, and each time he said he'd quit and work on our marriage. But he never did."

The demise of Mona's marriage was inevitable because *good intentions are not enough.* Even though Morgan professed a desire to change, in reality that was just a stalling tactic. Mona became alternately furious and vindictive. Here she cared immensely, wanted to *save* the marriage, and Morgan just sat back and "yessed" her. Maybe he *did* love her. But he was *more* intent on pleasing—or destroying—himself.

The marriage was doomed because it embodied the three Marital Failure Factors: (1) Refusal to recognize the problem: Morgan insisted that marijuana was not addictive and that their marital distress was "normal"; (2) Refusal to take one's spouse seriously: He placated Mona by saying he'd change, but he remained uncommunicative and unresponsive to her; and (3) Repeated relapses into dependency: His addiction switched from being an open form of "relaxation" to a secret habit, despite pleas from Mona and three different therapists.

I am not an expert in the field of substance abuse. But I do know that the effects of alcohol and "hard" drugs can be devastating not only to the user but to an extended network of family, friends, and co-workers. I can only suggest that any wife or husband who observes a spouse using such substances or even acting suspiciously *not* just sweep it under the carpet or make assumptions. Get help. This is urgent and imperative, not just for the sake of your marriage—which in extreme cases may not be able to survive—but for the physical and emotional health of your partner and yourself.

PSYCHOSIS

Mental illness ranges in severity from mild and infrequent to perpetually present and impossible. Certainly, when your spouse is on the extreme end of this continuum, and therapy and other measures have failed, you may have to save and salvage your own life. You also must spare yourself from martyrdom if the process of recuperation is so burdensome as to cause intense, unrelenting stress on you, without prognosis for improvement. There should be no valiant heroics just for pity or praise. Anyone who would tell you to "stick it out" after a reasonable amount of time, and after you've seen to the needs of your spouse, is not principled—*they're punishing you*. You deserve support and sympathy, nothing less.

PHYSICAL OR MENTAL ABUSE

The agony of physical and mental abuse was chronicled by Charlotte Fedders in Laura Elliott's book *Shattered Dreams*.[1] In blatant, wrenching terms, she reveals the secret anguish of her life with John Fedders, former chief enforcement officer for the Securities and Exchange Commission. Her shocking experiences attest to the fact that abuse is prevalent across all socioeconomic groups, and that even well-educated and aware women find it difficult to break out of an abusive situation.

With admissions like Fedders', some of the shame of living with abuse has been dispelled. The most achieving women—married to well-respected men—can be so mired in low self-esteem that they accept themselves as the cause of their own abuse. In addition, abused women often justifiably fear the financial and physical insecurity of abandoning a familiar life and therefore stay, ever hoping that their husbands will change. The causes and particulars of each case of physical and mental abuse are far too complex and personal even to be touched upon here. But the problem is often serious enough to not only warrant divorce, but to require it.

There are many gray areas. What constitutes "mental abuse"? When is a slap permissible and when is it intolerable? In the days before no-fault divorce laws, "mental cruelty" was often listed as grounds for divorce and was used as a catch-all for many types of unpleasantness, sometimes in situations where there was very little discord at all. The problem is that people are too quick to label nasty interchanges, insults, or breaches of agreements as "mental cruelty." And with the current sensitivity to the serious and important topic of abuse, those who want out may use the term "mental abuse" when it is not really appropriate. I urge anyone with suspicions of physical or emotional abuse to immediately seek outside help. While it is true that some perpetrators of both physical and mental abuse can be rehabilitated, no one should ever remain—no matter what the reasoning or explanation—where physical or mental well-being is in jeopardy.

EMOTIONAL AND PRACTICAL NEEDS TO DIVORCE

Sometimes a relationship becomes so unfulfilling and miserable, over such a long period, that the only way the constant tension and agony can be relieved is to divorce.

It happens. But not nearly as often as people make it happen.

The trouble is that the popular mind-set switches into a combative "I won't take it" mode the moment you *begin* a fight. You get embroiled in that one sometimes extremely volatile argument, and it becomes so intense that it overshadows all your areas of compatibility. Never mind that you have shared ten years and two children and furnishing a home and building bonds with your neighbors; never mind that you have the same religious and political outlooks, or you like to do the same things on Sundays. You're positive that this issue, whatever it is, is so fundamental and basic that you could never compromise.

Or you take this one disagreement and make it the basis to examine everything else in its negative light. "If he could feel this way about this subject, then he must be nuts!" From that perspective you see that all the other borderline behaviors you let slip by in the past were really manifestations of this unbearable character trait and further evidence that you're right and he's completely ridiculous. And so you walk out, pay him back, let him see that you simply won't allow this kind of attitude or behavior. At this moment, all the good stuff is intentionally forgotten. The repulsive idea or action takes over and looms so menacing and intolerable that the good stuff doesn't matter.

It happened to Jan Storer, a magazine writer and the new wife of Bill Jenkens. At thirty-six, Jan had a fairly extensive reputation writing for many prestigious magazines. Bill, a successful shopping center developer, had paid for their lavish wedding and then moved Jan from her apartment cluttered with papers and travel souvenirs into his spacious farmhouse-style "rancho" on the outskirts of Los Angeles.

"What an opportunity," Jan thought upon marrying Bill. No more need to do the dumb stories she knew she could sell but which she found excruciating—the poignant Christmas tale of a family meeting long-lost relatives; the miracle mother whose bout with infertility led triumphantly to a houseful of disgustingly happy children. Now she could pursue only the ideas that interested her. Finally she was free to enjoy her craft.

Jan wrote a series of articles on women executives for a women's monthly magazine that was such a big hit that a major publisher approached her to do a book combining the stories and capsulizing the executives' recipes for success. Jan was thrilled and started compiling her interviews.

Midway through the project, she found to her delight that she was pregnant. During her expectant months, she was often preoccupied with thoughts of the coming baby, preparing her home, and spending what she considered to be precious private time with Bill. She'd promised her finished manuscript to her publisher in January; in December her baby was born and the book was only halfway completed.

Luckily, her publisher was understanding and did not pressure her. But Bill started grousing, at first teasingly and then rather cruelly. When the editor of a hugely popular national magazine called Jan for a juicy assignment to interview a major political candidate, she jumped at it, anticipating the break of her career. But Bill forbade her to take the assignment.

"How dare you tell me how to run my business affairs!" Jan fumed. Bill became even more stubborn.

"No magazine work until you turn in the book!" he insisted. "You've got enough to do feeding Jason, keeping the house going, and getting that book done," he told her with finality. "No articles unless that book is in!"

Jan couldn't believe this was the once-supportive man she had married. But here he was, acting like a male chauvinist, not only relegating the household chores to her but telling her how and what to write. She was on edge because of his incessant pushing about the book anyway, since he kept implying that she was incompetent and would never get it done. "I'll write what and when I want to!" she screamed.

"No you won't!" he screamed back. "You're married now. You have to listen to me!"

Jan couldn't stand it; she rushed to the door, grabbed her purse, and leapt into her car. She drove to her girlfriend's house. Luckily, Lynne was home.

Luckily only for Jan, because Lynne in short order was subjected to a tantrum against Bill's condescending management. Their relationship had to be based on mutual respect, Jan ranted, or else it could never work. And now Bill had proven that he didn't respect her, that he would treat her like a child rather than a competent professional able to make her own decisions. She wanted to stay with Lynne for a few days with Jason to decide where to go from here.

In one afternoon, Jan moved in her word processor, Jason's crib and high chair, and three-fourths of her clothes, and Lynne became distressed. She asked how long this move would last. Needing to prove her self-sufficiency, Jan immediately went apartment-hunting and found a vacant place just two blocks away from Bill; she could move in immediately.

And so began a series of events that led to Jan's swift divorce. Angered that she would take such a drastic move, Bill sought female companionship, beginning that first night Jan left for Lynne's. Convinced that his carousing proved his lack of devotion, Jan too began to date. The couple's tit-for-tat battle of pride built hostility upon hostility until it was impossible for the couple to retract their actions or their words. Fueled by anger, it was easy to call a lawyer, and surprisingly easy to file the divorce papers. Bill, determined to be the playboy, didn't seek custody of Jason. Jan, whose role was supercompetent professional, needed to "do it all" by assuming child care as well as the national article and book.

Without Bill riding her, Jan set up her own schedules and finished both the interview and her manuscript triumphantly.

But in this private war, both sides were losers. Their relationship crumbled needlessly. When stunned friends asked why they were divorcing, Jan's past answer was: "Because Bill didn't want me to have a career." Bill's reply was: "Because she walked out on me. I don't know why she left—she just had this ridiculous point she had to prove."

"Do you regret getting divorced?" people would ask. "No," both would reply.

From my own vantage point as a psychologist, I could see a different perspective. A bit of dialogue probably would've revealed Bill's expectations about the role of mother and his difficulty reconciling it with the profes-

sional Jan he loved and respected. Jan also held role-
based conflicts, and the couple could have forged new
patterns of interaction that were less stubborn and more
observant of underlying expectations and motives. When
the problem arose, it might have taken just one or two
hours with a therapist, or even an evening with a percep-
tive and understanding mutual friend. But once Jan
slammed the door, Bill's pride took over and he could
not appear vulnerable by apologizing or seeking the help
of a counselor. And once Jan was at Lynne's front door,
Lynne had no choice but to support her friend.

Yet in their minds, both Jan and Bill persuaded themselves that their divorce was the end result of a deep-
seated, global problem that was unresolvable. They
choked back their love because of infuriating moments
that compounded themselves. When Jan heard the premise of my book, she wholeheartedly endorsed it: "Yes,
people head for divorce court too fast; they should make
every attempt to stay together." Then, just two minutes
later, when I asked her about her own divorce, she replied, "Well, we were one of the exceptional cases who
are better off apart."

It happens too often.

So how do you know if your situation is one where you
truly *are* better off, or if, with enough determination, you
could rebuild a love-filled, satisfying relationship? Norman Sheresky and Marya Mannes in *Uncoupling: The
Art of Coming Apart* define that point like this: "When
you feel you can function better without your spouse than
with him; when you'd rather be alone or with somebody
else than with him usually; when your children would
profit if one parent is gone; when there's no fun left."[2]
This definition of the time to part is unsuccessful because
it is too loose and global and can be made to cover just
about any period of marital stress—including predictable, normal ones. *Every* marriage undergoes times of
flux and estrangement; every wife thinks sometimes of
glory she lost because at the moment it seems her husband stood in her way. What does it mean exactly for
children to "profit" if one parent is gone—a prospect I
find difficulty to imagine unless the situation is extreme?
I'm afraid that Sheresky and Mannes's definition could
be seen as another easy out.

Abigail Trafford, in *Crazy Time*, writes that loss of equality in a relationship is cause for its demise. A healthy relationship has partners switching dominance and submission as the situation calls for it; a doomed marriage has reached what Trafford terms "Deadlock": "In Deadlock marriages, the power balance between husband and wife mimics the psychological dynamics between parent and child, lord and vassal, lady and servant, overdog and underdog, oppressor and oppressed."[3]

I agree only partially with this view of when divorce is inevitable.

Yes, people get into "deadlocks"; the balance of power can become unbearably stuck. Yes, there are periods of time when you like your mate and his company more than at other times. But even under this conditions, people don't *have* to break up. Both Sheresky-Mannes and Trafford make it sound as if the partners in a marriage have no choice, that their marriage jumps into the gutter before their eyes and they just stand back helplessly and watch events take shape. These writers' definitions imply that the two people involved have little self-determination or power. *Whap!* Suddenly "there's no fun left." *Bam!* A three-ton boulder gets plopped on the marital scale, weighting the once-genteel husband's balance and making him into an ogreish dictator. Not very likely.

In most cases, there is a slow, and probably not steady, decline in the quality of the relationship; a series of problems or discontentments get swept under the rug until the carpet bulges and bursts. At every whisk of the broom, a decision is made to damage the relationship, though that decision may be unconscious or repressed.

Most people know their lives are in decline, that their lover hasn't wanted sex in weeks, that the daily routine has gotten mechanized, that they become less interested in their mate's career, his dreams for the future, his feelings about the moment. It's a lot easier to simply ignore these warning flags. People who get divorced usually do.

NOT THE MARRYING KIND

There's also the theory that certain personality types simply can't successfully stay married. One of the first therapists to advance this idea in a popular book was Edmund

Bergler, M.D. Writing from a psychoanalytic perspective in *Divorce Won't Help*, he described "neurotic marriages" in which people trapped in their neuroses set up patterns of behavior that perpetuate those neuroses. Normal people, he wrote, don't get caught up in self-destructive patterns of behavior; neurotic ones can't help it, and therefore divorce won't solve their problems—only postpone them to subsequent relationships where the same needs surface again and again.[4]

Some of the statements made by Bergler in 1948 seem antiquated, if not downright offensive, given women's subsequent advances and the sexual revolution. But it's true that many people, due to their early family environments, have learned unconstructive ways of relating or have needs that are inappropriate and deleterious. And now that divorce is "no-fault" and easy to obtain, we can look at those "repeaters" and see that they must be responding, at least in part, to inner directives rather than merely a string of irascible mates.

Bergler's iridescent pearl of wisdom is that the problems in marriages stem from behaviors and needs originating deep in the personalities of the two individuals, not from external and reasonable circumstances beyond either partner's control. But unfortunately, nowadays we can't say, "You've got a lousy personality trait that you ought to work on," or "You need to change your communication style," or "You're being rotten to your mate." Under the banner of being "nonjudgmental," the trend is to say that you and your warring mate are "just different," not pointing a finger at one person who had untenable needs or behaved abysmally.

It's a crime that it's now out-of-bounds to correct someone for his moral failure. You can't say she was wrong because she had an affair and wanted out; you can't say his desire to "find his own space" is a ridiculous and unacceptable fantasy. And certainly never impugn someone's character, as Bergler does, by saying that they're basically weird or sick and therefore, unless they get help or otherwise understand their patterns, they will continue their lives in a helix, spiraling back to the same mistakes ceaselessly.

Another approach is taken in recent research on temperament, which suggests that people are born with different kinds of dispositions. The "easy baby" will grow up to follow his calm inclination; the "difficult" baby will need more care, channeling, and discipline to achieve the same end in our restricted and mannerly world.

The temperament you were born with sticks with you throughout your life. You can fight your natural inclinations and even get into habits that are contrary to them if you want to. If you recognize these natural proclivities, you can sort out which problems originate in controllable personal characteristics and which are manifestations of the two of you together. In either case, you can do something about the problem.

Similarly, some people come through their childhood and adolescence easygoing, content, and agreeable. Some might even call these people passive to a degree, since they're equally pleased with any of several options in a given situation and they have no need to enforce their opinions most of the time. These people, due to their dispositions, have a better-than-average chance of making their marriage a success, because they are less likely to be disturbed and therefore less likely to be argumentative and feisty. They get along well with strong-willed people without harboring resentments or eventually exploding; they are also smoothly compatible with other generally placid types. On the other hand, even the most even temperament is no protection against a spouse's cheating, or his magnifying some other flaw in order to ruin what could be an enduring alliance.

WHEN IT'S TIME TO SAY GOODBYE

My idea of the point when separation is unavoidable has four components, all of which must be present over a period of *at least* several months:

1. Your day-to-day relationship is so punishing, distant, or unbearable that your functioning is impaired.
2. You strive to be apart from your mate as much as possible.
3. You would unhesitatingly choose to be alone for the rest of your life rather than to continue on with your partner.

4. Your basic values have diverged irreconcilably (e.g., he values monogamy, she insists on diversity; she adheres to religious tenets, he has conflicting religious requirements; he refuses to have children, she believes marriage means having a family).

If you fit all four of the above criteria, you should get a divorce. If you fit only one, the situation is likely to be savable, with assistance. If two or three are applicable to you, divorce may be your only answer, but I would still urge you to take plenty of time and seek a counselor who views divorce as a regrettable last resort.

ACCEPTING REJECTION

Sometimes the most difficult thing to do is to accept the fact that you are one of the cases with no choice but to divorce. You want to stay married. You still love your husband or wife; you see there's plenty you still share. You're willing to make changes—almost anything!—because you believe in marriage, you want your family intact, and because this is a person you do not want to lose. The prospect of divorce makes you cry; the idea that your spouse doesn't love you anymore crumples your spirit.

If you've offered him this book and he won't accept it; if you've pleaded that she get counseling with you but she adamantly refuses; if you've adjusted everything he's ever criticized about you and he scarcely notices—keep trying. At least for a while.

One of the most common reasons why a husband (or wife) ends a marriage is not that love has completely withered, or that life with the same person has become unbearable. Rather, he's found somebody new and exciting. Somebody with whom he can be compatible and start again, feeling younger and sexier and refreshed. Someone who makes him laugh and gives him good sex and has lots of intriguingly unknown life experience to tell him about. Not necessarily anyone better than you are. Just someone different and compelling.

Barbara Gordon, in *Jennifer Fever*, calls much-younger ego enhancers "Jennifers," after the name that has been most popular for baby girls over the last fifteen years.

"Jennifers are sought by the man who *knows* in his core, in that inner place called wisdom, that the only antidote for mid-life angst is a young woman in his life. In his life, on his arm, but preferably in his bed." "Jennifer fever" has killed marriages in droves.[5]

So he dumps you, his wife, and runs to her and they get married. And often they really do make a go of it, and the first wife is simply left to fend for herself with bitterness, financial hardship, sole responsibility for the children, and much pain. Lenore Weitzman in *The Divorce Revolution* paints a dismal portrait of the divorced woman under the "no-fault" laws that make leaving marriage simpler. She notes that judges often see work for newly divorced mothers as "rehabilitation," though two-thirds of the women surveyed did not work during their marriages. While 19 percent of their husbands remarried within one year, only 4 percent of the women did so, suggesting that significantly more husbands than wives had lovers waiting in the wings.[6]

I'm certainly not saying that whenever a man makes moves toward a lover you should get divorced. Definitely try to stop it. Don't stoically sniffle back your tears and mutter, "If that's what you want." Be belligerent, insistent, factual, persuasive. Use the approach that you know from your years together works best. Surprise him. It's definitely worth all you can muster. For encouragement, read ahead to Chapter 11: "Throwing In the Towel."

But you probably ought to start your own process of emotional divorce if he's determined to *marry* someone new. Be careful: You have at your fingertips access to many deceptive emotional games to keep yourself entangled with your mate, and you are desperate to try them all. Chances are, as soon as your husband decided the time was right to leave you behind and left you to set the stage for Number Two, in his mind you became the "ex." Once you're in that position, you can begin the destructive games Catherine Napolitane with Victoria Pelligrino wrote about in *Living and Loving After Divorce*. They see these as primarily male maneuvers, but I think women take advantage of them too:

1. "Look who I've got with me," in which you/he bring around your alluring new lover;

2. "Look how I've changed," where you show off improved exteriors;

3. "See if you can get the money," where you play tag with dollars due;

4. "The kids love me more than you," and

5. "Let's see if he/she's still interested in me," where flirtation with the "ex" is merely a tease.[7]

Don't get caught up in these tempting links to your spouse. Cut free, get the divorce, and do your best to have no more contact. You're going to be damaged—one of the basic premises of this book is that divorce has disastrous consequences—but the more alert you are to likely fallout, and the quicker you force yourself to accept the finality of his or her rejection, the less agony, you'll have to suffer.

A marriage cannot work if there is only one person committed to it. And the surest sign that your partner will never return is his or her repeated, firm statement—coupled with the attention of a replacement lover. "It isn't fair!" I hear abandoned husbands and wives moan in my office. But they know the response: "Who said life was fair?" And unfortunately, you're not going to make it fair by hanging on to your unwilling mate. More likely, you'll only turn a potentially cordial (and more profitable) relationship into a hateful, miserable battle.

ESCAPING THE EXTREMES

So the situations where divorce is advisable really fall into a list of extremes: Chronic Addiction or Substance Abuse, Psychosis, Physical and Mental Abuse, Emotional and Practical Needs to Divorce, and Accepting Rejection. If this list is reminiscent of the pre—"no-fault" assignments of blame that many found so constricting and hateful, remember that it is not a list for lawyers but for your personal introspection.

And remember that these *are* the extremes. Very few marriages fall into these dire categories, certainly far fewer than the one-in-two marriages per year that ends in divorce, and many less than the more accurate statistic that only one in fifty of the marriages existing at a given time dissolves.

Divorce should be viewed as an escape from an impossible situation, not simply a matter of personal preference at the time, and certainly not as part of a "healthy" national trend toward serial monogamy. Our inner equilibria and the stability of our society depend on it.

NOTES

1. Elliott, Laura. *Shattered Dreams: The Story of Charlotte Fedders*. New York: Harper and Row, 1987.

2. Mannes, Marya, and Sheresky, Norman. *Uncoupling, the Art of Coming Apart: A Guide to Sane Divorce*. New York: Viking Press, 1972, p. 6.

3. Trafford, Abigail. *Crazy Time: Surviving Divorce*. New York: Harper and Row, 1972, p. 8.

4. Bergler, Edmund. *Divorce Won't Help*. New York: Harper and Row, 1948.

5. Gordon, Barbara. *Jennifer Fever*. New York: Harper and Row, 1988, p. 8.

6. Weitzman, Lenore. *The Divorce Revolution*. New York: Free Press, 1985.

7. Napolitane, Catherine, and Pelligrino, Victoria. *Living and Loving After Divorce*. New York: Rawson Associates, 1977, p. 16.

CHAPTER 9

The First Three "Reasons" For Divorce: Grabbing the Gusto

Remember the classic beer commercial several years ago that urged viewers to "go for the gusto"? It showed Sunday sailors, daring hang-gliders, and other risk-taking adventurers, hearty individualists to be admired not only for the brew they guzzled but for their ability to live life intensely, to the fullest. No "wussies" here—these folks were exemplars of bravado.

The message? Grab the most out of life—no matter the danger or side-effects. Or, as Valley-speak would have it, "Go for it." It seems a lofty and desirable sentiment. So if there's a chance to experience something novel or enhance sensual pleasure, we're half-alive fools if we don't devote whatever energies it takes to pursue that possibility.

Of course, we may be wrong. We may in fact diminish our character, shrivel our worth, or even physically kill ourselves in the process, but hey—haven't the last decades taught us that reason and caution needlessly restrain us from "maximizing our potentials"? Unfortunately, our values have changed such that stability and predictability are to be subjugated to the pursuit of the unusual and extreme.

Novelty has become exalted over the past several decades. It's reflected in all sorts of cultural phenomena, including those related to marriage. Fashionable hemlines shift up and down drastically from one season to the next. Every dozen weeks a new diet book climbs the charts. Self-help gurus publish ''ultimate'' guides for fulfillment that replace those of the months before. (You'd think that if the weight-control and personal growth theories worked, there'd be no need for replacements!) Products with ''New!'' splashed across their labels sell better than the tried-and-true.

And for you fitness buffs, remember when tennis was ''in'' for a few years, then racquetball, then roller skating or skiing? Remember how, and with each new sport's popularity, the previous rage declined? But in our eager consumerism, we bought those roller skates and tennis racquets and now they sit, with our Trivial Pursuit sets, dusty in the closet. The point is that those of us who refuse to jump on the latest bandwagon, whatever our interest or fancy, are, at the time, branded eccentric stick-in-the-muds, obviously naive to the advancement of the human race.

Whether we subscribe to it or not, this mentality carries over to our relationships to a startling degree. Fidgety and ever alert to the smallest signal to change, we vigilantly examine every potential crack in our closeness. ''Ah-ha! There's a difference between us!'' we mutter, scrutinizing our motions with a magnifying glass. ''My, what a disturbing fact. We aren't in perfect sync! Our relationship seems to have a flaw.'' Pretty soon our occasional mutters become annoyed complaints. And we suspect that somewhere else, with a more ideal mate, such imperfections simply won't exist.

So we scurry toward enticing possibilities of finding someone perfectly matched, of a passionate affair promising ''happily ever after,'' of achieving that perfect freedom, independence, sexual fulfillment, career success. We rush out into the world, overly confident that its options are infinite and therefore that utopia is accessible. This attitude is completely erroneous and unrealistic, and somewhere in the backs of our minds we know it. But such an uncomfortable truth is easily repressed in this age of gusto-grabbing.

Certainly there are some people, in these more conservative political times, who may say that gusto-grabbing is on the wane; that with the prevalence of sexually transmitted diseases, heterosexuals are becoming more cautious, more selective. And more traditionally monogamous.

But the data don't support it. The primary mongers of the heterosexual AIDS scare, William H. Masters, M.D., Virginia E. Johnson, and Robert C. Kolodny, M.D., were roundly and publicly denounced by their medical colleagues. Masters et al.'s 1988 book, *Crisis: Heterosexual Behavior in the Age of AIDS*, claims: "The AIDS virus is now running rampant in the heterosexual community."[1]

Gratefully, this is wrong. One of the many voices criticizing the work of Masters et al., that of Michael J. Fumento, writing in *The New Republic*, notes that "Only about 2 percent of all diagnosed AIDS cases in this country have been attributed to heterosexual transmission . . ." and of those, "about 85 percent of heterosexually transmitted cases occur in the partners of i.v.-drug abusers." Those cases, he continues, are passed on by anal sex 95 percent of the time. All in all, the chances against heterosexuals acquiring AIDS through regular intercourse, he says, are "astronomical."[2]

Even *Cosmopolitan* magazine devoted a cover story to the fact that modern women with straight male lovers needn't worry.[3]

Women seem to have heard this message, maintaining their passions in the wake of AIDS, according to a study by the Alan Guttmacher Institute. In fact, between 1982 and 1987, the number of American women aged eighteen to forty-four who indicated they were sexually active actually *rose* from 68 to 76 percent. "Young women, whose levels of sexual activity appear to be increasing, may choose to participate freely in sex," the report speculated, "because young people believe that they will not get AIDS and that they can determine someone's sexual health by his or her appearance."[4] AIDS may be the best publicized and deadliest disease in recent memory, but those who would grab lusty gusto are not daunted by the furor.

EXIT LINE #1: "WE'RE NOT WELL-MATCHED"

What a lame euphemism for saying your mate isn't good enough for you anymore! Of course, you don't want to sound personally insulting, so you conveniently blame your departure on differing genes or dissimilar sleep patterns or the wrong birthdate—things out of your partner's control. What you really mean is: "You're not up to my standards, and I could find someone more (fill in the blank here) sexy, attractive, young, exciting, bright, achieving." You don't want to be cruel, so you let your spouse down easy: "You can't help your I.Q. or propensity to wrinkle or that piercing cackle just like your mother's. But still, I deserve better, and I've got to leave you to find this ideal person, who's probably waiting for me right this moment."

What a seamless way to let everybody off the hook. Your partner's not maligned because you simply require a characteristic that he or she doesn't possess. And you're not the villain because your divorce is merely a matter of uncoordinated needs, not whether one of you is bad or good, desirable, or unattractive. Saying that you're "different" doesn't cast anyone in a negative light. It allows you to throw up your hands and plead, "What can I do?" Blame fate, heredity, temperaments, or time, but never yourself.

This exit line is bunk because obviously you once were so convinced that you were matched for life that you got married. Lots of people fall back on "I was blinded by love," or "We were so young then," but face it, you may have been eager or inexperienced but you weren't stupid. And the longer you stayed together, the more convincingly you proved that you were similar enough to make it work. Every day you spent together happy shows that despite whatever innate differences you have, you *can* love each other; that these contrasts don't have to stand in the way of your closeness. Unless suddenly you want them to. Unless now you decide to point your finger at them and say they're forcing you to negate the veracity of what you proved before.

Lots of couples come to me for premarital counseling touting their differences. They claim they're going to make it over the long haul precisely *because* they're not cookie-cutter clones; precisely *because* they have things they can learn from each other. The fact that you have gaps in your habits or backgrounds can be the source of tremendous growth; this heterogeneity can give you self-esteem unreliant on the characteristics or behavior of your partner. "They" say opposites attract, and I say the contrast with your partner in certain skills or abilities or interests can stave off boredom and bring efficiency to your relationship.

Success Story: Carol and Mark Hamlin had big differences in their paces and temperaments. He liked to sleep long and late; she was up at the crack of dawn and never seemed to slow down until she retired hours after Mark did. Mark took the world in stride. He didn't get upset when he tried to succeed but got rejected; he simply shrugged it off and tried again. Carol, on the other hand, was higher strung and needed others' assurance of her usually stellar performance. Carol was the "star" of the couple, a partner in her medium-sized law firm at age twenty-eight. Mark was very proud of her, and when she did legal "homework" into the night, he brought her coffee and cheered her on.

The relationship worked because both got something— Carol got adoration, support, and assistance. In turn, Mark got Carol's gratitude, her competence in organizing and carrying out innovative activities, and the material benefits of her glory. On weekends and many evenings, when neither was working, they wanted only to be together, planning little field trips, intimate dinner parties for their friends, overnight getaways, and even quiet rent-a-video dates at home. Each one allowed the other to function in his or her own style—they were dramatically different and yet complementary.

Ruined Relationship: Edward and Polly Graham met sixteen years ago when Edward worked as an intern on the Minneapolis newspaper Polly's grandfather published. A tall, strikingly handsome college senior, Edward had impressed Polly, then attending a prep school for girls, when he wrote a probing interview of her grandfather, reaching into the family's history and even asking her a few questions to give the piece depth. It never ran in the paper, of course, but it earned Edward his degree in journalism and sparked the romance that culminated in their marriage four years later.

Cameron Price wasn't happy that his daughter was marrying Edward, however. Edward was certainly a go-getter and obviously talented as well. But he came from a family fraught with problems: alcoholism and accompanying periods of unemployment, lack of formal education, and divorce. Polly's dad opposed the marriage at first and demanded that the couple wait until Polly finished her degree and Edward had worked for a while at a decently paid job. But by the time the couple met these requirements, Polly's dad was already won over by Edward's tenacity and performance.

Two years after their marriage, Polly and Edward had their first child, a daughter, who became the apple of Cameron Price's eye. Polly brought Stephanie over to see her grandparents frequently, and they filled the child's room with giant stuffed animals—and her bank account with funds for her college education. Edward was working as a ghost writer and doing quite well for himself. Polly, who'd earned her bachelor's in library science, worked part-time as a children's librarian for the city.

She became involved in charity events to benefit the library and then joined the auxiliary, working to fund a children's playhouse. At first Edward didn't mind, but when Polly attempted to involve him in fundraisers, he found himself increasingly uncomfortable. "There were all these ladies in big hats with long fingernails munching on mushroom salads," he says bitterly. "I wanted my wife home with our daughter, not wasting so much of her time organizing tea parties." He felt that true charity began at home—and Polly always seemed to treat Edward's struggling family with disdain.

Polly's view is significantly different. "He went berserk, ranting that he didn't marry a princess, that he wanted me to just be a normal housewife. Well, for one thing, I *was* a normal housewife. And for another, I refuse to be insulted and bossed around like that." Polly was comfortable in a milieu where Edward felt like an interloper. She was used to debutantes and white gloves; he was used to stale peanut butter sandwich dinners eaten alone. He didn't like this upper-crust gentility and demanded that Polly leave her "phony, money-centered world."

After the divorce two years later, Edward reflected, "It was a case of incompatible backgrounds. I was from 'the wrong side of the tracks.' " His statement suggests that their marriage was doomed from the start, as if their differing types of families precluded any chance of success. The real problem was that neither partner continued to want it to work. Edward had learned early to fit in with the fast-paced publishing crowd—in fact his assimilation into that world was so seamless that he was heartily welcomed, even by Cameron Price. Polly had never been asked to give up her family and friends—so that was certainly not the problem.

Instead, Edward was reacting to Polly's expanding interests: he was no longer the only focus of her life. In a sense, their relationship's demise is a stunning irony: Because he really craved more of Polly's affection, Edward began resenting anything distracting her from him. He wanted her so badly that he ended up driving her away.

A pathetic paradox—loving so much as to want possession and control, and yet also wanting your love to be happy and fulfilled. He wanted to be reasonable. He wanted only the best. He *didn't* want to admit that his love could be selfish as well as altruistic.

But thanks to the spit-it-out "honesty" left over from the sixties and seventies, Edward just unloaded on Polly, who, understandably, unloaded right back. This behavior kept the issues away from the real, underlying problem and onto such reactionary volleys as "You can't do that!" and "Who says?" Edward had no time to contemplate that he was simply jealous of the activities that pulled Polly away from him. He never had a moment to focus on the depth of his love, rather than the depth of his hostility. And Polly could do no more than defend the life she'd always known.

EXIT LINE #2: "I MUST PURSUE THIS OPPORTUNITY FOR THE LOVE OF MY LIFE."

Affairs: According to various sources, between 30 and 70 percent of married men succumb to them; between 25 and 50 percent of wives so indulge. Several authorities, including Blumstein and Schwartz in *American Couples*, have found that women tend to do so more seriously, often falling in love and using the affair as a springboard out of marriage and into the new relationship. Say these authors of their extensive survey results: "These data confirm to us that women have difficulty engaging in casual sex—or they have sex outside their relationship only when they are looking for a way to get out of it."[5] A 1986 *Ladies Home Journal* survey found that 83.4 percent of women who were unfaithful wives got divorced.[6]

Recognizing the devastating effects of a wife's dalliance, Dr. Joyce Brothers sternly warns: "The woman who wants a lifetime marriage should remain faithful. The odds are against the woman who fools around. If you need a challenge, give yourself the challenge of making your marriage more exciting."[7] Her no-nonsense admonition follows by several years her own opposing stance. In the more permissive ambiance of 1975 she wrote that "in certain cases under certain circumstances" the ego lift a middle-aged woman gets from an affair could rub off on her marriage. "Now I have reversed my position," she writes in 1984. "What worked in the early and mid-1970s for a handful of women is too dangerous for the woman today who wants a lifetime marriage. It is a case of the cure being more harmful than the disease."[8]

The 1985 film *Twice in a Lifetime* chronicles the effect of a man's philandering on his dull but devoted wife and their grown children. The involvement of Gene Hackman's character with a bar waitress (played by Ann Margaret), and his subsequent separation and divorce unfold under the guise of helplessness—"What can I do if such a fabulous opportunity presents itself?" After all, the choice would be between a pleasantly safe but uninspiring continuation of his familiar life, and the stimulation of beginning anew with someone offering adoration and fresh challenges. This particular film was honest enough to show both the positive and negative aspects of this decision—the growth forced onto the rejected wife, the pain suffered by the errant father. And it also wisely hinted that perhaps all this anguish could have been avoided if the Gene Hackman character and his barmaid had simply never met.

Based on the lighthearted çamaraderie of a back-slapping barroom environment, Hackman could hardly have been expected to resist. "Everybody does it" may be enough to rationalize your misdeeds. It may put you in extensive, if not good, company. It may allow you to discard spousal trust with less guilt. But we don't like to notice that it's also a self-serving device to mask the inevitable harm you're doing your marriage. I cannot stress too much that if you have any regard for your partner, or if you place any value on the growth, accomplishments, and outcomes of your wedded years, you'll summon up the self-discipline and self-esteem to resist tempting situations. You'll spare yourself and everyone you care about enormous grief.

But let's say you've already become involved, fallen in love, and become convinced that your lover would make a better mate than the one you've already chosen. What do you think is really going to happen? What makes you think that in five, ten, fifteen years—or whatever time you've spent with your present partner—this currently exciting lover will seem any better or different to you than the person you found so arresting so many years ago? Why should your new relationship be any more immune to change—to the rigors of aging, to settling into monotony, or to finding independent interests?

In fact, some authorities warn that if you marry your lover, your chances for a lasting marriage are actually *lower* than if you'd stayed put. Paul Glick and Arthur Norton explained in a 1979 U.S. Census Bureau booklet that second marriages dissolve sooner and more often than first unions: half of first-marriage divorces came within 7 years, but half of second-marriage divorces occurred in only 5.3. While 38 percent of women married for the first time were expected to eventually divorce, 44 percent of those on the second go-round were predicted to feel their marriages crack.[9] It's true that other evidence is contradictory, suggesting that second marriages may be no more prone to divorce than "firsts" (so says an *Insight* magazine cover story of October 13, 1986). But when stepchildren are involved in the second union—as they are very likely to be—the risks increase. At best, even if you leave your first marriage child-free, you're still faced with only a nerve-wracking 50 percent chance of marital survival.[10]

It's true that an affair, especially a long-term one, can make you feel optimistic. You seem so compatible and attracted to each other. You can talk about anything. Sex is fantastic. You seem to share the same interests and values. But what delusion tells you that your lover will indeed even want to marry you once you're free? Eric Weber and Steven S. Simring, M.D., note in *How to Win Back the One You Love* that "although 70 percent of those who divorce have an extramarital lover, only 15 percent actually marry that person."[11] Things do change when you shift the status of your relationship. Yes, what you and your lover have now is beautiful, and what an opportunity, if only you can be together so things can continue unimpeded. But only illusion cons you into thinking everything will remain the same as it is now.

Because nothing remains the same. No relationship stagnates to the point of complete stillness; no passionate joining retains its original heat. And one factor is *sure* to change. Once you've disentangled yourself from your marriage and settled into your new life, you won't have the sneaking around, the clandestine meetings, the romantic secrecy that existed during your affair. And that factor, whether you want to admit it or not, contributed to the excitement and intensity of your budding relationship. With that factor removed, a cohesive element of your dynamic together disappears—which has a deep impact on the whole of your relationship.

Once you're remarried, you adjust how you relate to your new partner. You relax. You let down your guard. You revert to the behavior you already know how to do. In other words, you start relating to your new husband in the way you've learned to relate to all husbands in your past. You swear you'll change—cast off the ho-hum, earnestly work on obnoxious habits, practice the consideration and attention you've cultivated during your courtship. But because your old "married" behavior is already ingrained and because you've practiced it for so many years, it takes a lot more effort and determination to stay reformed. Relaxing into practiced patterns is so much easier and more automatic that you can't help but slip back into the "old you." And your relationship pays the price.

Before long, you start noticing that what once was a glorious and titillating *affair de coeur* has become a nuts-and-bolts partnership replete with all the day-to-day nuisances and decisions that plagued your first marriage—and characterize any marriage. You've let the first one die—

but looking back, couldn't you have rescued it if you'd tried? Couldn't you have prevented the waste of all those years and emotions by simply turning around and saying, "Okay, enough; let's rekindle what we once had"? But people who get into affairs only say "Enough," and then only say that to themselves. To them "enough" is an exit line to that ego-massaging new flame rather than the spur to tackle a more difficult but ultimately more rewarding task at hand.

Just as people use the excuse of possible lost opportunity to end a marriage, they also use excuses to allow themselves to enter and continue affairs. Often these excuses are just means to feel off-the-hook by blaming circumstances or hormones rather than internal failures. Everyone's heard the old male sexual release argument—he needs this fling because his wife doesn't give "it" to him at home. Then there's the classic: "My wife doesn't understand me." Women stereotypically lament that they're "taken for granted." What this really boils down to is the need for intimate and personal attention.

Daniel Dolesh and Sherelynn Lehmann surveyed 275 couples in which one partner had had an affair for their 1986 book *Love Me, Love Me Not: How to Survive Infidelity*. Half of the respondents said they strayed to cure loneliness or bolster sagging self-esteem; a quarter went after emotional excitement; and another quarter claimed they broke their vows for sex.[12] So by simply giving your "old faithful" spouse more attention and adulation—even if forced at first—you can probably head off his or her need to get this reassurance elsewhere. Such a simple prescription to spare yourself and your marriage trauma or destruction. And most on-the-lookout spouses intuitively understand it. But they choose to ignore their marriage, opting instead for selfish short-term gratification.

When forced to consider the impact of extramarital liaisons on their marriages, philanderers can now rely on trendy pop psychology. Over the past several years, liberal self-help authors have offered would-be philanderers a good excuse to pursue outside attraction: "I was only trying to help my marriage." Supposedly a brief affair can be a pick-me-up for an ailing relationship, the means to improve life at home. Joyce Brothers' 1975 statements weren't the only words compromising monogamy, by any means. These plentiful sources still mistakenly and destructively suggest that an affair can (almost harmlessly!) jolt offended husbands and wives into correcting their shortcomings. It can, they wrongly claim, shock complacent individuals—both cheater and victims—so much that they realize how precious their relationship really is and miraculously begin to cherish its irreplacable value. This is ridiculous.

Obviously, your mate already values your marriage, including its sexual exclusivity—that's proven just because he or she honors the pledge of faithfulness day to day. Even though things may have settled into a predictable routine that you find boring, that same routine may feel comfortable and rewarding to your mate—and so he or she doesn't have a clue that you're disgruntled. Just knowing about your dissatisfaction and fathoming the possibility of your adultery would probably be enough of a jolt to merit immediate change and improvement. You don't have to act on your feelings in order to perk up your marriage. Verbalizing them strongly and directly would send anyone who previously thought he had an intact marriage into instant distress.

Excuses aside, people become involved. They get divorced and remarry. Let's project ahead a little and evaluate the basis of such a relationship. If you do marry your paramour, you probably know many things about him or her from hearsay: educational background, career progress, philosophy of life. Your lover tells you, and you take him at his word. You also know several other characteristics that you can directly observe from your own experience with him or her: kindness, attentiveness, attractiveness, sexual chemistry. But note that all these qualities are transitory; they're certainly not reliable predictors of future behavior. However, there is one value you know your partner holds, because it's been demonstrated: *He or she has no compunction about stealing someone out of a marriage.* In other words, the one fact you can verify is that your intended is a homewrecker.

Conversely, the first thing your new mate learned about you was that you're willing to be unfaithful. He or she knows that you can be deceptive to one you've promised to honor. That you're great with excuses. That you can be distracted away from commitment. That sensory pleasure or ego gratification are bait that you'll follow. These are of no consequence to the mistress or lover also flushed with loin-driven passion. But when your divorce is out of the way and you have to confront long-term commitment, you can bet that these thoughts will simmer beneath whatever lush interpersonal facade you create together—forever. No matter what you swear, there's bound to be some damaging doubt inbred in those second-wedding vows. You promised to be faithful before—how does spouse number two know that you won't be lured away again?

So if you become embroiled in a wildly rewarding and exciting affair and feel compelled to follow it through, consider that this irresistible "opportunity" may not offer you as much as you believe. Consider that it could be your own weakness and ego needs that are propelling you toward divorce rather than the reality of your new relationship. Consider that in five or ten years with your now-passionate flame, you'll simply be another divorced person who married his lover—five or ten years ago. You'll be a conventional established married couple. And you'll be in a similar position to the one you're in now.

Don't discard something you've vowed to honor and hurt people you care about unless you're absolutely sure that the new partner unquestionably surpasses the old. And how do you know? To a large extent people choose their mates based on the reactions and feedback of outside sources like family, long-time friends, and business associates. But if you've been sneaking around, creating a fantasy paradise, observing each other in an isolated, limited context, how likely is it that you can truly see what's to come? What kind of legitimate "opportunity" are you really passing up?

EXIT LINE #3: "I NEED MY . . . (INDEPENDENCE, SEXUAL FULFILLMENT, CAREER, WHATEVER)"

While it's true that marriage does put limits on spouses, nearly everyone considers these tradeoffs extremely worthwhile. After all, Simenauer and Carroll report in *Singles: The New Americans* that "only a tiny percent of those who have never married intend to stay single for life."[13] Indeed, more than 90 percent of the population does eventually marry. My own survey of two hundred separated and divorced people confirms that even those who left their marriages for freedom, independence, sex, etc., believe that this quest can be satisfied relatively quickly—and will last just until they find someone new.

Which shows how shallow an exit line this one really is. To say that you have to separate or divorce to find freedom, independence, good sex, career advancement, or any other ideal is to say that you cannot strive for mutually acceptable levels of these within marriage. It's to discard the institution and the partner as inflexible, unyielding, and stubborn. If you need more time alone, negotiate it with your partner. If you want to plow ahead with your career, work it through with your mate. If you crave better sex, be creative with your lifetime lover and if necessary, get therapy.

If you require variety—well, you should have thought of that before you made your commitment. Since you did decide to get married, you must've once believed that you could be true to one person. You must've once felt that dedication to a particular individual was desirable and worthwhile. To now abandon that position and shrug helplessly, throwing up your hands before they reach around a succession of bodies, is to allow yourself to sink morally, to make yourself a less laudable person. We, as a society, admire loyalty and faithfulness and abhor the cad.

It's more acceptable and less wrenching to tell your partner that you just need your independence than to confess that you've taken up with someone you find more alluring. Often someone engaged in a flirtation or affair offers this bland, nonincriminating excuse in order to more gracefully exit from the marriage. Or, in a variant scenario, guilt about cheating motivates you to separate before consummating a liaison that's already begun on an emotional level. You can't bring yourself to devastate your partner with the truth about your overpowering chemical attraction for another person. So you conceal your situation with these more benign—but no less hurtful—words.

To your chagrin, your spouse, panic-stricken, may quickly grant you your claimed needs. "You want more independence? Take Sundays to yourself! You want more sex—okay, I'll read Masters and Johnson and wear sexy lingerie! You want to advance more in your career? All right, I'll fold your shirts when you have to fly off to Toronto to present your paper at the convention. And I'll type your paper too." But since this strong need is merely a cover, you ignore every overture, perhaps responding with, "I'm just fed up; I've got to go off by myself." This pablum is transparent to anyone with the slightest intelligence, though you dearly hope it isn't.

But let's say you're not just feeding your spouse a line, but are sincere in desiring the freedom to pursue a different life. You're not leaping into another relationship, instead simply yearning for a life of rugged individualism, of nonconsultant decision making, of release from compromise. You believe you need that breathing room, or the sexual experience you never accumulated before. You see escape from your marriage as entering daylight after traveling in a long, confining tunnel.

You're probably deluding yourself. Jean Brody and Gail Beswick Osborne interviewed couples who divorced after twenty years or more of marriage in *The Twenty-Year Phenomenon*. You'd think that these veterans of long marriages would have the strongest urge to make up for lost time by indulging in all the freedoms typical marriages preclude. And yet every man they interviewed reported that divorce left him confused—he didn't know what he wanted anymore.[14]

That you even desire solitary self-fulfillment shows a nonmarriage mentality. This exit line reeks of selfishness—"I need my freedom." I need my (private) career focus. I have to get my kicks with a busload of broads (or hunks). What kind of immature thinking is that? Maybe you think you deserve it. You've been smothered in marriage for a long time, and you can't let your whole life go by without experiencing more. This is only "Me Decade" egocentrism.

Judith Bardwick, in her book *In Transition*, summarizes: "The 1970s have been marked by a number of attitudes that, not surprisingly, increase the likelihood of divorce. We can predict a higher divorce rate when the criteria of success in marriage change from family integrity, security, and contentment to happiness in which people are to grasp opportunity and feel vital; when compromise is judged to be a sign of inadequacy; when 'doing your thing' and 'getting yours' are legitimized, so that relationships are continued only as long as they gratify one's own needs.''[15] Even if you were socialized much earlier or born after the hang-loose years, you have undoubtedly been affected by its dangerous and unhealthy tenets—or else you wouldn't consider using its platitudes to justify your divorce.

It used to be that people delighted in an identity as part of a couple. They thought it enhanced their status to be married. Now, people think they need to fulfill themselves as unconnected individuals. They think it's better to be self-confidently single than self-confidently married.

It's true that in some marriages one partner dominates the other. The person who is continually overridden and subjugated can deservedly require increased self-esteem. And frequently the only way to accomplish this is to separate, to remove the pressures of the dominating partner, so that the squashed personality has a chance to establish itself and blossom. I fully believe that the root of almost all psychological problems faced by normal people is low self-esteem.

But separation will not necessarily bring increased self-esteem. Building self-confidence is a lifelong job for *everyone*, no matter how self-assured they appear. Everyone is insecure at some times, in some areas—it's a matter of degree. Diagnosing the seriousness of the problem, obtaining counseling, and involving the oppressive spouse in the process will bring beneficial results more easily than having to face the world alone and build self-confidence. There's more distress in separation and divorce *combined* with enhancing one's identity than in overcoming low self-esteem alone.

Jason and Karen Lewis were the classic case. Married in their early twenties in 1973, they'd assumed rather traditional sex roles. Jason was a star, a syndicated columnist whose political writing gained him both praise and notoriety. He'd always been a whiz-kid, and Karen soon gave up any loosely held plans of a career in decorating to help Jason to the top. She ran errands, did his Xeroxing, typed the transcripts for his interviews. She was devoted, and while Jason was verbally appreciative, he was unrelentingly domineering. There was nothing that Karen didn't have to clear with him first—the color of the paint in the kitchen, the menu she planned for dinner parties they'd host. Pretty soon she unconsciously realized that any ideas she had that deviated from what Jason wanted were sure to be rejected—so she modified her tastes and behavior to please him. His desires became her own.

In return, Jason considered his wife "part of the team." His career was their joint effort, and he thrived on the unwavering support and assistance Karen gave him. He trusted her. She could be counted on to take care of the home front; she'd cover all loose ends. He knew that she made possible his blooming success. When he saw other women who were more dynamic, who accomplished things on their own, who had longer legs or more sculpted features, he felt attracted to them. He'd flirt. He'd tease with lunches, romantic rendezvous, and occasionally, "meaningless" physical contact. But he never considered leaving Karen. He never considered splitting up such a perfectly functioning "team."

Then Karen walked out. Jason was shocked. She'd never given any serious sign of dissatisfaction. They'd always had a fine sex life. They were engaged in projects that gave them a sense of purpose, a *raison d'etre* that mattered to the whole world, not just to themselves. You may recall that Abigail Trafford in *Crazy Time* calls this sudden crack in the relationship "deadlock." She says that this pattern occurs in all marriages that end, and it centers on just this kind of imbalance of power. The imbalance can last for years, as it did for the eleven years Jason and Karen stayed together. But when the dominated partner feels the weight of responsibility to his mate (or, conversely, when a dominating partner shifts roles and become oppressed), the relationship is bound to falter.

If suddenly you've been hit by deadlock and simply must withdraw, you have a choice. You can work on yourself and your relationship within the marriage. Or you can say you need to move out. You can say you can't put up with this anymore and have to create your own identity, on your own terms, away from your mate. You have to have some privacy, some freedom, perhaps some extended therapy.

That's what Karen did. She took an apartment ten minutes from Jason. He helped her build her shelves and set up her stereo. He was respectful and apologetic. He wanted her back, he told her, but she would have none of it. After her therapy sessions, she'd call Jason and rail about all the occasions he'd stifled her, made her feel like all her opinions were the wrong opinions, made her feel that her role in life, not just in his profession, was secondary. She'd wanted to please him so much that she'd swallowed any self-esteem. She no longer had even wanted to stand up to him because she simply couldn't. Now she hated him for imprisoning her personality and individuality and for quashing her ambitions.

Jason's sympathy lasted about two months. He listened to her tirades, cried when she cried, said he was sorry, so sorry, and he'd try to reform. "No!" Karen screamed. "You can't reform, because you're so positive that you're right and the rest of the world is wrong!" And it was true. After a while Jason kind of liked living alone. He lost twenty pounds without Karen's cooking, by just drinking beer and eating ice cream out of the carton. He ogled women and had a few sexual experiences. He thought he'd been given a whole new life, a fresh start. He liked his freedom to pursue women, to pick them up and bring them home to his own bed.

Meanwhile, Karen was getting her built-up resentment out of her system. She saw Jason regularly, continuing to vent her hostility. She couldn't stand it anymore, he drove her crazy. She had to stand on her own, and she'd get smug satisfaction when Jason's work went down the tubes as a result.

But it didn't. And after a few months, Jason realized he now could find someone even better than Karen, someone accomplished who would probably be just as devoted and give him just as much attention. Maybe the new one wouldn't type his transcripts, but any secretary could do that. Jason, realizing his liberation, soon allowed himself to fall in love.

Karen had her own agenda to follow—releasing her feelings, coping on her own, pursuing all the activities that Jason had prohibited. She bought a car Jason hated.

She decorated her apartment in colors and fabrics Jason would've nixed. She had a few sexual experiences of her own. She went back to school to pursue a degree Jason had ridiculed. She relaxed.

Then she realized that she missed Jason. She had built a comfortable, secure, and rewarding life with him, and she wanted to return to it now, refreshed and renewed. But it was too late. Jason's "infatuation" had become serious. Jason said he still loved her. But he didn't want to give up the possibilities he saw with this new, more achieving woman. And this woman knew what she'd found and had no intention of letting go. Karen suggested reconciliation. She said that all she'd wanted was some time on her own to "get my head together," some breathing space, a hiatus for sorting out all the feelings that had built up over eleven years of domination. Now that she'd accomplished that, she realized the good aspects of their relationship, not only the bad ones that had stared her in the face like an ogre over the months she contemplated the break. Jason was caring, he was sweet. But the tradeoff was too much for him—and Karen watched the new woman invade her once-secure territory, watched as her life was dismantled, until eventually the divorce papers were signed and Jason married again.

Karen had taken the solidity of her marriage for granted. She'd seen Jason's eyes roam, and yet he always came home to her, always assured her he'd be there when she needed him. But once she made her grandiose "plea for help" as she later termed it, Jason took her at her word. She said she wanted out. She said she couldn't live with him. She said he was impossible, that he had buried her identity to the point that her sanity depended on separateness. So she got it—for the rest of her life.

The moral of this story is that you'd better be prepared to spend the rest of your life alone when you depart for that self-defining private space. You'd better be prepared for the truth—even if you do change your mind and return, even if your shocked and betrayed partner wants you back. Things can never be the same. The security and ease of your relationship cannot be easily reestablished. Suspicion is inevitable.

NOTES

1. Masters, William H., M.D., Johnson, Virginia E., and Kolodny, Robert C., M.D. *Crisis: Heterosexual Behavior in the Age of AIDS*. New York: Grove Press, 1988, p. 7.

2. Fumento, Michael J. "The AIDS Cookbook." *The New Republic*, August 8 and 15, 1988, pp. 19–21.

3. Gould, Robert E., M.D. "Reassuring News About AIDS: A Doctor Tells Why You May Not Be At Risk." *Cosmopolitan*, January, 1988.

4. Parachini, Allan. "Women, Sex: AIDS Having Little Impact." *Los Angeles Times*, July 28, 1988, p. 1, p. 9.

5. Blumstein, Philip, and Schwartz, Pepper. *American Couples*. New York: William Morrow & Co., Inc., 1983, p. 313.

6. "Twenty-Nine Secrets We Know About You." *Ladies Home Journal*, August 1986, p. 89–98, 161.

7. Brothers, Joyce. *What Every Woman Ought to Know About Love and Marriage*. New York: Simon and Schuster, 1984, p. 277.

8. Ibid., p. 276.

9. Glick, Paul, and Norton, Arthur. *The Joy of Being Single*. Prepared at the request of the U.S. Bureau of the Census, 1979, p. 215.

10. Diegmueller, Karen. "Breaking the Ties That Bind." *Insight*, October 13, 1986, pp. 8–13.

11. Simring, Steven S., and Weber, Eric. *How to Win Back the One You Love*. New York: Macmillan, 1983.

12. Dolesh, Daniel, and Lehmann, Sherelynn. *Love Me, Love Me Not: How to Survive Infidelity*. New York: McGraw Hill, 1986.

13. Carroll, David, and Simenauer, Jacqueline. *Singles: The New Americans*. New York: Simon and Schuster, 1982, p. 324.

14. Brody, Jean, and Osborne, Gail Beswick. *The Twenty-Year Phenomenon*. New York: Simon and Schuster, 1980.

15. Bardwick, Judith. *In Transition*. New York: Holt, Rinehart and Winston, 1979, p. 120.

CHAPTER 10

Four More Reasons for Divorce: "Got to Get You Out of My Life"

Some people are pulled out of marriage; some are pushed. Those who utter the three reasons for divorce discussed in the previous chapter are lured by the pulls of freedom, excitement, or potential with another person.

In contrast, some disgruntled mates are pushed away by some intolerable condition at home. He's moody. He's slovenly. He nags. She's always on the phone with the TV on full blast. She's crabby. She doesn't care about her appearance.

In the last chapter, we looked at a few of the magnets drawing people out of a perfectly acceptable—and certainly repairable—union. Now we'll focus on problems that may be even more serious—conflicts endemic to the relationship itself.

EXIT LINE #4: "WE'RE ALWAYS FIGHTING"

Okay, perhaps you do share a common core of compatibility with your mate; but lately, preserving it just doesn't seem to be worth the effort. You say black; she says white. You say jump, he says "do it yourself." There's friction. You each feel forced to stand up for yourself. It's difficult to admit when you're wrong and harder still for your partner to simply give in gracefully.

So you don't look forward to coming home. Maybe

you invent excuses to go out, stay late at work, or stop off before you get home. Maybe you're tempted to find a mistress or lover who will just adore you and not force you to put on your combat gear. It becomes less and less important that you and your spouse have a lot to share. The fights center in those areas of commonality. The children are doing badly in school—whose fault is that? Your career isn't going as well as it had, and your once-supportive spouse is suddenly full of criticisms. Your house is falling part, but suddenly your suggestions are met with indifference rather than interest. It's enough to make you furious, and to force your mate to respond in kind.

While it's true that arguing is exhausting and embittering, and that these jousts leave permanent scars on any relationship, they only have to mean the *end* of your marriage if you want them to. Sometimes people exacerbate or provoke fights precisely *because* they want out. They want their partners to do the actual severing to minimize their guilt about leaving, or perhaps so they don't have to actively make the choice.

If your partner says "you're impossible," then you think you're the victim—you've been pushed out by someone whose taste or tolerance simply refuses to accommodate you. You can always defend your divorcing with the protest that you only stood up for yourself, you only asserted your honest, sincere feelings, and based on those, your short-tempered spouse chose to terminate the whole relationship.

Playing along with arguments can be a most effective way to passively destroy your marriage. Doing things that you know will irritate your spouse, often under the guise of "good intentions" or "only trying to help" is a clever means to set up your exit scenario. Your mate responds predictably with anger; you too are then "forced" to respond, and soon the tit-for-tatting becomes an endless battle. *Voilà!* You're separated and your conscience is clear—probably more clear than it deserves to be, since people who use this tactic tend to repress their underlying motivations.

This is just one example of an agenda hidden in arguing. Before you discard what seems to be a rocky and explosive marriage, carefully examine whether this or another goal lurks beneath the apparent cause of your cross-fire. Here are some possibilities:

1. *Arguing is stimulating.* If you regularly alternate ups and downs, you could be trying to bring some action or stimulation into a relationship you've let languish. By lapsing into arguing, you feel there's something brewing, a spark, even if it's negative, that characterizes your marriage. You've developed roles in the relationship that in a painful yet effective way give each of you a reward.

This logic may sound more like justification to separate than reason to stay together: "If all we've got is disagreement, then what's the point?" But that's not all you've got. You have a shared history, a publicly formalized relationship, a status and position together that shapes how you relate to the world, and how your family, co-workers, and even brand-new acquaintances relate to you. You've simply fallen into a destructive pattern—but it's one that can be reversed.

There's power in the ability to rouse your mate to fury. There's reassurance that he or she still cares enough that what you say is inflammatory. Blow-ups can give each of you a rush of adrenaline, a surge of excitement that actually keeps you going in the status quo, as disturbing as it may be, just a little longer. "At least we keep working on our relationship," you say to yourself.

Many couples require therapy to undo well-ingrained habits of bickering. But the basis of turnarounds in therapy or on your own is self-discipline to focus on your mate's positive behaviors and relax about irritable ones. If you left the marriage and started dating, you'd miraculously be able to do that—with other people, in the context of a first date. Everyone's an expert at "looking on the bright side" during infatuation. But who's to say you wouldn't fall into the same old destructive pattern later?

2. *Arguing to play your role.* Are there certain aggravating scenarios that seem to get replayed over and over? If so, each of you may be getting a personal ego boost by enacting unspoken roles within your nuclear family. For example, if you constantly fight over the children, you could be reestablishing the importance of the mother or the authority of the father, so that both of you feel renewed significance.

Another role often enacted is the family member who is *helpless* and requires the others' protection and care—that person may "fit in" and gain attention and security by constantly getting sick or injured, or perhaps becoming substance-dependent. Someone else in the family may habitually be the rescuer, gaining his own ego strength by responding to this need with heroic competence or caretaking ability. People play against one another in significant symbioses that are often difficult to recognize. Arguments may be the vehicle for enforcing these patterns—to cease arguing then means a traumatic restructuring of the entire family.

3. *Arguing as a power play.* One of the classic pop psychology pronouncements is that marriages fail because the "balance of power" is off kilter. One partner nearly always makes the decisions; the other responds predictably. Abigail Trafford, in *Crazy Time*, suggests that this tilt is set early in the relationship—when things change and roles reverse, dreaded "deadlock" sets in and the union crumbles. Arguing reassures you that you have power—and the outcomes of your spats tell you just how much. Even the *process* of arguing, no matter who wins, involves standing firm, being assertive, and even perhaps being ugly—but that ugliness is in itself one means of leveraging and feeling power. Every struggle proves that at least for fifteen minutes or half an hour or a night of sulking, even the most dominated spouse can be center stage. Even when you lose the argument, you have the satisfaction of knowing that you stood up to your challenger.

4. *Fighting to make up.* Another possible reason for fighting could be the aftermath of your duels. If your battles usually end with kissy cuddling and cooing, then perhaps one of you is intentionally setting up these confrontations in order to gain the end result. They're a bid for attention, caressing, sexual release, or another kind of positive response that you would not otherwise initiate. And it might be too difficult to simply ask for attention because of fear of rejection. What an irony if a need for affection ends up the cause of divorce!

5. *Fighting as a distraction.* If you conclude your bouts by retreating to your separate corners in simmering resentment, the aim could be some short-term motive.

Avoidance of sex? Steering clear of another subject, something even more loaded than the source of your argument? Once you get into the habit of relating through bickering, you've eliminated means to address other superficial or fundamental issues. After your tirades, you return to your separate corners, raising the family, tending to career matters, "performing" together as a public duo, blending into the extended family. You lead parallel lives that only seem to intersect briefly when you have something to argue about. Conflict is your norm. And yet all the problems you scream about are merely a mask for a sexual dissatisfaction, an unspoken desire, or another matter that could be resolved.

So you're sick and tired of it, all this bickering and pouting and yelling. Call a truce, and take an earnest look at the positive side of what you share. Lies and lures of the singles world notwithstanding, it's not that easy to find someone who understands your quirks, who wants the same things out of life, and who shared your past strivings, experiences, and connections.

EXIT LINE #5: "WE'VE GROWN APART"

What a pitiful condition, when you and your spouse feel like unfamiliar roommates who have come to share a flat. You have different schedules, dissimilar jobs, disparate preferences for leisure activities. You once were so close—but lately it's been weeks since you even discussed the mechanics of your days. What's left to bind you together? It seems as if you might as well confess that you're estranged and act on it, once and for all.

Sounds simple, but it's not. You made your real choices a while ago—to relax your interest in each other, to loosen your grip on the relationship and let it slide. *New* lovers are vigilant: they want to know everything about each other; they want all the secrets and "penny for your thoughts" momentary reflections. Once couples solidify their commitment, they may gradually lose this attentiveness, languishing in comfortable feelings of security and permanence.

Sometimes a spouse will come to her mate and ask directly for permission to pull away: "I want to go back to school." "I want to take a vacation by myself this year.'' Imagine the reaction of an infatuated lover—hurt, disappointment, insecurity. But once you "feel married," i.e., stuck together, what's the risk? Your passion has cooled. You've made the commitment, you've experienced years of time-glue. So you say okay, or maybe you protest: but in the end, you begin that steady pulling apart that leads you to admit that nothing holds you together anymore.

Since you made a *choice* to disengage, why can't you *choose* to rekindle what you've lost? Why does this feeling of emptiness have to conclude in separation and divorce, rather than revitalization and renewed excitement? You've probably been sucked in by the advertising and movies and music around you. You've seen far too many of your friends get divorced, and you think that once the staff of your microcosm disburses, you are next. You've read pop-psych articles about putting pizzazz back in your marriage, and you think all those rules sound a little silly, a little simplistic, given the complexity of modern relationships. You dread the process of therapy, of negotiation, of slogging through all the little hazards you passed on your way to indifference. On one side you see all this emotional work, this reconstruction of something that appears to be totally demolished. On the other you see a "fresh start," unlimited opportunity, and in your fantasies, a more adoring, exciting, and perfect spouse. If that's your perspective, there's no contest as to which you'll choose.

The problem is that your vision of the future as a divorced person is unrealistic and skewed. You're skipping over the part where you spend the first six months to two years as a zombie, or at least engulfed in divorce-related tasks. You're forgetting the kind of financial devastation divorce brings. You don't realize that no matter how hard you try, you won't be able to easily disentangle emotionally from your spouse, especially if you have children linking you together. You deny the impact of your move on those children and others around you. And you've been duped into believing that singles life is an easy and desirable way to live and that finding a replacement mate is a snap.

"We've grown apart" sounds so benign, so blameless. You're both wonderful people. You get along just fine.

You may have raised beautiful children and found satisfaction in everything you've tried. It's all so lovely you could read about it in *Better Homes and Gardens*, and now you'll have your civilized parting and dignified disengagement and continue to be friends forever.

Who are you trying to kid? When you cite this exit line, you admit that you *want* your marriage to end. You've probably had an affair or two, perhaps a serious one that's tugging you away this very moment. You can't admit it; you employ the utmost discretion. You've always found useful the old standard, "My wife (or husband) doesn't understand me," and you've been working to make sure you weren't lying. By clamming up when he asks you about your day. By planning activities and business retreats that didn't include her. By encouraging her to get involved in her own cliques and fancies and applauding when she did something independently from you. So you both lead minute-minder lives, and you're so busy it's astounding, and now you can turn around and point to your date book and say, "See? We really *don't* spend any time together," and shake your heads and move on.

You're saying that this "We've grown apart" line is easier and better than the truth. And I'm saying that it's a cop-out. Unfortunately, few people who become embroiled in intense or long-term affairs have the courage to turn back to their marriages once calculated decay has been fostered. The new life is waiting, and the pending husband or wife is impatient for official status. If you've completely closed your mind to reconciliation, good luck; you'll need it. There might be some brutal surprises ahead.

For one thing, when you announce that you've "grown apart" your partner may try to prove you wrong—and try to get you back. She may buy all those marriage enhancement paperbacks, enroll you in Marriage Encounter, and start therapy. He may believe you when you give the "growing apart" excuse, and because this is one exit line that he can do something about, he may work to change the situation with a vengeance. Then you'll have to reveal the truth, and things get sticky. You can resist all you want—you can refuse to go for counseling, get sick for the Encounter weekend. You can find new meetings to attend for work, or praise her independent achievements even higher and louder. But "growing apart" is a lame reason to discard a marriage, and sometime there's going to be a showdown.

But let's say you're clean—you're *not* involved outside the relationship, but life simply seems stale. If you both have just allowed the marriage to stagnate, and you concur that there's not much left, even though you're not in affairs, keep reading this book—you should stay together. Divorce is not just another "transition" to endure like childhood chicken pox, military service, or college education. The effects are far-reaching, not localized; they're enduring, not ephemeral. Getting a divorce will inevitably scar you, bring you loneliness and a lowered standard of living. Once you get a divorce, there is no way to recapture what you've lost. Even if you should somehow rediscover each other and remarry, it will be on new footing. You cannot simply forget pain that passes between you during a divorce. Better to recognize the pain you're causing now just by being passive and address it, before it becomes debilitating in divorce.

Exit Line #6: "You're Driving Me Crazy with Your Despicable Habit"

This is the divorce excuse grounded in revulsion, annoyance, or disgust. You've reminded him a zillion times to pick up his dirty clothes, but he still refuses to do it. You've rushed in to fill the gap dozens of times when she fails to make arrangements, meet repair people, accomplish something basic in her work. She's got an unbearable cackle. He walks around with toothbrushes sticking out of his cheek and leaves the crushed-bristle ruins in cubbyholes throughout the house.

Jared and Carolyn divorced because of the pins. They certainly weren't the only thing—Jared had been having affairs for years, on and off during their twenty-three-year marriage. The first fling happened when Carolyn was pregnant with their oldest child in 1956 back in Newark, where they grew up and lived until Sanford was six. It was just because she was out of commission, Carolyn thought to herself when she discovered Jared's philandering.

Carolyn was crushed by his infidelity but carried on valiantly—at least Jared always came home. By the couple's fourth child, Jared was into his fifth affair. Each had lasted only a few months, then the sexual fervor cooled and the demands of his work as a financial consultant would take over once again. Carolyn came to recognize these periods, and she always sighed in relief when they subsided.

Carolyn rationalized that men had sexual needs that simply had to be expressed. But she denied that her *own* behavior contributed to Jared's wanderings. She was the ultimate slob, and while Jared was far from neat, he constantly complained of boxes blocking the hallway, a garage full of second-hand junk Carolyn had rescued from front lawns on trash days, and piles of unread, yellowing magazines cluttering nearly every corner.

Jared often voiced his objections to all of these things, but Carolyn continued her miserly pack-ratting. She did love Jared and showed him affection. She wanted to go through all the magazines and get the crates out of the kitchen, but with four children . . . The kids consumed her time and her identity, and with all the scavenged oddities everywhere, her home became an uninviting place.

It was the pins that finally motivated Jared to move away from his wife and four teenage boys and in with his latest lover Claudine. Claudine was no great intellect; Carolyn was bright and inspired. But how many times had Jared asked Carolyn to pick up the pins she left on the living room carpet after pinning patterns? How many times had he worried that some barefoot boy would step on one of the sharp implements and puncture his tender foot? The pins became symbolic of Carolyn's unwillingness to change; symbolic of her annoying idiosyncrasies against which Jared felt powerless. Carolyn said she couldn't help it—her own mother had been so compulsively neat that she simply could not control her overreaction toward slovenliness. This was her nature, that's all, and if Jared could stand it all these years, why should he walk out over some silly pins stuck in the carpet?

Rarely is it really a single habit or characteristic that causes the breakup, but often the disgusted spouse zeroes in on one, such as the pins. It's the camel's proverbial last straw that led to his collapse; and in a marriage, when an irritating condition persists with no effort to show good faith, no sign of regret or possibility of change, the load threshhold of the marriage, like the camel's, is reached. Jared really had all he needed—the tacit acceptance of his affairs by his wife, an adoring family, a skyrocketing career. But he only enjoyed and needed two out of the three; and so, when he thought the boys were old enough to handle it, he got out.

But what happened? His affair fizzled, and Carolyn, devastated, begged for his return—to no avail; he bought a condominium. He didn't really care about the furnishings—an old steel desk, a folding table, a few dilapidated chairs and scratched-up bookcases. There were papers in piles and books lying on their sides. The kitchen had two forks, three mismatched plates, and a few battered pots, but Jared didn't care. Everything was the way he wanted it. At last he could run his own life without Carolyn's quirks getting in the way. At last he could have some peace.

But he got lonely. He missed the boys and dreamt up excuses to have them over, to call them, to reunite them like they were a family again. Of course he'd invite Carolyn, who couldn't tear herself away emotionally anyway. He wanted to play Pater again and gain that sense of control, but the gaiety only lasted until the boys, now in their twenties, went home. Then he was left with his consulting ''homework'' and his silent condo.

Sure, he tried to find another relationship. He'd go hiking with women he'd meet through business. He'd get them in the sack and they'd have a great time, but he could never include them in his family get-togethers because Carolyn would get too jealous. Jared didn't want to marry a woman with children of her own, children that would make him a stepfather and would mean new connections away from his own brood. Jared couldn't let go of his family, but despite desperately trying, he also couldn't duplicate the camaraderie and closeness they'd had. Most of the time he accepted it stoically, but even eight years later, there were times, when the weather was right for a family hike and picnic, that he'd let himself cry.

I met Jared ten years after he left Carolyn, and he was still grasping for the family he'd headed in his young adulthood. Carolyn was bitter but harbored continued hope that when Jared "got this craziness out of his system," he'd come home and they could reunite. Jared is now sixty, Carolyn fifty-eight. Three of the boys are married; one has a baby. And yet both Carolyn and Jared are stuck in a time warp, unable to disentangle, unable to fully accept reality because they find it too depressing, too much of a waste. They are obviously a couple who should not have divorced.

Carolyn admits that she doesn't sew anymore. She still accumulates piles of magazines, however, and rationalizes that she's better off apart from Jared so she can collect her *Family Circle*s and *Woman's Day*s without guilt. But on the other hand, she occasionally laments that she doesn't know why Jared doesn't just come back to her and make them all a family again.

Too many people fixate on particular annoyances and allow them to balloon into generalizations about the relationship as a whole. "You never . . ." "You always . . ." "This is just symptomatic of your ridiculous insistence on . . ." Carolyn left pins on the floor and the house a mess, but she was devoted and provided Jared with what he obviously valued most in life—a family structure in which he could lead and shine. Jared let her sloppiness get to him and failed to address any underlying problems, and the sad part is that both Carolyn's disorderliness and his deeper concerns could've been overcome. If Jared wasn't satisfied with his sex life, he could have conveyed its importance to Carolyn. If he needed ego strokes, he could have said so directly (perhaps with the aid of therapy) rather than ruminating on her absorption with the children and her collectibles.

No problem is one-sided, and Carolyn was at fault as well. By accepting Jared's philandering silently, like a martyr, she devalued herself and her marriage. And her refusal to improve her housekeeping in the face of Jared's continued rantings was an unconstructive means of retribution for his disloyalty. Neither partner wanted their marriage to end, but neither could get past the hurts and irritations to realize it. In the end, both continue to suffer.

I do believe that some habits are simply intolerable. I also believe that some people refuse to confront the seriousness of their continued actions—they deny that they may be in the wrong. They deny that they may be using their behavior to manipulate their partners. They may be using such actions as a means to reinforce existing feelings of low self-esteem, as proof that they ought to hate themselves. There are layers and layers of motives behind actions that seem clear-cut on the surface. And similarly, we can endow simple behavior with layers of motives that don't really exist, as a means of legitimizing them.

FAT AS A WEDGE BETWEEN SPOUSES

Take obesity. Many wives become fat after they have children, knowing—though not wanting to admit—that their husbands will find them less sexually desirable. They're under new stresses and can't help it, and they refuse to look in full-length mirrors anymore because they abhor their own shapes. But they eat anyway; they want love but consciously, though uncontrollably, make themselves less loveable. Overeating is one "despicable habit" that is often cited in exit lines—by both those who leave and the ones left behind. Overeating and size carry such—pardon the pun—enormous importance in our vision-driven culture that people simply accept that a food-obsessed mate is a candidate for disdain.

I know about this syndrome from vast experience leading a workshop I developed eight years ago called "Free From the Fat Mentality." In it I help clients—who range from anorexically emaciated to morbidly obese—to get back in touch with natural body signals of hunger and satiation and to deal with psychological push-pulls with food directly and constructively. I've worked with thousands of people and followed up with dozens who afterwards choose to pursue solving their underlying problems in private therapy. I'd project that approximately 50 percent of men and 70 percent of women in the general American population suffer from the "fat mentality," in which their feelings about themselves are inextricably entwined with how they are relating to their bodies and food.

Does any of the following sound familiar? Food becomes a neck-up tranquilizer, a private indulgence that is an effective outlet for stress. Control over food becomes symbolic of your mastery of the world. You fall into a cycle of good intentions, giving in to temptation and the self-hatred afterward that sometimes becomes the focus of your life, the definition of your self-esteem. That this internal process has the added effect of changing your spouse's reaction to you and undermining your whole marriage is simply an additional burden justifying further your self-flagellation.

But understanding what's going on—as many people do—doesn't keep the marriage together. When a man (for the sake of argument—of course this happens in the reverse as well) sees his wife gain and maintain weight, he may be understanding at first, but far less so as time goes on. Even with the best intentions, he often becomes less attracted to her. He may feel that she doesn't care enough about him to do something about it. He abhors that she probably doesn't care enough about herself to do anything about it.

Pretty soon he gets angry. Then, realizing the futility of his ire, he slowly withdraws his emotions. And other women begin to look better and better by comparison. His attachment becomes more sentimental than romantic, and sensing this, the wife hates herself even more, driving her back to the comfort of food. All understandable. But it's abominable that this situation then becomes a cause of divorce—when neither spouse really wants it. Both want the marriage to work, both still feel or could rekindle love. But instead of banding together to see the wife's overeating as a joint problem that could be addressed through teamwork and support, they retreat into their own interpretations and reactions.

I've given this particular marital disillusion a lot of attention because physical appearance is a much more crucial part of marital satisfaction than most people dare to admit. They know they're supposed to say they got married for better or worse; that their love isn't just based on fleeting physical beauty but on enduring intimacy and deeper, higher connections. It's embarrassing to admit that other men or other ladies turn you on now that your own spouse is looking a little less presentable. In a sense, it signals failure on your part—you once could attract a nice-looking partner; now, after knowing you, that same person thinks so little of you that he or she has gone to seed.

When physical deterioration ruins a marriage, it usually does so in a sexist and blatantly unfair manner that everyone disdains and yet acknowledges at the same time. In the norms of our unfair and biased society, even post-liberation, men are still allowed to go bald and become soft; they can acquire "distinguished" graying temples and "character" lines, and all women, including their wives, simply adore them. But women are offered far less grace. When that pert homecoming queen gets wrinkles and gray hair, when she shows the effects of having three children, men not only see a less sexy stereotype in their wives but are gripped by fear that they too are old. It's easy for them to then test their appeal, to find someone eager to prove their virility.

Insecurity about oneself is an internal psychological problem. Insecurity about the foundations of a marriage due to physical changes is similarly something that goes on inside one's head, not on the perimeters of one's body. Unfortunately, far too many men refuse to realize this and seek the external solution of separation and fresh romance. Negative reactions to a partner's weight, graying hair, or aging countenence reveal a flaw "in the eye of the beholder" rather than grounds for a speedy exit. Coping with your hang-ups about physical changes or characteristics is a matter of inward searching, unceasing communication with your partner, and often, counseling to help you see that threatening your marriage is perhaps the worst way to solve the problem.

EXIT LINE #7: "I NEED TO BE APPRECIATED!"

Lack of affection and recognition is distressing to any spouse who still loves his or her mate, because it implies that the partner's once flowering ardor has cooled. Why would any caring husband decline to caress or hug his real soul mate? How can a secure relationship deteriorate into ho-hum routine? What do women want, Freud wanted to know. Those who bother to get married want a little recognition, a little appreciation. With those basics, marriage brings adequate reward.

I came across a newspaper advice column headlined: "Is Boredom Enough Reason for Leaving?" The writer, Virginia Doody Klein, says no. "Marriage is a partnership," she declares, and the bored partner has the ability—and obligation—to spark the other person into excitement—basically by bringing more excitement into her own life. Relying on one's spouse to be the source of everything grand and interesting just makes *you* seem helpless and boring too. If you're bored, you've got to *do* something about it—and there are a lot less risky and drastic things to do than break up your marriage.[1]

On the other hand, lack of affection in most cases is a serious and legitimate complaint. People enter marriage for lots of reasons—for the benefits of family, for continuity, for a context. They want to perpetuate their values, and by choosing marriage and children are living the very values they hold. They want to accomplish something in the world, and marriage gives them the "safe haven" from which to operate.

But people also get married in order to receive and give love. They need personal rewards, such as assurance they're desired, assurance they have a valued place in the world. Yes, I've heard plenty of men admit that once they've settled into marriage—once they've gotten all that "mushy" stuff out of the way—they see little need to repeat all the endearments and adoration required during the courtship period in order to "bag" a woman. Marriage for them is far different from being single. Once wed, they don't need to be "on the make," and certainly not to their wives!

And yet, for many women—most women—their love relationships are by far and away their greatest source of satisfaction and validation in the world. So when husbands and wives come to live as if they were alone, without that sustenance, they question the point of the arrangement.

Just about every magazine article or newspaper column about maintaining a happy marriage says that demonstrating affection is a crucial ingredient. A September 1986 "Dear Abby" newspaper column included the following letter:

"Dear Abby:

"What does a man do when he approaches sixty, has a beautiful wife and fine children, but still feels the need for more excitement?

"I decided to renew my acquaintance with a woman with whom I had had a very romantic encounter many years ago. I reminded her of the thrilling romance we had, and in no time at all we were reliving those days with renewed passion. The effect on me was phenomenal, but the effect on the woman was even more amazing. She loved it!

"You see, the woman I renewed my acquaintance with was my wife!"[2]

Sounds so very simple, and it is, if the partners are willing. The problem arises when attempts to motivate your spouse are futile. When those little love notes left on his pillow arouse no more reaction than the bill for his dry-cleaning. When a Sunday brunch of his favorite pancakes and eggs is consumed behind a raised newspaper. And especially when your requests bring defensiveness rather than agreement.

When you hit that impasse, it's time to shake a few shoulders before you give up. Write a letter to your partner detailing your distress. The written word always carries more impact, especially if you rarely use letters as a means to communicate with your mate.

Bring in an outsider. Sometimes simply telling your spouse that you'd like marriage counseling is enough to jolt him into improvement. Spending money on therapy may hurt enough to inspire change.

The problem, however, could also be yours. It's a matter of expectations. You're being duped by our culture if you think marriage should have ongoing passion of the same type you shared when you first met. The proper and ultimately most rewarding progression of love and marriage is beyond chemistry, to comfort and familiarity. True romance comes from increased closeness and intimacy, not getaways to Rio. You probably loved the period of your relationship when you felt frequent thrills and titillations, and you miss that now. But if you're at all adult and realistic, you'll accept that the kind of love you gain over time is far more valuable and irreplaceable.

You're also likely to be disappointed if you choose to view your mate's passivity as entirely a function of his personality, his lack of development, his indifference to calling you from the office daily. Carol Tavris, in an article in *Woman's Day* magazine, notes that who you blame for your situation can largely determine your happiness. She reports on the research of Dr. Ayala Pines, a social psychologist at the University of California, Berkeley, who says that happy couples focus on the *situation*, while unhappy duos point fingers at *each other*.[3] It's one thing to say that your partner forgets your birthday and hardly notices you because he's consumed by his job which, after all, pays the bills. It's another to say his absent ardor is a hopeless manifestation of his lackluster and uncaring personality. In the first case, you can maintain your regard for him and direct your ire at outside circumstances. In the second, you end up hating your partner, throwing up your hands, and, ultimately, walking out the door.

NOTES

1. Klein, Virginia Doody. "Is Boredom Enough Reason for Leaving?" *Los Angeles Times*, February 10, 1986, Part V, p. 2.
2. Van Buren, Abigail. *Los Angeles Times*, September, 24, 1986.
3. Tavris, Carol. "How to Put Romance Back In Your Marriage." *Woman's Day*, April 1986, pp. 88, 90–91, 179.

CHAPTER 11

Throwing in the Towel

The last two chapters have focused on the most common exit lines used by people who initiate separation. A first group of departers want something better—a more exciting lifestyle or a more exciting spouse—and so reach for "the gusto" by destroying their marriages. A second set of terminators are fleeing from trouble they perceive in their relationships, problems they'd rather escape than fix. But what about those who *don't* want the marriage to end—the other halves of divorcing couples who get left behind? How do they explain why they are alone?

The following three replies to questioning observers that are detailed in this chapter may very well be legitimate. Sometimes there's nothing to do but accept it when your spouse walks out. You can't simply lie in front of the tires when your mate's pulling his car out of the driveway stuffed with suitcase and golf clubs. There is such a thing as being abandoned, as being slapped in the face, and I again acknowledge that there are times when rejected spouses have no alternative but to admit defeat.

On the other hand, such admissions often come prematurely, spurred by anger and pain. It's ego-protecting to sound so final, as if the whole issue of marriage or divorce is settled. In reality, however, the case is often still wide open, and the relationship can be saved.

Exit Line #8: "If He Can Do That To Me—Good Riddance!"

Everyone's patience has a limit. Let's say he stays out regularly at bars, knowing that every night you're waiting up for him, growing more and more hurt. Or perhaps it's an affair, or overzealousness at work, or anything that shows his allegiance is anywhere but with you. You've screamed, pleaded, and tried the silent treatment: and maybe he says he's sorry, but still he does it again, ignoring your wishes, your needs, and following his own selfish desires.

But then, there's a showdown. You tell him that he's got to shape up, or he won't have a wife to return to. You've got your pride after all, and you can't take being treated as if you didn't matter, especially when what you crave is to be the one thing that matters the most. This is it, the ultimatum, and you show him passionately, emotionally, that the "next times" are over.

He finally understands. He sees the light. He feels like a fool and hopes you'll forgive him. You do.

And then there's a "next time."

Now it's up to you—do you carry out your threat? Do you phone the lawyers and pack up the canary? You're justified in doing so, and fueled by fury, you put into action all the contingencies you've dreaded but steeled yourself for.

He's shocked. He can't believe his secure world is actually crumbling due to his lunkheadedness and stupidity. Now he's making changes, trying to restore equilibrium, trying to win you back. He dropped his lover, or cut back his hours at work, or joined AA and comes right home after work. But you've already said that last time was his final chance. Now you're so livid all you want to do is pay him back for giving you so much pain.

Desmond Locklund, a forty-year-old magazine writer, phoned me from a coffee shop six blocks away from my office one Tuesday night last winter. He'd been driving around for hours after his wife had confronted him with the fact that she'd taken a lover. He had to see me, he had to make his plan of action.

When Desmond arrived, he laid it all out calmly. He'd

seek joint custody of their year-old daughter. He could stay with friends for a couple of weeks. He'd already phoned his lawyer from the coffee shop, and the lawyer was drawing up papers he could sign the next day, dividing property, laying out child support, putting together terms. If Joselyn had a lover, that was it. Joselyn wasn't that perfect anyway. Her hips were too wide—and she didn't turn him on anymore. She was dynamic but uneducated, and she couldn't hold her own very well in a philosophical debate. He could do better. The marriage was over.

Desmond didn't want to consider anything else. His pride was so wounded that he could only see running away from the entire relationship. How could he have anything to do with someone who could do that to him? What nerve she had slapping him in the face by taking a lover! Sure he still loved her, but since she was so involved with someone else—well, he'd be just fine.

As anyone who ever read Desmond's writing knew, he was a very opinionated man. Once he got an idea into his head, he could articulately defend it, whether he was ultimately right or wrong. He always sounded so reasonable, even when he made his readers angry. His platitudes were impenetrable.

While impenetrable platitudes worked well for his reputation as a writer, they destroy relationships, which are always filled with nuance and complexity. The way he saw it, if his wife was wrong, then the relationship was wrong. If she could betray him, then the marriage had been permanently violated. Now all he had to do was retroactively look for flaws in his wife and their interaction that could justify this unilateral decision.

This generalizing and rashness blinded Desmond to his wife's true message. Joselyn would have gladly given up her admirer, if only Desmond were willing to say that he'd change. She wanted his attention and devotion—and said so by grasping for attention and devotion from a source willing to comply. But Desmond's pride allowed him only to end the marriage.

Because he's a celebrity of sorts—or simply because he's a man—Desmond will find a new partner. But because he distances himself from blame for the failure of his marriage, the quality of his new relationships are likely to be the same.

What a waste. The maxim "pride comes before a fall" applies to Desmond. He's too proud to allow Joselyn to call the shots; he's too proud to admit his own role in her infidelity. He's too proud to say that the marriage means enough to him to tolerate being cuckolded. He sees her behavior as symbolic of a kind of one-upmanship in which she has just proven her low regard for him; now he has to react in kind and prove his similar disdain for her and the union they'd created. It's lamentable that their child has to be hurt in the process, he'd admit, but there are some principles—such as a man's need to be honored and respected—that come before the feelings and suffering of others. Above all, Desmond is principled. I wonder if his principles will comfort him in his present difficulty and in the years of bitterness to come.

If you're feeling hurt by your partner, it's because you still care about him. So by retreating or by reaching for retribution, you're not only wounding your mate but destroying yourself. You further dismantle the relationship you wish were whole.

It's true that your anger deserves acknowledgment. But the drama of playing tit-for-tat or walking out only leads to the unhappy ending that in your heart you despise. Yes, you're hurt. You cannot just forgive and forget. The cliché to swallow your pride seems simplistic and wimpy. But what do you have if you discard your marriage? How will the situation improve?

Jewish tradition teaches an unusual but effective means to deal with anger: Give a gift to the object of your rage. At first, this approach sounds hypocritical. It runs contrary to the "follow your feelings" mentality popularized in the 1970s. But recent research shows that letting your anger loose only exacerbates bad feeling. Controlling it minimizes the trauma. And by extension, going the other direction—i.e., giving the target of your ire a gift—smoothes over your hostility and allows you to function to your own benefit. I'm talking here about a material gift (a book, a piece of clothing, etc.), something solid that you physically procure. This item is a concrete expression of your intention for yourself not to feel such harmful emotions. Once you give the gift, you gain a measure of serenity, and with it the patience to rebuild a worthwhile relationship. Don't let short-term stubbornness or pride cause you lifelong regret.

EXIT LINE #9: "I CAN'T MAKE HIM WANT ME"

When your partner says he's "fallen out of love" or that he needs space or has taken a lover—any one of the many lines you've just read about—you can admit defeat with this explanation—or fight. You don't have to accept it when your partner tries to convince you that you have nothing in common or that the passion has died. And while it's true that ultimately you can't force someone to love or stay married to you, you can certainly make it difficult to leave, physically and emotionally. This sounds somehow unfair or devious, but it's really not at all—in fact the purpose is to prevent disaster.

The problem is that when you're rejected by your partner, your self-esteem plummets. And when you feel unwanted and unloved, when your partner implies that your value is zilch, you tend to believe it. After all, if someone who pledged his whole life to you can turn around and say you mean nothing, after all you've been through together, well, maybe he has a point.

So for you to say, "Wait a minute, you're throwing away the best thing you've got, something precious and worth saving," makes you feel like a hypocrite. How can you tell your partner how great you are when you don't believe it yourself? How can you summon up the *chutz-pah* to sound self-assured and confident when you're reeling from a debilitating blow to your self-esteem? It's much easier to slump into helplessness and accept the situation as it's presented to you: he doesn't love you; it's his decision; you can't get into his head and change his mind.

It's easier to use this line than face the difficult task of trying to win back your mate. Unfortunately, when you take this easy route, you also provide your partner further justification for his exit. "She's just accepting what I tell her, so she must want me to leave," he can figure.

Or, he can point to your behavior to prove your inferiority: "I know she still loves me, but look at her—she's just whimpering around, depressed. Why should I want to stay with someone like that—someone with so little spunk and gumption that she won't even fight to keep me?'' Either way, you look pathetic. The ''I can't make him love me'' line is great for inspiring guilt in your partner—but lousy for saving your marriage.

I remember Marty Logan, a thirty-eight-year-old real estate syndicator, who played around during the thirteen years of his childless marriage to Sybil. Of course he knew he shouldn't have strayed, but somewhere deep in his soul was the conviction that Sybil wasn't his match, wasn't the romantic ideal he should be paired with. She was devoted and sweet and really did nothing that Marty could condemn. She kept his home immaculate, cooked outrageously rich gourmet meals for him, and considered her ''career'' to be helping Marty with his accounting and other paperwork. But in her devotion, she became too familiar, too bland to earn Marty's respect and pride. The ladies he pursued had the dramatic allure Sybil lacked—one was a concert pianist, another a professor of political science, a third a sculptor.

When he finally left Sybil for a film studio executive, Marty was consumed with guilt. He gave her the house and a generous allowance. He helped get her investments so that she would never have to work. He visited her regularly and came through in small emergencies, such as fixing her car and clearing out the clogged rain gutter. And whenever he spoke of Sybil to his new wife, he always preceded her name with the adjective ''poor.''

Because when he announced his departure, all Sybil could do was cry. She cried at lunch with her girlfriends. She cried when she worked alone in the garden. And she cried in my office when she came for counseling with Marty. ''What have I done wrong?'' she wanted to know, her brilliant blue eyes crowded with tears. ''Why wasn't my best good enough?''

In one session I couldn't turn her thinking around. She hated Marty for what he did, but passively accepted his assessment that the marriage was washed up. It never occurred to her that Marty could be wrong—that she was a great wife, and that he would be the loser if he opted out. Her low self-esteem was so pervasive that all she could do was wallow in her defeat—and Marty, pointing to her depression, kept saying that he simply needed someone more dynamic, more upbeat, more glamorous. She relied upon the classic line: "I can't make him love me," Sybil sniffled. "All I can do is let him know how much he's hurting me."

After listening to an hour of this lamenting, I could understand why Marty had problems with her. Now, whatever I hear "I can't make him love me," I want to shout, "Maybe you can!" But then, you'd have to start acting like a different person—one your spouse would desire.

Robert Weiss, writing in *Marital Separation*, asserts that there is hope for your marriage even after separation. Based on research evidence, he projects conservatively that for every separation that ends in divorce, at least one separation leads to reconciliation. But that can happen only if someone—you—refuses to let go.[1]

Okay, it's true that nothing can stop someone when he's determined to leave. But how many people walk out with 100 percent conviction? If there is the slightest quiver in his voice when he announces his departure, you've got something to hang onto. With the right course of action, you *can* get him to love you again.

EXIT LINE #10: "HE'LL BE HAPPIER WITHOUT ME"

This could be the martyr's theme song. Just think of all the self-deprecation implicit in these words: "He can do better." "I'm not that great to be married to." "I'm not good enough for him." "What he can get elsewhere is better than what he has with me—or what we could have together even if we work to improve our marriage." Pretty pathetic. But I don't think most divorcing folk who use this line are expressing sincere feelings of inferiority. Usually, they're trying to say—or ask for—something else.

The rejected spouse who lets go of her mate *tsk-tsk*ing, "he's better off without me" *does* have low self-esteem, of course—to an unusual degree. But when you tell others of your separation with these words, you're not just maligning yourself but expressing hostility—and at the same time forcing your listener to bolster your ego. When you say, "He'll be better off without me," friends shift uneasily and have to respond, "No! your *ex* is the big loser, not you! You're terrific and he's just a fool to leave!''

It's strange how often unfaithful spouses mournfully mouth this line. "She'll be happier without me," they say wearily, supposedly confessing that their wrongdoing makes them unqualified to continue fulfilling their vows. They reason that after such transgressions (entered willingly, of course!) no good or noble spouse could ever maintain respect. No, 'tis far better to free the poor soul to find a more worthy mate, sighs the philanderer, silently concluding, ". . . leaving me free to pursue my affair."

I have absolutely no pity for people who want to slink out their responsibilities, no matter how they try to rationalize it. And this exit line certainly does a poor job of justification. But why *can't* you just admit you've sunk to the depths of depravity and hope it's nobody's business but your own? Why *can't* you quietly sidle off into the sunset, leaving your befuddled ex-partner to find someone else?

You need this modest-sounding exit line because you can swear all you want that your life is your own, but that's just too bad—no matter what you say, *it's not*. You can never negate the fact that you married someone— promised you'd be bound to that other person for life. Attempts to arouse sympathy for yourself or your benighted spouse—such as saying he'll be happier without you—don't detract from what a louse you are for cheating. No matter how immoral you've become, you have an obligation to face your mate squarely and explain your actions.

What you've just been reading may have made you angry. It suggests that you, or perhaps the person you still love, has acted like a jerk, a louse, a slimy sort who, for selfish reasons, behaves abominably. It suggests that people use lines to disguise true motivations; that they really intend to quickly cut off long-term associations rather than withdraw in a kind-hearted, orderly fashion. When I pick holes in the exit lines you use to justify your divorce, I question your good will, your honesty, your integrity. Maybe it's appropriate that you feel uncomfortable.

The problem is that when you're in the middle of an

affair, or when your marriage seems so confining or unbearable that it feels like the walls are squishing in on you, you are likely to compromise your usually high moral standards. It becomes much more simple to begin acting in a way you would otherwise disdain. It's a kindness for someone close to say, "Wait a minute, at this point you are acting in an uncharacteristically louselike manner." I work on the premise that healing a relationship that has existed for years in good standing is better than destroying it. And negating the ten exit lines I've described in the last three chapters, as harsh and difficult as that is, encourages that beneficial end.

NOTES

1. Weiss, Robert. *Marital Separation.* New York: Basic Books, 1975.

CHAPTER 12

A Few Good Reasons to Stay Together

As we've just seen, the ten most commonly accepted reasons for divorce in many cases are simply excuses for giving up a repairable marriage. The "exit lines" you've just read justify avoiding growth-producing confrontation. They legitimize running away with an extracurricular lover. They allow you to sever a bond that is probably irreplaceable with the rationalization that the connection between you is—at this moment—weaker than it was before. It's amazing how readily friends and family accept the pronouncements of loved ones determined to separate. "Okay, if that's the way you want it. If that's the way it is," they shrug, eager to avoid any uneasy explanations.

But if you say you don't want to get divorced—if, for example, you're the one who's left behind and are trying to convince your partner to stay—you won't receive the same kind of unquestioning support. There's a double standard operating in our society today, and it's a standard that honors for marriage and at the same time honors divorce. It sanctions leaving for the most inane reasons, among them "needing more space" and "going through an identity crisis," and yet also accepts those seeking to keep the marriage together.

The unspoken logic goes that as long as marriage functions perfectly, fine; but if there's the slightest crack in the relationship, then it is obsolete. The notion of "dis-

167

posable marriages'' includes those, like plastic Baggies or Pampers, that are slightly soiled and therefore worthy only of the trash can. It occurs to few people to wash the Baggie or recycle the mountains of plastic in the diapers because these conveniences were designed to be discarded. Similarly, though marriage was not created to be a phase, many people are entering into it believing that it should last only as long as it feels good. Once the ecstatic patina of the relationship wears off, the union is as soiled and unwanted as the dirty wrap off the baby's bottom.

This assumption leads to a particularly cynical attitude toward anyone known to have a troubled marriage who decides to stick it out. One of my clients, Alan Meyers, in just that position, described his conversation with an old-time buddy at his high school's twentieth reunion. Alan and his wife of fifteen years, Rebecca, had two girls, aged five and seven. A lanky, balding man of thirty-eight, Alan was nonetheless handsome, with a thick mustache and enthusiastic brown eyes. Rebecca and he had just seemed to find different worlds over the last few years. She was totally consumed with the children, and her work part-time even involved giving piano lessons to a host of seven-year-olds.

While he was genuinely fond of his daughters, Alan had become engrossed in the office-based world of his engineering consulting company. On his days off, he looked forward to a game of tennis or a sail with his business partners, half of whom were women. Rebecca, on the other hand, when she wasn't filling her weekends with piano lessons, preferred to take the kids on field trips, often with a couple of their little friends in tow. Their times together had become a *mélange* of amusement parks and girl scout activities, and when Alan suggested time off without the girls, Rebecca responded as if he were shirking his familial duties, saying that only a ''bad father'' wouldn't want to see his offspring on the few days he's available to them.

Inevitably, Alan became more and more unwilling to break tennis dates he purposely set up on weekends with co-workers. He wasn't the type to be unfaithful—he took his upbringing and commitments too seriously—but be began to feel more and more depressed. His sex life was down to an every-Friday-night routine, and his midweek amorous inclinations didn't fit in a schedule so filled with activities. Alan felt ignored, despite the adoration of his daughters and a wife who praised him for any and all of his paternal demonstrations of affection and playfulness.

It had been twelve years since Alan had last seen Steve Blum, his best friend through school in California's San Fernando Valley. Steve looked fantastic in his rented tuxedo; the years had not lined his jogging-in-the-sunshine complexion. Steve's second wife was a knockout, ten years younger, though she and their baby, six months old, weren't all Steve boasted about. Alan joined in Steve's praise of fatherhood—the girls were gorgeous and full of surprises. And what about Rebecca? Still as cuddly as ever?

Alan paused a moment too long, and looked down into the melting ice of his Bloody Mary. Steve caught his hesitation immediately. "What's the story, old buddy?" he whispered with paternal concern.

"Rebecca's just fine, just fine," Alan responded, trying to brighten. But Steve's curiosity wouldn't quit.

"You can't fool me, Alan," he insisted. "I know you too well. What's the problem?"

With that Alan haltingly revealed his frustration with Rebecca's focus on the kids. He felt left out, he felt unimportant. "Nothing's new anymore, like it used to be when we were younger. I love my family—but I have a wife-and-mother, not a lover anymore."

"Then get out," Steve urged. "I did, and look at me now, buddy. I've got a beautiful wife who loves to go skiing with me. She doesn't mind leaving the baby with the housekeeper. She puts me first. You can do it too. There are plenty of women out there just dying for a guy like you."

Alan immediately regretted telling Steve about his long-suppressed feelings. Things weren't that bad, he reassured him. He really loved his little girls, and he would go crazy missing them if he left—and it would totally break their hearts, not to mention Rebecca's and both their family's.

"You've only got one life to live, buddy," Steve persisted. "Do you want to live your life for them or for you? You think you can just change Rebecca's personality like that? No way. You're doomed to many years of the same, my friend, unless you get out now—or take somebody on the side.''

Alan was shocked to hear his once-closest friend talk like this. They both swore to their high school sweethearts of undying love, of romance worth keeping forever. How could he betray these noble ideals so easily?

"The past is past," Steve said casually. "We learn from our mistakes. I wasted precious time with Sally, and it sounds like you're doing the same with Rebecca. I'll tell you something else, my friend, if it'll make it any easier . . ." Steve leaned in close to Alan's ear. "I never thought Becky was all that much to look at anyway, if you know what I mean.''

Alan was shaken. Steve had nonchalantly brushed off his reasons for keeping his marriage together. The girls, the feelings of his wife and family, the fact that they still shared a close bond—all seemed to matter little. All that Steve cared about was immediate excitement, a trim body to bed, and somebody he could bend to his will.

I had to assure Alan that his reasons for staying with Rebecca were not only sound but excellent. They proved that there was a basis of rationality upon which to rekindle the more transitory kinds of rewards that sex and mutual rapture represent. Steve had a good life, of course, according to his present standards. But perhaps the development of his present standards—as opposed to the till-death-do-us-part values he shared with Alan in high school—was necessary in order to rationalize the major changes in his life. He couldn't very well tell Steve to put effort into saving his marriage when he had refused to do it himself. Alan was relieved that he wouldn't have to upend his marriage and lifestyle in order to be "fulfilled." A few sessions later, he and Rebecca, who was surprised when she learned of Alan's discontent, had made several changes in their routine and communication. In only two months of devoted attention, the couple was able to reestablish the closeness they'd lost.

The point is that nowadays, the only reason to stay together that's indisputably accepted is that you're "in love." (You can grouse far more than Alan did to Steve and get away with it if you simply cap your complaints with, "But I can't help it—I love her!")

What "being in love" usually means is that each spouse has his or her personal romantic expectations met, even if those expectations are unrealistic. A problem arises when there comes even a brief time of disappointment. No mediocrity is allowed into an anticipated lifetime of passion. A wife has to be unflaggingly adequate, if not great in bed, for her husband to waste even another night with her. A husband has to be unqualifiedly supportive of a wife's career for her to consider him worth even the smallest emotional investment.

The truth is that every marriage has periods when one or both spouses aren't getting all—or even many—of their needs met. These periods may last weeks before either partner notices anything even vaguely amiss, and by the time the situation is verbalized, resentment may have crept into their everyday interaction. In this post-1970s time of emotions ruling motion, too many partners don't ponder the prudence of their reactions before acting. And yet, we apply standards to our marriages that we would never consider applying to other relationships. We accept that other relationships can't stay steadily rewarding, but marriage must be consistently satisfying. "Down times" do not mean that you'll never have the "up" times again.

Seven Good Reasons to Stay Together that Have Gotten a Bum Rap

The following reasons not to split are usually labeled "bad" reasons to stay together. You shouldn't remain married "just" for the sake of the children or because you don't believe in divorce—that might mean doubting the importance of your feelings as the immediate basis of action. Over the past several years the one thing we've been taught not to doubt is our feelings. Never mind that the pursuit of "high" feelings led to minds permanently numbed by drugs. Never mind that generations of families were irreparably torn apart because teenagers had to follow their feelings and rebel against their parents. Never mind that marriages crumbled because personal feelings were allowed to dictate behavior rather than courtesy and dignity—and commitment to one's spouse.

The "bum rap" the following reasons received is due

to a warped sense of values that place selfish feelings above higher, and ultimately more healthful, goals. The problem is that we've come to view feelings as solid and immutable, when in reality, we can shape them and choose them moment-to-moment. The kinds of reasons for staying together that have recently been branded "bad" are those factors that take into account the impact of one's marriage on others, and its outside ramifications.

GOOD REASON #1: "WE SHOULD STAY TOGETHER FOR THE SAKE OF THE CHILDREN"

Naturally, a divorce is less cruel to children than subjecting them to extreme ongoing parental malice and discord. I would never suggest that a venomous couple stay together solely because they have children—they do the child no favors, exchanging their physical presence in the same house for guilt, tension, and misery. Children are extremely resilient, and certainly an intolerable situation of substance abuse or of physical or emotional torment must be ended. Judith Wallerstein, in her classic five-year study following divorcing parents and their children, *Surviving the Breakup*, suggests that while divorce has profound negative effects on children, "sticking out" an oppressive situation does not improve offsprings' prognoses.[1]

With that in mind, let's look at the kind of person who would admit that he stays in a less-than-perfect marriage because providing a two-parent family for his children is of paramount importance. This is someone who values stability. Someone for whom consistency and reliability mean a great deal. Someone like Leslie, whom I interviewed for this book. A thirty-nine-year-old former teacher who now cares for her three children, aged eighteen months, three years, and six years, Leslie has been married to Rick for fifteen years. I met her in a workshop I was conducting for those with weight problems.

Her story: "I know that Rick has a lover. He knows I know but still plays the game of pretending she doesn't exist. He's had two long-term affairs over the past eight years, and I know he's ashamed of it and doesn't want to end our relationship. So what do I do? Confront him and force him to end it? Frankly, I'm afraid he'd choose her over me. It does tear me up at times, especially on the nights he doesn't come home. I know he does go to conferences—he's an English professor and presents those boringly long research papers—but I also know he takes her with him. Actually they get away with it because she's also a professor in his department, and there are so many plausible professional reasons why they could be together.

"It might be one thing if he was satisfying to me, but frankly, since my first pregnancy, I've used food to cope with my distress over it all. When Rick comes near me, my own self-loathing makes me create a physical distance. I love this man, but I'm so ashamed about my size [she was forty pounds overweight] that I don't want him to touch me.

"Still, we have one thing that we're together on 100 percent—the kids. We both adore them. To see Rick playing with our baby on the floor, rolling around, and the baby with his silly little laugh—it's worth everything. Talking with the kids about 'Daddy this' and 'Daddy that' is important to me too. And his help—he takes our eldest to Indian Guides and that gives me a little breather. And the three-year-old goes to swimming lessons with Daddy. When I see how the kids react—how they idolize Rick and seem to blossom when we go on outings as a family, I know I could never take that away from them. And of course I compare my kids to those of my friends who are divorced. Those kids do suffer, no matter how much my friends pray they don't."

I respected Leslie because her argument wasn't one of martyrdom or irrationality. She knew she had problems that needed addressing, and she knew her marriage was in trouble. But rather than simply abandoning everything in search of some personally rewarding abstraction, or out of retribution or pain, she looked at the totality and decided that because of her children, the situation was worth saving.

Sociologist Lenore Weitzman, whose 1985 book, *The Divorce Revolution*,[2] examined current divorce laws and attitudes, commented to me in an interview that "the real message of my book is how valuable marriage can be, and how devastating divorce is.'' She notes that in the throes of hatred for a spouse, many people, and men in particular, don't realize how painful separation from their children will be. ''There is a definite loss in the relationship with children that is inevitable, no matter the cost of custody.'' She says that the attachment of parent to child is persistent, and ''that loss is pervasive.'' Dr. Weitzman's point is not only that divorce wallops children, but that it also deeply hurts *parents*, who see the nature of their relationships sadly and profoundly changed. While escaping one situation that causes them pain, divorcing parents create for themselves another.

At least if you stay married, there is the option to work actively to improve the situation. Equally importantly, if you love your children you will want to spare them the crushing impact of this event. Wallerstein found that divorce ''is predictably extremely stressful to most children and adolescents and that the physical separation of the parents, which was regarded by most youngsters as the central divorce event, precipitated a wide range of feelings and behavioral changes at home, at school, and on the playground.''[3] This observation implies that the emotional separation that may be present in a less-than-ideal marriage does far less harm than when one partner actually moves out. Given such consequences, it's certainly worth giving your marriage several chances.

GOOD REASON #2: ''I WANT TO STICK IT OUT''

Of course, the story would be almost pitiful if Leslie simply continued to suffer in silence, knowing of her husband's infidelity and reacting by drowning in a sea of calories. Instead, she decided to join my workshop, change her self-image through therapy, and eventually confront Rick. An upbeat ending to a common story. But what about the thousands of other women (and men) whose mates are philandering and who prefer not to ''rock the boat'' by addressing it? Are their husbands justified in walking out to the eagerly passionate arms of their lovers? Is divorce so horrendous that a life of daily wounds and secrets is preferable?

Obviously it's much healthier to deal with marital strains and crises directly. Obviously, in the best of all possible worlds, the husband (or wife) would see the error of his ways and in a stroke of magnanimous civility, cast off his lover and appreciate anew the allure of his original and true love. In a burst of apology, he would sweep his wife off her feet and their romantic fires would be rekindled once again.

Rarely do events unfold so neatly. Relationships are far too complex to prescribe categorically the best solution for everyone. With that caveat aside, I believe that preserving the marriage, even if it has lapsed into a benign routine that exists mainly for the benefit of the children, is preferable to divorce.

The decision to leave is always based upon a balance of the value of factors affecting your well-being. If there comes a point when your personal gain outweighs what you think will be the impact on the children and other outcomes, then you leave. The variable is the amount of value you place on each of the influences on your decision. Leslie placed a high value on her children's happiness; balancing against it was a chronic lack of fulfillment. An acute dose of emotional pain can upset the balance—unless the importance of preserving the family outweighs it.

In Nora Ephron's 1983 book *Heartburn*, the character of Rachel Samstat finds herself in a position similar to Leslie's—while seven months pregnant with her second child. A cookbook author, she minces onion but no words with her husband, heartbroken as she is to discover his tarrying. He swears repentance, and Rachel's desire to keep together the cozy family she has created helps her to believe that her mate has reformed.

But later the evidence betrays him, and Rachel feels forced to pack up her son and the new baby. Her emotions culminate as she contemplates bashing him with a Key Lime pie from across the dinner table:

> "I still find you interesting, even if right now you are being more boring than the Martin Agronsky Show. But someday I won't anymore. And in the meantime, I'm getting out. I am no beauty, and I'm getting on in years, and I have just about enough money to last me sixty days, and I am terrified of being alone, and I can't bear the idea of divorce, but I would rather die

than sit here and pretend it's okay, I would rather die
than sit here figuring out how to get you to love me
again . . .''[4]

That's the key. You've got to want to figure out how to
get him (or her) to love you again. I maintain that is a
good reason to stay.

"Sticking it out" means slogging through the pain of
the moment in order to achieve a better state afterwards.
It may mean even stoically waiting out a husband's self-
limiting affair, knowing that his primary commitment is
to you and to his family, even though the marriage does
not meet his present (hurtful and selfish) need for excitement.

Too often women who wait out a husband's affair are
condemned as martyrs or self-hating fools who have such
little self-esteem that they even accept emotional beating.
In some cases, this scenario may be true. But the majority deserve praise for their unshakable devotion to their
families and their husbands, and for their ability to see
past the immediacy of the situation to a broader scope
and greater outcome. They may not be handling events
in the 1970s' "let it all hang out" style, but this too is
to their credit, since an open-mouthed method risks the
good will they seek to preserve.

GOOD REASON #3: "WE SHOULD STAY MARRIED BECAUSE WE'VE BEEN TOGETHER SO LONG"

On the surface, this reason not to separate seems crazy.
What have past events, "water under the bridge," got to
do with the future? Why get sentimental over a symbol
for time passed, dates on a calendar, something that is
basically just a statistic?

But look beneath the words "we've been together so
long." Here are two very good reasons to work it out.
Firstly, the phrase implies that there was a significant
stretch of *simpatico*, which proves that the marriage *can*
work well, even through long-term pressures. The couple
enjoyed a basic compatibility, a shared world view. Such
a similarity is formed through years of birthdays, Christ-

mases, births, and career ups and downs and cannot be forged in any other way.

There is *value* in shared history. It should not be discounted simply to rationalize an immediate desire, or even to correct what has developed into a current problem, especially when you cannot be so sure that any new relationship you enter into will be as workable, even in the short term. In other words, you're giving up a known and proven success for the mere hope of one.

And secondly, the longer people are together, the more close and indelible the relationship becomes. It's inevitable, even if the time spent together was not always pleasant, even if the bad times outnumbered the good. Destroying the intimacy that years bring is definitely worse—emotionally, spiritually, financially, practically—than dissolving a brief partnership, asserts Robert Weiss in *Marital Separation*. He notes that it takes two years for a marriage to become integrated into one's identity. But after that time, the attachment is solidly ingrained.[5]

So ingrained, in fact, that Weiss devotes a large part of his work to the "disruption of identity" that occurs with divorce. The painful process of redefining yourself as separate from your spouse is fraught with ongoing distress, the symptoms of which include difficulty in choice and planning and "obsessive review" of events from the marriage.

Weiss explains that once you've been together a long time, it's impossible to simply cut free and start again. The persistence of marital bonds after separation, he writes, "is unique because of its resilience . . . its extrordinary ambivalence."[6] The destruction of such powerful links is not undertaken by the wise—or those who see tranquility in their futures.

In fact, psychologist Constance Ahrons of the University of Southern California found in her study of 98 divorced couples in the Binuclear Family Project that almost everyone interviewed wished they had better relationships with their ex-spouses. (Because of the children, all were forced to have contact throughout the five years of the study.) Of those Ahrons followed, half carried such anger with their "ex's" over the years that their interaction invariably was fraught with conflict and hostility.

The other half of Ahrons's subjects had civil, if not cordial, relationships five years after their divorces, though they were still bound together not only by their own connection but by the needs of their children. Sixty-four percent of the women and 52 percent of the men in her study said their relationships now were better than at the climactic separation. So why not reconcile? Ahrons notes that presently there is no socially acceptable way to preserve the positive aspects of a relationship postdivorce. This means that there is societal pressure for those who have separated to *remain enemies*—which is one more force causing needless animosity and misery.[7]

Given Ahrons's results, if you have children, you can expect to remain associated with your ex-spouse *no matter* the state of your relationship, amicable or not. You will be involved for the rest of your lives, so you might as well keep that tie a positive one, with as much regard and affection as possible. You know that things can be good between you, because they once were. And the best context for maintaining the continuity of your relationship and retaining the benefits of the time you've already invested into the union, is . . . your marriage.

GOOD REASON #4: "WE SHOULD STAY TOGETHER BECAUSE OUR FRIENDS AND FAMILIES WOULD BE DEVASTATED"

Anyone who disagrees that this is an important reason to stay together is living on Mars. Only on Mars can you live in a vacuum, with no neighbors to watch you or care about you, save possibly for some little green men. I don't know where people get the absurd idea that their marriage is their own business, and that whether their marriage survives or dies is of consequence to no one but themselves. Unless it's from the same admittedly fantasy-based brain lobe wherein resides Wishful Thinking.

And even that queer region of the brain has its lapses. Because on the one hand, when we want to slink clandestinely into divorce court, our Wishful Thinking lobe says: "Make a dash for it; no one's looking; your marriage is your own business." And on the other, when planning a grandiose wedding for four hundred guests, it says: "I'm going to build a network of caring friends, family, and co-workers, an extended family!" In other words, we want conflicting things: a large cocoon of concern, and distance from those around us. How is this possible? The answer is that it's possible because we want them at different times.

When we're anticipating that lavish wedding, we want people we know to revel with us; to take our personal joy for themselves and reflect this happiness back to us. When the first, second, and further children come along, we similarly want those events to be of consequence to people beyond just ourselves. But when our marriage is a shambles, we keep our voices down and our pasted smiles handy, perhaps with the exception of one or two confidants needed for emotional support, until the moving van pulls up and it's impossible to hide the truth anymore.

And we only have to hide it because the wedding and baby showers, the July Fourth barbecues, and the charity fundraisers chronologically all come first; because more than our privacy we want those personal connections; because isolated is lonely, and attached is cozy and secure. We carefully construct those friendships, preserve and treasure them. We feel badly when we have a spat with a neighbor; we are careful not to hurt the feelings of the cousin with the ungainly daughter.

And even in these most unfriendly times, when bicoastal marriages and business opportunities mean that the "average" family lives in the same domicile just a few years, we work desperately to keep up connections. The new phenomenon of "networking groups" goes beyond the "old boy network" to actively solicit involvement with others. The urgency of people working to form "communities"—even for the most bizarre of commonalities—shows our need to come together. Each strand in our web of relationships is spun intentionally, dedicatedly, to be strong, to endure more than a wisp of winter wind.

In preparing this book I interviewed dozens of divorced people. Ann Boker, a thirty-five-year-old sociology professor, recounted the effects of the end of her thirteen-year marriage on people she cared about: "My sweet parents, who had always been so proud of me, were devastated. They loved my ex-husband like their own son, and they couldn't understand what would make me leave this gentle, loving person. It made me feel worse than I already did. My ex was torn up by my leaving, and now my parents were siding with him. And why not? How could I explain to them that I felt that Randy was more of a brother than a husband? My parents had always supported everything I wanted to do—but now they simply couldn't.

"And our friends as well. We'd been together so long—we were the couple everybody expected to outlast them all—and now I ruined it. Their whole image of what marriage should be like was destroyed. They each took me aside to ask me what was wrong—why couldn't we fix it? I have to confess now that we could have fixed it—but I had this idea of romance and passion, which, now that I'm single, I don't get much of anyway."

Why is the breakup of your marriage so tragic for your friends and family—and why should that be a good reason to stay together?

To answer the first question: because not only are they *your* context, but you form *theirs*. They have gone about constructing their network of extended family as carefully as you have; they form their world view on the continuity and soundness of their choices. When a piece of their world goes out of whack, they suffer—they must readjust their circle; their images and ideals are tarnished. This disruption gives them distress, because in constructing their microcosm, they banked on your permanence. They counted on you and now you've let them down. In a sense, you're telling them that they were wrong to place their faith in you.

These people who love you believe that your marriage *should* continue to work, as it has over the years you've stayed together. They know you; they know your spouse. They're not basing this assumption on whimsy but on experience. They danced at your wedding and saw you commit yourselves, perhaps even under the auspices of religious institutions that have served them well throughout their lives.

There's a reason why pastors quote the Biblical passage admonishing man not to put asunder what God hath joined. It's a reminder that once you make a covenant in the most holy and solemn context possible, then it's not God who allows it to go sour—but the participants in the relationship themselves. If your family or friends have a religious basis for their distress over your breakup, perhaps they're recognizing that it's merely your own lack of commitment that brings this jubilantly begun union to a close.

But why should the suffering of family and friends over your shattered marriage be a good reason for you to remain together? Because this network of closeness you've carefully constructed around you is *valuable*. It's something you cannot replace. It may seem as if your friends will stick with you through any changes you make; but, as I discovered in my interviews, that's simply not true. You lose friends; you lose the respect of both friends and family. You've failed at something fundamental that reflects on your loyalty, your interpersonal skills, your trust in someone else—all essential ingredients to good friendships and family relationships as well as a solid marriage. Even if you think you're the same person as before the separation (and of course you're not), people will *view* you differently. The terms of your relationship with family and friends shift, and you not only lose your husband or wife, but you lose the essence of the relationships you're counting on to get you through the divorce.

You're also pulling the safety net of love and support out from under your soon-to-be ''ex'' and from the children caught in the detachment process. Others cannot act toward them in the way they did before, leaving aching, rejected spouses and chagrined children only awkward relatives with clumsy communication to support them. There's no safety net of associates for people getting divorced, since the fabric of their lives—the casual, easy conversation that marks close relationships—is often impossibly rent.

GOOD REASON #5: "WE SHOULD STAY TOGETHER
BECAUSE I'M AFRAID OF THE CONSEQUENCES
OF GETTING DIVORCED"

The mistaken logic of the 1960s says to listen to your feelings no matter what they tell you, because only by following your gut rather than your brain can you be "natural" and "authentic." I'm not sure why being "natural" and "authentic" are such exemplary characteristics, but somehow in our "liberation" ethic, they were urgent necessities. But with the wisdom of maturity, we can look back and see that simply following our feelings got us into a lot of trouble—including drugs, sexually transmitted diseases, and wasting precious years wandering, trying to "find ourselves." Many of us in the baby boom are only now becoming adult enough, in our late thirties and early forties, to have babies ourselves. We say we're glad we waited, that we benefited from all those years in exploration or graduate school, that our backpacking forays to Europe were educational, and that doing drugs and sex were things we're happy to have gotten our of our systems. But aren't these just rationalizations for behavior that we realize was selfish and destructive?

Part of our growing up in the last several years has been to realize that our behavior *does* have consequences, and that these results ought to be considered *before* we act. In this spirit, the wiser ones among us look at the trauma, expense, disruption, and other outcomes of divorce and, with rationality and clearheadedness, usually decide it's not worth it. Why break up a broken but repairable relationship when there's no guarantee that the next one will be any better? Why scuttle the family, traditions, and familiarity you've painstakingly created in order to start from scratch, building the same thing? Aren't there enough troubles and inconveniences to deal with without adding the consuming agonies of divorce?

I'll admit that when you're suffering, when you're in emotional pain and you simply want relief, it's difficult to think of long-term consequences. You're not in the mood to go to the library and find out that you'll end up 73 percent worse off financially (if you're a woman) or that the chances are that even if you're awarded "joint custody" you'll seldom see your kids (if you're a man). You don't want to hear that you'll be emotionally out of commission for the next several months to two years, when you feel emotionally drained *this moment*. You just want to escape. Never mind to *what*.

Of course some people coolly and calculatedly plan out their withdrawal from a pesky marriage when they stand to lose substantial sums. According to an article in *Inc.* magazine entrepreneurs can go to extreme lengths: "One business consultant in a Chicago suburb, anticipating the breakup of his marriage, considered such tactics as entering into separate bank accounts, establishing new trusts, investing in side ventures, prepaying his taxes, and indulging himself in bigger but less obvious perks—all of which are divorce shelters that are unlikely to be traced by a valuator. In the end, he decided it wasn't worth the energy to be so furtive. His strategy, rather, was to convince his wife that the business was more stagnant than prosperous.

" 'It was pretty simple,' the consultant recalls. 'First of all, you keep your mouth shut. You say nothing at home—nothing positive, anyway. Even if you land a big contract, you say things are only okay at work, because you don't want that stuff thrown back in your face in court. Then, at the end of each quarter, you put everything in the worst light possible, and you tell your accountant you expect him to do the same. It was tiring, it was stressful, and I don't know that I'd do it again. But it worked.' "[8]

The goal: divorce. The tactic: devious. The result: a decree and lots of guilt, possible tax evasion prosecution, and fear that if ever the "ex" finds out, there's hell to pay. You can't blame the guy for wanting to preserve the monetary fruits of his hard work. But you can blame him for dealing dirty. He focused on one consequence of divorce (loss of his business) and ignored other, more significant, outcomes (loss of self-esteem, stress, vulnerability, engendering his wife's hatred). What a smart guy: he may have been stressed and exhausted by his single-minded dedication to obtaining his divorce, but at least his bank account never suffered. Does that sound like such great planning?

Good Reason #6: "We're Staying Together Because I Don't Have the Heart to Hurt Her"

Bravo! At least there's someone with a little compassion in the world. Someone who is thinking about the other person as well as his or her own station. What a good starting point for healing whatever rift is separating you. You care about your mate. She obviously cares about you, or else she wouldn't be so pained by your departure. You've got the makings of fine, rekindled love, if only you'll give in to it.

It's true that a relationship built only on pity may not be the most rewarding to you. Obviously you see problems; obviously there are aspects of the relationship that are making you deeply unhappy. Or maybe it's not what she *is*, but what she isn't, or hasn't got, or has never had the inclination to do. I'm not saying that you should just learn to live with it—but rather learn to *work* with it. Don't just throw up your hands and say "He'll never change," because he *can* change if given the right motivation. And don't give in to your own weakness and say you'll never change either, unless you simply prefer to be divorced and refuse to make an attempt.

That this reason to stay together has been scorned is another manifestation of the destructive "looking out for number one" philosophy that pervaded the early 1970s. Robert Ringer's best-seller capitalizing on that concept emphasized that you deserve to get what you want, and that people are too afraid of stepping on toes to find real fulfillment.[9]

Now we've come the other direction, and I'm continually amazed at how many people think that their pleasures and desires are their "rights." People craving cigarettes feel that their "right" to smoke takes precedence over the "right" to clean air. People have a "right" to see TV shows that privately owned stations prefer not to air. Others say their "right" to display their sexual proclivities or preferences should not be breached by those who wish they'd keep such activities confined to their bedrooms.

All this is happening simultaneously in a culture where etiquette books have enjoyed a phenomenal comeback and women are again pleased when their dates pay for the evening or help them on with their coats. Conflicting messages, yes. But perhaps there has to be a time of confusion as the pendulum moves toward a more moderate position.

What this means is that we are now rediscovering the fact that by being considerate and caring for the feelings and characteristics of others, our lives run more smoothly. By stepping back from your marital difficulties and beholding the depth of your partner's commitment and love, you see that such a gift is precious. Perhaps the flaws you perceive would become apparent in anyone new you chose—but could you be sure that the love a new spouse felt would be as sincere and enduring?

If you feel little passion for your partner and stick around because you care about his feelings or out of a sense of obligation, what happens? Do you become filled with resentment? Do you live unhappily ever after? The answer is, usually, no. You get used to it, then you rationalize it, then you relax with it and make the most of it. The result of this process is that you come to love your partner all the more—remember the section earlier when I described what happens when you give a gift? The receiver is grateful, but it is the *giver* who becomes more deeply attached. When you give the gift of your continued allegiance, you become more solidly committed than if you stayed with your partner out of lust or daily pleasure alone.

A teacher of mine married a feisty woman forty years ago. Two years after their marriage, she contracted polio, which left her unable to walk and with permanent, severe respiratory problems. As time went by and her once-valiant attitude wore thin, she became harder to live with. Her sense of humor became sarcastic. She became demanding, then finally complaining. She turned from an active optimist to a depressing pessimist, and whenever I visited her, I left weary with defeat.

My teacher lived with her ailment for thirty-eight years—supportively, unflaggingly reliant. He pushed her wheelchair, made sure she read the newspaper and had visitors by the score. Many of the visitors, myself included, made the trek to their palatial home more out of gratitude to our teacher than to visit the grousing wife, who kept telling us how her demise was imminent and her improvement a myth.

I considered it the most selfless devotion that my teacher never complained, never withdrew. Once, I asked him how he could stand putting forth so much effort for what appeared to be so little reward. "I do it because I'm obligated to," he replied matter-of-factly. He took his marriage vow seriously, never considering that he could be rid of all the heartache and inconvenience simply by getting a divorce.

And yet, he was no martyr. The inner strength and moral benefits he received were apparent in his gift for teaching, in his amazing ability to synthesize deep and difficult texts into messages helpful to all who studied with him. And he was the one who told me how, after thirty-eight years of caring for his wife, he had become so connected, so attached, that he loved her all the more. He was fiercely protective of her, blinded by his bond to the extent that he could not understand why others deemed her difficult. He became immune to her complaints and focused joyously on her small triumphs.

My teacher didn't think about whether or not he should love his wife. He took his responsibilities as "givens," acted as if he were in love with her, and—*voilà*—he felt more intimacy and love than if he had only responded to his wife's benevolence. He couldn't hurt her, couldn't leave her defenseless. He stuck around out of just the sort of charitable tie that a kind heart provides. That means he's a great husband, not a chump. And a happy husband, too.

GOOD REASON #7: "I'M STAYING IN MY MARRIAGE BECAUSE I CAN'T FACE BEING ALONE"

The touchy-feely gurus of the sixties and seventies might have denigrated this reason to maintain your marriage because it implies that you're "chicken"—too scared to face the frightening parts of yourself, too scared to take a risk. You're a wimp, a sissy, willing to "settle" for what you've got rather than reach for something that may be fantastic.

Don't let these insults get to you. The reality of the

situation, as discussed earlier, is that it isn't that easy to
find someone suitable who's willing to make a lifetime
commitment to you. It isn't even that simple to build a
network of women friends for the support you need; it
isn't such a snap to fit companionship into your life.
Without ongoing attention, your social calendar remains
empty, and you face the prospect of many lonely nights.
Even with enormous effort put into scheduling, you're in
for many dejected evenings on blind dates, at uncomfortable parties and bars, or on platonic forays that are
really second-choice events. You get the picture.

The problem isn't just the short term. If you're a
woman in her mid-thirties, the selection of eligible men
is small, especially if you live in major cities like Los
Angeles and New York. William Novak, writing in *The
Great American Man Shortage and Other Roadblocks to
Romance*, informs us that women outnumber men in the
United States by 6 percent, which was about 6.5 million
people in 1980. He points out the "double standard" of
age, in which men chase much younger women, leaving
the older ones even slimmer pickings. He also cites Dr.
Paul H. Gebhard, director of Indiana University's Institute for Sex Research, who says women's choices are further depleted by men's more frequent homosexuality (13.4
percent of men versus only 4.5 percent of women).[10]

These statistics mean that the likelihood of wasting
lots of valuable time on aborted relationships and difficult encounters is enormous. People now talk about
emerging from one love affair after another as if they
were trains weaving in and out of mountain tunnels. They
also speak matter-of-factly of "dry spells" of up to many
years without an interesting prospect for a long-term relationship.

The question remains as to why being alone is so bad.
It sure beats a tormenting marriage, one where you dread
coming home every day, or where you find the company
so repulsive or intolerable as to be an excruciating burden on your life. But people who give this reason for
staying with their mates are not in these extreme situations. They're the ones with the wives who have aged
poorly or put on weight. The ones whose husbands have
begun to take them for granted. The ones who have come
up in the world, at least in self-esteem if not in monetary

wealth, and realize they really desire someone more dynamic or accomplished or energetic or prestigious. With enough coaxing from (themselves divorced?) friends, these people on the edge of their marriages can be pushed to separation. But something keeps them coming home.

That "something" is an intuitively correct, often unspoken belief that it is better in every way to be married than to be alone. I'm not insulting those people who are single, just presenting the reality that I hear in my clinical practice every day: if given a choice, singles would prefer to be married. Jacqueline Simenaur and David Carroll's study *Singles* affirms this: "Even though the single population is expanding in this country, it is not necessarily because Americans seek the single lifestyle per se, but because *they find it so difficult either to stay married or to find an acceptable marriage partner*. This is a fundamental distinction and cannot be stressed strongly enough."[11]

Popular culture acknowledges that marriage makes you happier, marriage keeps you saner, marriage allows you more security, marriage makes you richer and more successful than staying single. I'll discuss these benefits later, but for now keep in mind that anyone who watches TV or reads *Newsweek* is aware that people who are married go further. In early 1987, presidential candidate Gary Hart kept insisting that he was happily married because he knew his constituency favored happily married candidates—to the extent that when Hart was "caught" fraternizing with Donna Rice he had to withdraw from the race. He later reentered it but has seldom laughed at the raft of jokes that grew from his indiscretion.

People who "can't face being alone" are not weaklings to be pitied for their lack of self-sufficency. Almost all could keep their checkbooks up-to-date, clean their apartments, hold down their jobs, and make decent social small-talk as well as the never-married achiever next door.

The problem is that when you've been married once, you get spoiled. It's *nice* to come home to someone else. It's *comforting* to have a shoulder to cry on or a listening ear to hear your day's woes. It's *fun* to go on outings with someone whose anticipation of the event mirrors your own. And it's perhaps the most rewarding experience any two human beings can know to raise children with a shared sense of pride and accomplishment, rather than the adversarial tug-of-war or even cordial but business-like resignation characteristic of divorce.

Those with children intelligently find the singles world unappealing. When you're used to vacationing as a family or completing all the little holiday rituals together, running the show solo is a steep come-down. Playing both mommy and daddy is not only exhausting but patience-testing, since you have no one to relieve you from your duties and no other source for moment-to-moment decision making, disciplining, supervising, and praise giving. If there's a choice between a not-perfect marriage, or even a spotty one and the prospect of raising your children alone, it's smart to prefer marriage. I've said this before, but it bears repeating: at least if you stay married you have the option to improve it; once you're divorced you can never reassemble your broken family to its original strength.

NOTES

1. Kelly, Joan Berlin, and Wallerstein, Judith. *Surviving the Breakup*. New York: Basic Books, 1980.
2. Weitzman, Lenore. *The Divorce Revolution*. New York: Free Press, 1985.
3. Wallerstein, Judith S. and Kelly, Joan Berlin. *Surviving the Breakup*. New York: Basic Books, 1980.
4. Ephron, Nora. *Heartburn*. New York: Pocket Books, 1983, p. 219.
5. Weiss, Robert. *Marital Separation*. New York: Basic Books, 1975.
6. Ibid., p. 83.
7. Stark, Elizabeth, "Friends Through It All." *Psychology Today*, May, 1986, pp. 54–60.
8. Wojahn, Ellen. "Divorce, Entrepreneurial Style." *Inc.*, March 1986, pp. 55–64.
9. Ringer, Robert. *Looking Out for Number One*. New York: Fawcett Crest Books, 1977.
10. Novak, William. *The Great American Man Shortage and Other Roadblocks to Romance*. New York: Rawson Associates, 1983.

11. Carroll, David, and Simenauer, Jacqueline. *Singles: The New Americans*. New York: Simon and Schuster, 1982, p. 356.

Section III

THE COSTS
OF DIVORCE

But what exactly does divorce *do* that's so bad? In *The Courage to Divorce*, published in 1974 with the divorce rate exploding, Susan Gettleman and Janet Markowitz claim that divorce, "stripped of gratuitous negative connotations, stands as inherently a 'neutral' institution, in itself neither good nor bad for individuals or for society." They suggest that divorce up until then had gotten a bum rap—that marriage was wrongly ascribed a more desirable and prestigious status.[1]

Somehow that conclusion just doesn't ring true to experience. Is it merely because Western civilization has been indoctrinated that over the past five thousand years it has preserved and honored marriage? Is it a sinister plot that keeps us dancing at weddings but somberly gulping when we learn of a divorce? Certainly those who are divorced deserve the same courtesy and respect as those of other marital statuses. But to say that the hordes now divorced represent the forefront of a proud new social structure is ludicrous.

They ache. They cry. They know the increased burdens of raising their children on the efforts of one person instead of two. They go on dates in hopes of changing their status, not because they are hopelessly brainwashed, but because they know the benefits of approaching life with a teammate, or at least approaching it with the *choice* of individual attack or dual effort. What's so bad about divorce, Gettleman and Markowitz asked? Plenty. Ask anyone who's been through it.

Or just read on.

CHAPTER 13

A Mind-Shattering Experience

Everybody knows that divorce makes people behave bizarrely. It's common knowledge that divorcing individuals act irrationally and inexplicably for a period of months or even years—a stretch, you'll recall, that Abigail Trafford calls "Crazy Time." Intellectually, we all understand this.

But when you're considering whether or not to leave your husband or wife, you put that knowledge away, perhaps assuming that your own behavior will be self-determined, if not excused, and you gloss over the immediate future to a long-term vision of something better.

This shortsightedness is a tragic mistake. The period when you're contemplating divorce is precisely the time to face squarely the reality of what you're in for. You need to know that you absolutely cannot go through a divorce emotionally unscathed, even if you have the most supportive, exciting, and compelling lover to go to. And you must understand that the pain you'll inevitably face is not just over a period of months—but definitely lasts years. You need to focus on next week, next month, with their emotional repercussions, as well as long-term psychological scars. Don't announce your separation without first considering all the facts, even if you don't want to hear them.

One of the most hard-hitting arguments in the case against divorce is the persuasive evidence that its effects are emotionally devastating. I'm only going to provide a sampling of them here; a whole sociological journal is devoted to the consequences of divorce; every issue of the magazine *Psychology Today* is rife with stories on it; whole shelves in bookstores are lined with optimistic volumes on how to overcome divorce's blow to regain your self-esteem, restore family balance, and find a replacement mate. The sum of this writing, however, illustrates that there is little you can do to your mind that is worse than divorce. The "Social Readjustment Rating Scale," which lists the life events most shattering to one's equilibrium, shows marital separation and divorce as the second and third most stressful situations (after the death of a spouse) that anyone can experience.

Lenore Weitzman points this out in *The Divorce Revolution*, where she also notes: "The psychological distress engendered by divorce is revealed by the fact that divorced men and women exhibit more symptoms (such as 'nervous breakdown' and 'inertia'), and in more serious degree, than do persons of other marital statuses. Divorced and separated people have the highest admission rates to psychiatric facilities, and this holds true across different age groups, for both sexes, and for blacks and whites alike.

"Divorce also takes a toll on the physical well-being of both sexes. Divorced people have more illness, higher mortality rates (in premature deaths), higher suicide rates, and more accidents than those who are married. In fact, the marital status of a person is one of the best predictors of his or her health, disease, and death profile."[2]

THE EMOTIONAL IMPACT OF DIVORCE: MUCH PAIN, NO GAIN

As I mentioned above, in the short term everybody expects a divorcing person to be traumatized—we write off all sorts of strange misbehavior with the sympathetic words, "She's going through a divorce."

As long as the problem doesn't persist too long, the symptoms of this transition period can be dramatic, and the world will simply let them pass. Unexplained crying jags in public bring consoling pats on the shoulder during the immediate postdivorce period; such a display two years later is treated sternly. Sudden weight loss or gain or an upsurge in smoking are all understandingly dismissed. Irresponsibility, forgetfulness, illogic, and carelessness bring more pity than punishment for several months. All of these behaviors are excused for a reasonable time as within the boundaries of normal emotional reactions.

That's fortunate, but the consequences of behaving in this way are still severe, if not in loss of business, cancellation of friendships, or disgust of relatives, then simply in terms of your own inner turmoil. What happens in your mind? Several writers have tried to explain the distress of divorce via stages.

Abigail Trafford describes the process most explicitly. First comes the Crisis, when the marriage falls apart due to a shift in oppression/submission she terms "deadlock." Then there's the "crazy time" full of ambiguity, while identity is half in, half out of the marriage. Long-undisturbed thoughts crowd your consciousness, including issues of separation from your parents and all the other conflicts you've encountered through the years. She notes: "To get through Crazy Time, you have to let yourself be out of control for a while—in order to gain control of your life."[3] You go through numbness, denial, fantasies of violence. Deep shock means immobilization for many; then there is anger and questioning your entire value system, tearing apart the basis of your notions of right and wrong.

Feeling consumed by anger, Trafford suggests, can last three years, even five years, and evolves into bitterness and spite. Even if yours is merely moderate anger, inevitable ambivalence colors your world, which is seen "through the prism of whether or not you should get a divorce."

Then there's depression: "At the core of divorce depression is low self-esteem," Trafford writes.[4] You feel like a failure and blame yourself for your family's problems. It's a self-fulfilling prophecy, she explains: you feel like a failure and therefore become one.

It's amazing to me that during this pain so few people admit they're making a mistake. If they can prophesy failure, why can't they prophesy success? Why do people wallowing in the abyss of negativity realize that going through this may not be simply a byproduct of ending their marriage, but perhaps important information that can help them revitalize a relationship that obviously still has deeply emotional components? Your feelings may be completely appropriate and insightful: You feel sad at the loss, because you're losing something valuable. You're depressed about being alone, because it's better to have companionship. You ache with nostalgia, because the times you had together were good. You mourn lost potential because the potential still exists. You have a right to go crazy.

Trafford says that this traumatic time can be seen as three phases: First the Hummingbird Phase finds you flitting away from anything painful and negative. Then the Foundering Phase brings confrontation with the pain and anxiety. Finally, during the Phoenix Phase, a "new you" rises up out of the ashes of your divorce. But, Trafford notes, it takes "at least five years" to reach that exalted point. Seems like an exhausting journey.[5]

Indeed, the five-year figure that Trafford estimates is conservative. From my own survey of two hundred separated or divorced people, the average time of recovery was seven years; many respondents wrote that twenty and thirty years after terminating their relationships, they are still reeling from the emotional wallop.

Other writers on the subject concur that recovery is a prolonged process. Elizabeth Cauhape, author of *Fresh Starts: Men and Women After Divorce*, writes: "It is easy to lose one's entire perspective on Time, when one feels that the divorce process will 'never end' or that one will feel overwhelmed 'forever.' "[6] Marcia Hootman and Patt Perkins admit in *How to Forgive Your Ex-Husband (and Get On With Your Life)* that it took each of them six years to recover from their divorces, and they trace the progression of pent-up anger to depression and resentment.[7]

"A VERY SPECIAL PRIVATE HELL"

One of the most eloquent descriptions I've read of the catastrophe of divorce is Joseph Epstein's book *Divorced in America*. The depth of emotional upheaval caused by divorce is evident when he writes: "To go through a divorce is still, no matter how smooth the procedure, no matter how 'civilized' the conduct of the parties involved, no matter how much money is available to cushion the fall, to go through a very special private hell."[8] That divorce is very special is indisputable; the separation is of the type unlike death where mourning is unacceptable and yet required. That it is private, an embarrassing episode one does not boast about on resumes and best refrains from discussing, adds to the frustration as well as magnifies the emotions. Largely, feelings must echo in your mind as they would in an unfurnished hall. You haven't felt these emotions before, and their confusing mix swirls around in your mind without reprieve, day and night. And finally, Epstein's comparison of divorce with hell quite directly conveys the hateful intensity and illusion of endlessness that the process engenders.

Characteristic of "separation distress" are desolation, apprehensiveness, anxiety, and panic, leading to tension, vigilance, insomnia, depression, and feelings of worthlessness, notes Robert Weiss in *Marital Separation*. He writes of a persistent need for attachment, a need well-established within two years after marriage—and one that is nearly impossible to extinguish.[9]

You may not think you're susceptible to such dramatic emotional reactions. Possibly you're leaving a marriage that has been so stale for so long that your divorce feels like a blessed relief. Or perhaps your lover awaits, and you anticipate that the passion you share will more than make up for the loss of a relationship not nearly as fulfilling. While having a lover to fill the loneliness and love-need gap will help you slide by confrontation of your feelings immediately, you will not be able to escape your psychological due altogether.

Fran McDougal figured she would suffer, but minimally. She sought counseling with me after seeing my book on deciding whether or not to marry, since her lover of three years had been hounding her to divorce and marry him. Fran, with her sun-kissed golden hair and health-club-toned body, was proud that people mistook her thirty-five-year-old face to be ten years younger. She was also proud of her accomplishments—though she'd married at twenty-five, she'd completed her doctorate in education and at thirty was a high school principal. By thirty-three she had moved up to a high post in the state education administration and quite smoothly made the transition to working mother. Her seven-month-old daughter was the pride of her life, though she was unsure if her lover or her husband was the baby's father.

This was a capable woman. William McDougal had always bragged about her stellar achievements, though he himself had floundered in a series of mediocre jobs throughout the first six years of their marriage. With Fran's urging, he finally returned to college, earning a master's degree in physical therapy at age thirty-three. It didn't bother him that Fran made twice his income or that he was the "tag along" at campaign events. The strapping blond man always garnered enough congratulations on his wife to make him feel good. She was his accomplishment and his sole investment in life.

Then why did Fran need a lover? "At first I did everything to dissuade Robert," Fran sighed. "But there he was, gorgeous, famous, rich. Everything William was plus everything I'd assumed I could never have. And he was pursuing me!" She laughed easily. "Here was someone in politics, someone who had been a lawyer and was really accomplished, someone who could have his pick of the hangers-on and the political groupies that are so abundant. But he wanted me.

"Ordinarily even this would not have been enough, though I admit I was excited. But this was someone decent—okay, you can say that his attention to a married woman wasn't decent—but he wasn't promiscuous, he wasn't gay; in fact he's a sincerely religious Christian, but one who doesn't flaunt his beliefs. Robert studies the Bible. He knows right from wrong, and even though he started out with the same honorable intentions as I did, he gave in to his desires. As a single guy, you fall into flirtatious habits, I guess. Anyway, we kept our meetings platonic for a whole year, and then we couldn't stand it anymore. Imagine my shock to discover this fantasy man was also a fantasy lover."

Fran wasn't apologetic for her own involvement, but now that she had come to love Robert more than she loved her husband, she was at a decision point. It wasn't fair to keep deceiving William, she believed, but how could she leave someone so devoted to her? And yet, how could she pass up openly leading the life she wanted?

I wanted to meet William; I urged Fran to hold off Robert until she could fairly assess the situation without his pressure. But when he handed her an ultimatum the next day, she immediately took her daughter and moved in. I saw her two months later.

Fran was a wreck. Her healthy body looked skeletal, her manner was fidgety and tense. "I love Robert," she insisted. "But I can't take William's trying to win me back. He writes me love poems. He sends me nostalgic old photos of the two of us backpacking through Europe. He even sent one of the three of us in the delivery room when I had Monica. It just tears me up. He calls me every day, and knowing he's crying every night makes me miserable.

"And of course I have to see him. He takes Monica most afternoons, and I have to see him clutching that little baby as if she's the only shred of me he can get. Why am I such a rat? Why couldn't I just keep our happy home the way it was, without all the complications? William doesn't know about my lengthy affair; he thinks it was something recent. And the fact that he cherishes me and thinks I was faithful to him until the end, is another punishment that just makes me crawl into a hole."

The Most Tenacious Connection

Mel Krantzler, in *Creative Divorce*, notes that divorce does not end your relationship with your ex-spouse. Your former mate had "the disproportionate power . . . to twist their vision of the present into a repetition of what they left behind," he writes. In Fran McDougal's case, William could roust up all her sweet, cozy memories of a flawless husband whose positive attitude had always been a constant beacon for her.

And she couldn't handle it. Robert was fantastic, she assured me. Everything she'd hoped, and even more fun, even more exciting. But the people she knew before were strangely silent when she entered a room with him; they remembered William and stared as if concurring that Fran was a rat. With Monica binding them, Fran knew that every time she saw William, her guilt and pain would be renewed. These feelings interfered with her dedication to her relationship with Robert.

Fran was a loser all around. During her affair she was able to separate the two components of her love life, but when the two collided, she could no longer deny what she had done. Fran prided herself on being a moral person; she had violated what she believed to be right and was reminded of it by William's kindness and devotion even in the face of rejection.

Fran never did choose between Robert and William. Instead, the story ended on Robert's initiative. He watched his once self-assured lover wilt under guilt and embarrassment. She became a depressed companion, a lethargic sex partner, and withdrew rather than blossomed under the new arrangement. He decided to call off their relationship rather than cause both a ruined marriage and Fran's decline.

With help, Fran realized that her reaction to Robert and William had actually forced Robert's exit. She couldn't consciously allow herself to turn away such a "good opportunity," but she could accept her failure in it. Robert's rejection was a huge relief; gratefully, Fran moved back in with William and began to rebuild the trust and comfort she had long enjoyed.

That process, by the way, was not just a matter of reconstituting original roles. Central to solidifying the relationship was a change in William's self-esteem and career direction, as well as a new recognition on Fran's part that her family took higher priority than her career aspirations or need for fame and excitement. These kinds of deeply rooted changes grow more easily out of crisis than tranquility, but still demanded difficult psychological transformations that were frustrating and slow—but ultimately rewarding.

And the moral of the story? Look at it this way: no matter which choice you make, to stay in a less-than-ideal marriage or to quit and pursue possibilities outside, you'll still have to make psychological changes. Either you need to rebuild your marriage and boost your attitude about its value and potential, or you will be forced into the far more consuming tasks of dismantling your marital connection, bridging any shaky transitional period, facing the singles/loneliness problem, and eventually starting from scratch to construct a new, untested relationship. Any rational person would want to avoid the total chaos and agony divorce brings.[10]

HURTING THE ONE YOU LOVE

But let's say you're a masochist. You don't care that you'll be a basket case, that you probably won't be able to carry on your normal life for up to seven years. Maybe there's something perversely challenging in trying to "beat the odds" and appear sane during an unequivocally emotional time—as if the dust of your wrecked relationship settles everywhere but on you. Ignoring the question of what such an attitude says about your mental health, there still remains the fact that by breaking up your marriage you are by necessity inflicting the distress and disruption on your partner. By either accepting his or her pronouncement that your problems are irreconcilable or by leaving on your own, you are imposing cruelty on someone you once loved.

Even if your spouse is in an extremely fragile or volatile mental state and would actually benefit from getting away from you, a divorce, with its overwhelmingly severe impact, is bound to be worse long-term than the heat of a temporarily negative phase in your marriage.

Unfortunately, when your partner is hot-headed or embroiled in the passion of hostility, his mind is not on the future. Imposing divorce is cruel, it's mean, it's often retributive. That may seem fine in the midst of angry parting, but later the relationship takes on a different shape. Looking backward from a distance, all the days even out—the ugly end carries no more weight in memory than the exciting and promising beginning of your relationship. All the "good stuff" comes back to mind, and it is then that the one who destroyed the union is hit by guilt and regret.

All is not fair in love and war—there are some actions that remain indisputably right or wrong, and those that are wrong can never become "fair" just because they happen to be in the context of your marriage. While this truth may never be verbalized, anyone with a basically decent core intuitively understands it and later suffers from remorse for having behaved destructively to someone so close to him.

BECOMING A LESSER PERSON

Divorce brings another psychological consequence that diminishes everyone's "decent core." Because of the inherently adversarial and selfish nature of separation and divorce, you by necessity lower your moral standards. Suddenly you're thinking only of what is in your personal best interest, and you not only disregard your partner but intentionally (though often unconsciously) act maliciously to further your emotional goals. In the milieu of divorce, you allow yourself to act despicably; your feelings are so deep and vindictive that the more pain you can cause your spouse, the better.

And it doesn't even matter if your once dearly loved partner left you or if you're the one to run away. You harbor feelings of resentment, jealousy, blame, anger, and bitterness that come to the surface no matter how civil you intend to be.

Lori, the lady who pedals on the exercise bicycle next to me at the gym, told me how stunned she was the day before to witness the confrontation of two divorced spouses outside the school where she'd come to pick up her five-year-old daughter. "They'd gotten divorced three years ago, and you could just see the anger smoldering," Lori began. "The father and the mother were both there. The mother told their little boy, 'Go get a Kleenex,' and the father said sarcastically, 'No Timmy, why don't you wipe your nose on your mother's shirt?' I couldn't believe it. But then the mother snapped back, 'Why don't you wipe it on your father's shirt?' You could feel the hostility. You've got to wonder what that poor child thinks.''

This is an illustration of crude psychological warfare; unfortunately, everyone involved is a casualty. I'm not saying that it's impossible to remain friends with your spouse; only that such a relationship is destined to be painful and delicate. Judith Wallerstein found that even remarriage does not blunt the bitterness of divorce—41 percent of remarried women and 30 percent of remarried men were "very angry" fully ten years later![11]

Constance Ahrons at the University of Southern California followed for five years divorced couples with children and found that the 12 percent she called "Perfect Pals" were able to focus on the children, putting their feelings about each other aside to enjoy a cordial relationship. Thirty-eight percent more managed to minimize their conflicts to preserve acceptable interaction. But half of her sample couldn't even avoid fighting when necessary for the business of shared parenthood. Sadly, all respondents, from the most clashing to the most amicable, told Ahrons that they wished they could have a better relationship with their ex-spouses. As this study shows, even good intentions often cannot bring peace between partners. And a very important relationship continuing in an unsettled and imperfect state undeniably takes emotional tolls.[12]

CRAZY IN OUR MIDST

An increased willingness to hurt your former spouse is not the only manifestation of your weakened character. The very fact that you allow yourself to act out all your emotional trauma in a publicly identifiable way shows lack of consideration of other people. You're feeling depressed; you oversleep and miss work. "I'm going through a divorce" is your excuse, and that's supposed to make up for the extra burdens on your co-workers and the last-minute hassles they have because of your absence. You're forgetful and leave behind important papers or even the chips-and-dip you'd promised to bring for the after-hours get-together. Your divorce is supposed to be explanation enough for lapses that let down others who trust you.

Face it, it's selfish of you (and symptomatic of moral slippage in our society) to expect others to patronize and accept this kind of irresponsible behavior simply because you're undergoing a popularly approved emotional phase. Before divorce lost its stigma, such behavior, even in this context, was inexcusable and cause for job loss and social criticism, if not self-imposed exile (via relocation or mental hospitalization) from the community affected by the disturbance. Now, I do not advocate a return to the days when prejudice ruined further the lives of divorced individuals, but I do want to point out the widely ignored—or rationalized—cost of divorce for everyone directly involved.

THE ALLURING VITALITY OF ANGER

With the guarantee that family and friends will accept connubially caused craziness, people sometimes go so far as to consciously or unconsciously exacerbate problems in their marriages. This stems from a constitutional need for emotional intensity or excitement, a trait Matthew McKay and Peter Rogers, et al., say in *The Divorce Book* is characteristic of "emotional addicts." The stress and uncertainty on the cusp of separation is stimulating and is an antidote for routine and boredom.[13]

Some people who pride themselves on the consistency of their lives in other areas intentionally inject their marriages with this kind of unpredictability. They may have been on their jobs so long that work has become second nature; they may have lived in the same place for decades. Their staunch support of particular political positions or their religious activities provide grounding against which they enact the drama of marital upheaval and renewal.

Such emotional junkies don't realize how destructive this is. Couples with this habit get into patterns of behavior in which they feed off of each other, encouraging new arguments by seizing on predictable areas of sensitivity. The up-and-down nature of these marriages brings the spark of vitality these people need.

The "down side," however, is that with each confrontation or "close call," part of the security and foundation of the relationship is eroded. A marriage characterized by repeated disturbance, even when that disturbance is meeting a basic need, eventually is compared with the "happily ever after" ideal. Sooner or later the trade off becomes too great; one or the other partner "has enough," and the marriage crumbles. The divorce process is in itself stimulating, so once it is instigated, the parties follow through. Then the emotional addicts move on to other relationships, where they continue their provocative habits and repeat their disastrous mistakes. Divorce, remarriage, living together, remarriage—a trail of addresses and people pursued for the exhilaration of contrasting extreme pleasure and pain.

Of course, in those cases, divorce is the wrong solution to the presenting problem as well as to the underlying need for tension. In fact, each successive separation seriously and permanently harms the participants. They get into a pattern of charging into relationships and then destroying them, effectively guaranteeing the emotional intensity they crave but preventing them from ever attaining a permanent love or stable family. They become the "foolish choices" that Smart Women fall for—the ones who come on strong and then either pull back or cause a rift; the ones who can never provide the tranquil, comfortable home every wise person wants.

It takes a more mature person to find intensity in the serious—albeit often difficult—task of *coping* with marital tension, sticking it out through the ups and downs. The tasks of starting and rearing a family, of planting roots in a community and maintaining a solid home provide daily challenges that should bring more than enough emotional intensity for a psychologically healthy person. It takes more cleverness and involvement to avoid conflict rather than nurture it, to overcome natural divisions rather than seize upon them.

Graduates of the seventies "Me First" orientation mistakenly view divorce as a beneficial "learning experience" and a means to psychologically develop. But though divorce, as any event, does foster growth, it is through a *negative* experience—distress—rather than the *positive* experience of successfully solving personal and interpersonal problems.

What a handicap: In the extreme, "emotional addicts" can't even make marital commitments, because a pledge of fidelity interferes with the means toward excitement. And yet if you ask them, these people claim that in their living-together arrangements, they have the same commitment as in marriage; or they say that marriage forces people who shouldn't stay together to suffer; or they say that this way, when people change, as they inevitably do, they can simply make the transition to somebody else more easily. At least that's what they *used* to say. I see plenty of these people in my workshops on deciding whether or not to marry. They've been through lots of relationships, and the message always is that their "musical mates" game was far more frustrating than satisfying. They want marriage, with all its security, exclusivity, and permanence. Through hard experience, these "emotional addicts" have been cured.

Eloise Markham and John Hiller were products of the seventies who bought the day's "hang loose" philosophy. They met in college at their local Western Illinois University in Macomb in 1970, which was considered a "party school" at the time for its lack of academic emphasis. They thought living together was more "honest" than marriage since, in the pop music vernacular of the time, love would keep them together better than a "piece of paper from city hall." Good grades and graduate school weren't on their minds much; they drank beer late into the night and after two semesters dropped out to "find themselves" by backpacking through Europe.

Their parents were distraught about their lifestyle but had no control. Eloise and John rebelled against their staid Midwestern backgrounds, and they embraced the pot-smoking and casual sex of the other Americans they encountered in their six months hitchhiking in Europe.

True to the stereotype of their generation, they moved to New York, rented a garret with another couple, and went through several occupational phases: weaving, working backstage at a playhouse in the Village, making bread at a "natural" bakery, and selling books.

After six years with John (and two dozen casual physical relationships with friends and acquaintances), Eloise fell in love with a co-worker at the bookstore. It was meant to be a simple "expression of friendship," she told me in retrospect, an extension of the closeness they had come to share, like all the other friendships that had included sex. John had given his approval to her relationship; after all, he had recently enjoyed a sexual fling with a waitress who had auditioned for a part at the playhouse. No big deal; why not take advantage of every opportunity?

But after two months with her new lover, "I decided to switch partners," Eloise explained. Another unformalized relationship: "It was great for two years; then he found somebody new. I hadn't been on my own before; I latched onto the first guy who expressed an interest and we lived together for the next two years, fighting most of the time.

"I still professed to believe in 'freedom,' but what had it gotten me? I thought it was better to 'really live' by experiencing every aspect of 'friendship' with anyone. Now all I have to show for it is a lot of terribly romantic stories, a feud with my mother, and a case of herpes. I haven't had one solid commitment. I saw the values of my friends changing all around me and I seem to have stood still—now the two bumming-through-Europe pals I still keep in touch with are married and have babies. They went to graduate school and got degrees and started careers. All along I thought they were 'copping out.' This isn't how the script was supposed to end."

DIVORCE WON'T SOLVE YOUR PROBLEMS

Eloise became a slave to her philosophy. Her belief that a sexually "open" and "honest" relationship was better than a traditional marriage collapsed when she realized that the joys of family life were passing her by. Only when she revised this underlying premise did she approach dating with the seriousness and integrity she needed to make a true commitment and work to see it through.

Eloise's is but one of a myriad of problems that brings people to separation and divorce. I've outlined most of them before: irksome habits, extramarital affairs, inabilities to communicate, drifting apart. They seem catastrophic at the time; divorce appears the sensible way to escape these pressures and move on to someone and something new. A "fresh start," as noted before, is an appealing lure.

You think that the "same old you" will simply be freer and able to express yourself in a more liberated setting. But you're wrong—it *won't* be the same you facing the world. Because divorce itself inevitably *changes* you—it diminishes your moral perspective, staggers you emotionally for months or years, forces a change in address or living standards, and eliminates the friendships of half the names in your address book. Still, there are some things that, unfortunately, it does *not* automatically affect: the patterns in your behavior that led to your marital problems in the first place. And those are precisely what need to be changed most.

When you run away from your marriage, you can't help but focus your attention on the rotten person you're leaving and the intolerable situation that person created for you. You're not concerned with what you might have done wrong, the role you played in your own misfortune. You're not confronting the actions you took to structure your past relationship, how habits you formed in relating to your mate helped cause your deadlock and breakdown. The most useful lessons you could be learning from your distress are about yourself, and instead the only self-discovery you pursue is how well you can make yourself dinner and find an adequate shoulder to cry on.

A quick zip from your first union to a rebound marriage or long-term affair is probably the single worst step you could take. And the most tempting one. It's certainly a relief to find someone asserting that you're desirable and worthy just as you are—no changes necessary! Your new love is so reassuring: You were just the victim of a crazy "ex," and now that you're free, all is well. The same old you can just begin again—to repeat the same mistakes and head for a second divorce. In a few extraordinary cases, the person you choose for your next mate picks up on the problems and negotiates your behavior with you. This makes your second marriage an improvement over your first—and forces you to look back and realize that you could have been happy with your former spouse—"if only I'd known then what I know now."

DOOMED TO REPEAT THE PAST

An "extraordinary" second spouse is like a built-in psychotherapist—how wonderful! But despite every intention to choose more wisely the second time, the likelihood is small that your second marriage will be to such a person. Your tendency will be to run to someone on the other extreme (emaciated if an old sore point was her weight; twenty years younger if his bugaboo was a crisis of feeling old). Or you may look for a replacement spouse who meets the same old deeply ingrained but unhealthy needs, perpetuating your problems.

Joseph Drexel, thirty-nine, left his wife of sixteen years

because he felt that their relationship was a void. "I got nothing from her," he shrugged upon moving out. "Our lives are parallel and I don't find her attractive, fun to be with, nice to talk to—she's not a problem really, but I want some companionship and encouragement."

He found his second wife at the health club, and all was fine until about a year after their wedding. Then she began complaining that Joseph didn't talk to her, wasn't interested in "anything fun," and didn't want to have children. Joseph thought the problem was his wife's complaining and sent her to a shrink.

Alicia Diaz, thirty-three, said her divorce after seven years was the result of her husband's inability to find a career and steady employment. His laziness finally got to her, she insisted, and when she had the chance to hitch up with a successful computer software manufacturer, she grabbed it, thinking that finally she'd found someone she could respect. But two years later, she was ready to leave; her new husband refused to buy her a house and eschewed vacations, preferring to reinvest his time, energy, and money in his business.

Ralph Resnick, forty, admired beautiful women. He'd flirt a little, but never had any serious involvement during his ten-year marriage. He assumed he was married for life and would never carry his actions to the point of really "cheating." So he was floored when his wife left him for her yoga teacher, saying she had to move out and "find herself." Heading a part-time, home-based T-shirt painting business had been identity enough for her for six years—and Ralph had been careful to give her plenty of praise for it too. But she moved out, rebuffing his pleas to return, and he panicked at the thought of having to face the singles world.

What do these three cases have in common? All of these individuals thought their divorces were the fault of their partners. All of them believed they'd done nothing wrong and that only the lacking personalities of their mates caused their marriages to fail. But Joseph Drexel had unspoken expectations about a "courtship" and a "marriage." During courtship, he would pursue a beautiful woman, they would enjoy romantic encounters, and in logical sequence, they would fall in love, become engaged, and marry. After that, he could relax. And "relaxation" meant taking his wife for granted.

Alicia Diaz also had detrimental expectations. A husband, to her mind, was not someone perpetually trying to get ahead—he was someone who had already attained a certain level and then turned around to share that achievement with his wife. Alicia's first husband didn't want to settle for an unrewarding career, so he kept looking; her second didn't want to settle for his particular level of success and so kept pushing. Both men loved Alicia and gave her affection, but she allowed herself to become disgruntled when neither could provide her marital vision of a grand house and two vacations a year.

Ralph Resnick sabotaged his marriage via his overly loose definition of "faithfulness" and "cheating." By being "flirtatious," he chipped away his loyalty to his wife, who, in the meantime, only wanted to feel that she was the most special woman in the world to Ralph. She took up with her yoga teacher to give Ralph a taste of what she'd felt—betrayal—and when that was ineffective in getting Ralph to commit himself to her completely, she felt defeated.

If they'd wanted to save their marriages, Joseph could have responded to his wife's "complaints" and been more attentive; Alicia could have examined her priorities and accepted the importance of achievement for her partners; and Ralph could have restrained his admiration for other women and expressed his affection to his wife. In all three cases, internal examination and changes in behavior would not only have saved their marriages but would have brought greater contentment with every aspect of their lives.

A MODEL FOR THE FUTURE

Even if you manage to recognize your own contribution to the problems in your marriage and work to change your habits the second time around, you are still followed by shadows of your first relationship. After all, how do you even *know* what you want to do differently? Everything with your new mate is in contrast to what you had; your every move is compared with what you did.

Your definitions of a "wife's" and "husband's" roles

were forged from only two sources: observing other's relationships, notably your parents', and the experience you had. Because it is more recent and you had a more direct hand in its shaping, your own first marriage is the stronger basis for every relationship to follow.

Comparisons are unavoidable. Dorothy Grover, thirty-eight, married her second husband Lloyd, forty-two, just a year after both of them were divorced. Dorothy felt she knew Lloyd's first wife, Gloria, since she moved into the same house Gloria had shared with Lloyd for seven years. When Dorothy married Lloyd, she found Gloria's old prescription medicines in the bathroom cabinet, her face buffer in the shower, and several of her casseroles in the freezer. Lying in Lloyd's bed in the spot where Gloria had spent many nights, Dorothy was overcome with the eerie knowledge that Lloyd compared even her most seductive moves to those of his first wife.

The second day after the honeymoon, Lloyd hovered expectantly in the kitchen. Dorothy thought this peculiar but went about her business, getting ready to go to her job as West Coast editor of a national women's magazine. Lloyd was a systems consultant to businesses—his hours were his own and this morning he could stay in front of his home computer until two in the afternoon. As Dorothy was wiping makeup across her face in a rush to leave, Lloyd exploded: "Well, aren't you even going to make me coffee?"

Dorothy was taken aback. "Why would I make you coffee?" she wanted to know. "I wasn't going to have any myself, and I'm late for work. Why should I make myself later by stopping to serve you coffee?"

The unmade brew was just the beginning of Lloyd's unfulfilled expectations. Dorothy didn't spend much time in the backyard, and the flowers grew scraggly and weeds crowded the once immaculate beds. Dorothy didn't always get around to finishing the newspaper, and the unread dailies began to pile up in the closet. Dorothy didn't want to make calls to restaurants when Lloyd was curious about when they opened; she didn't automatically fold his shirts when he was packing for his occasional consulting overnights away.

Gloria, on the other hand, always made him coffee in the morning, and a fancy breakfast too. Fanatically thin,

Gloria took pride in Lloyd's consumption of the Eggs Benedict she produced just for him. Gloria would spend afternoons in the yard, manicuring the lawn's borders and planting seasonal posies. Gloria read the paper every day, and one or two paperbacks a week as well, which she immediately filed in the library alphabetically. Gloria always handled the dinner reservations, phoning around to see when Lloyd's latest "finds" would be open. And Gloria neatly readied Lloyd's belongings before each business junket.

Gloria, of course, was not employed outside the home. Gloria's entire identity and emphasis was the plot of land Dorothy had inherited—the home that bore her stamp in every corner. Dorothy couldn't—and didn't care to—measure up, and it irked Lloyd. He was grateful, of course, that Dorothy was an achiever, self-confident and intelligent; that she was beautiful and had an even temperament, and he called these things an improvement over his first marriage. But why couldn't she make him coffee in the morning? Such a little thing, and she was so stubborn!

Dorothy was having problems with Lloyd as well. Her first husband was argumentative and testy, and the two had endured a contest of wills, but at least he was egalitarian. He went food shopping for himself and didn't expect her to make his meals. If he needed information, he picked up the phone; he wouldn't think of asking Dorothy to do it. He encouraged her to achieve and was proud of her money-earning capacity; Lloyd belittled her profession and kept nudging her to take (his) days off to accompany him "exploring."

Instead of negotiating their roles, both assumed that the aspects of their former marriages that they enjoyed would continue. And of course, they both were bound to be disappointed. Dorothy withdrew more and more, wary of a repeat of her confrontational first marriage. Lloyd pointed to aspects of the house that were deteriorating and invoked Gloria's name as the ideal of how a wife should care for her home. Their fights grew more frequent and intense, until one night Dorothy grabbed her purse, jumped into her car, and drove the sixty miles to the home of a friend in Ventura. After six hours, she realized that her marriage was crumbling, called Lloyd tearfully, and agreed to come home—on the condition they enter therapy. It took a year of counseling for Lloyd and Dorothy to see how the expectations left over from their first marriages had nearly destroyed their second.

The point for anyone contemplating separation is that your first marriage, and subsequent marriages too, follow you forever—the parts you liked as well as the parts you'd just as soon forget. In fact, the resentment from those painful parts even more surely affects the kind of relationship you establish later.

But the tendency is to deny this. My divorced clients say their miseries could never occur again. Why not? Because they arose from the idiosyncrasies of a crazy former spouse. Or because they won't allow it to happen, period.

Sounds plausible, but then I ask how they can prevent a recurrence of something they know only too well. Some say they're working on it through therapy or close monitoring and communication with their new partner. The rest surreptitiously structure their relationships to exclude the possibility of the dreaded situation ever arising again. In either case, the first more healthy attitude or the second equally effective but less direct approach, your divorce forces you to reshuffle your priorities, values, and habits in reference to your dissolved marriage.

Marcia Hootman and Patt Perkins in *How to Forgive Your Ex-Husband and Get On With Your Life* write that the "central theme" of their book is that "stifled anger turns into resentment that not only affects your physical and mental well-being, but also predetermines new relationships."[14] Stifled anger: another link between your left-over feelings for your spouse and all the new relationships in your future. When you end your marriage without airing your grievences, you implant the resentment that Hootman and Perkins claim will dog you throughout your romantic life. The only hitch is that if you *do* express those feelings, you're more than halfway to healing your marriage anyway. So why not give it a try?

ONCE IS QUITE ENOUGH

Though sometimes we can't tell by our actions, we do learn from our mistakes, often unconsciously. And the facts can be quite sobering. Here are a few of the lessons we learn from divorce:

1. *We learn to doubt that any relationship can be truly permanent.* We remember the passionate intensity with which we swore that this was true love and that it would last through eternity. Even though (or perhaps because) these earnest pledges were uttered in the unbounded energy of youth, we were unable to make them stick—all the more reason why any vow we make at a more jaded advanced age is sure to be made with greater suspicion.

One of the foremost signs of this wariness is the popularity of "prenuptial agreements," contracts separating possessions—and thus planning the divorce—long before the wedding. Well-known divorce and "palimony" attorney Marvin Mitchelson told the *Los Angeles Times* newspaper: "I've never seen a marriage survive a prenuptial agreement . . . they create tremendous distrust to start with and can make someone feel very insecure. It's a negative way to go into a relationship."[15] But that's just the point—with the prevalence of divorce all around, and especially with the fresh stinging of your own divorce hovering in your consciousness, the core of your soul knows you could divorce again.

2. *We learn that even the most sincere testimonies of love can be reversed.* So we hesitate when the moment seems ripe to make such claims. In the tenderness of our first marriage, we unleashed our emotions and offered our faithfulness. We believed they were offered to us by another person. But we learned that somehow the commitment wasn't equal, or that the commmitment was a fraud. It takes years of pain to untangle from such connections; entering them again is something we approach with extreme caution. We feel at great peril.

3. *We learn that the most vulnerable partner is the one who hurts most,* and so we hold back, preferring our new

love to be more vulnerable, to give more, to initiate, lest we part with some of our power and strength.

4. *We learn that we have scars, and these scars are not attractive to others who want to know us.* And yet, they cannot be erased. So we watch the reactions of others, wishing they would see only our present selves. They see a "divorcée." That means a trail of "ex" relatives, a string of bonds that have been officially but perhaps only partially broken. That means owning material possessions with auras of romantic associations; photo albums of good times and fond glances for someone they don't want to consider. We can try to camouflage these scars, but when a new friend gets close enough to really care, the marks are revealed.

5. *We learn that striving to please the other person doesn't always pay off.* It's true that this lesson can be learned from parents, early romances, and friends. But never do we try harder to please than in the early stages of a marriage: and for many, in the last stage. So when we fail, we start to think of ourselves first; we get reclusive, self-centered, and guarded. And our personalities undergo metamorphoses to which we don't like to admit.

All of these "learning experiences" are not "growth promoting," as claimed in the buzzwords of the sixties and seventies. Instead, these lessons are the psychological *costs of divorce.* This kind of knowledge makes subsequent relationships more tenuous and less wholehearted, and leaves us more cynical, hardened, and sarcastic—so that it becomes that much more difficult to love again. All the hoopla and hype about sampling experiences and "trying it all," even if you must discard well-proven standards along the way, is false. Quite simply, there are some things in life for which once is too much.

A BLOW TO SELF-ESTEEM

One of the most inescapable and destructive lessons of divorce concerns how we view ourselves. If once we were competent, self-assured, and accomplished, with divorce we publicly disprove this success and proclaim our failure. Art Carey, in arguing for marriage in a world of unlimited intimacy, notes that his divorce "was my first major, public failure" in *In Defense of Marriage*.[16] As "a person used to winning all the prizes, for whom everything came easily" like many of his "baby boomer" cohorts, this assumption became a particular problem. After all, this generation, used to wielding power, takes failure poorly—Carey suggests that such a blow could sink baby boomers' self-esteem irretrievably, a huge cost to bear.

Conversely, reviving a failing marriage brings a feeling of accomplishment that *bolsters* self-esteem and developmental progress. If your marriage is rocky you have a choice: divorce and suffer lowered self-esteem, or heal your marriage and increase your feelings of worth. No matter what you do, your self-esteem will be affected.

Judith Bardwick, in *In Transition*, agrees that divorce damages self-esteem: "In addition to any social judgments of failure in a major adult task, divorced people confront their own sense of failure, wondering whether they are guilty of not doing as much as they could have or should have, along with the despair that they have been deselected as the uniquely wonderful person in their spouse's life."[17]

I especially like the term "deselected," which implies that you were once carefully chosen from the eligible crowd, but upon second thought demoted to no one special—"deselected," as one spits out a watermelon pit upon finding amidst the fruit that it offers no nourishment or taste. Realizing that you're not loved anymore—when you still cherish and adore—renders you insignificant and silly and pulverizes your self-importance. This realization affects everything you do—career, platonic friendships, living arrangements, relations with kin—not simply the width of your smile or the length of your come-on in singles bars.

NOTES

1. Gettleman, Susan, and Markowitz, Janet. *The Courage to Divorce*. New York: Simon and Schuster, 1974, p. 18.
2. Weitzman, Lenore. *The Divorce Revolution*. New York: Free Press, 1985, p. 349.

3. Trafford, Abigail. *Crazy Time: Surviving Divorce.* New York: Harper and Row, 1972, p. 51.
4. Ibid., p. 112.
5. Ibid., p. 124.
6. Cauhape, Elizabeth. *Fresh Starts: Men and Women After Divorce.* New York: Basic Books, 1983, p. 50.
7. Hootman, Marcia, and Perkins, Patt. *How to Forgive Your Ex-Husband (and Get On With Your Life).* New York: Doubleday, 1983.
8. Epstein, Joseph. *Divorced in America.* New York: E. P. Dutton, 1974, p. 19.
9. Weiss, Robert. *Marital Separation.* New York: Basic Books, 1975.
10. Krantzler, Mel. *Creative Divorce.* New York: Evans, 1973, p. 50.
11. Kelly, Joan Berlin, and Wallerstein, Judith. *Surviving the Breakup.* New York: Basic Books, 1980.
12. Stark, Kelly. "Friends Through It All." *Psychology Today*, May 1986, pp. 54–60.
13. McKay, Matthew, and Rogers, Peter, et al. *The Divorce Book.* Oakland: New Harbinge Publishers, 1984.
14. Hootman and Perkins, p. viii.
15. Krier, Ann Beth. "Prenuptial Pacts: Bliss or a Miss." *Los Angeles Times*, August 19, 1986, p. 1, pp. 26–27.
16. Carey, Art. *In Defense of Marriage.* New York: Walker & Co., 1984.
17. Bardwick, Judith. *In Transition.* New York: Holt, Rinehart and Winston, 1977, p. 125.

CHAPTER 14

The Money Morass

While it's true that fights about finances divide married couples, money matters aren't usually the primary cause of divorce. *Insight* magazine's October 1986 cover story mentioned infidelity, dissatisfaction with self, immaturity, and lack of appreciation as reasons for the soaring divorce statistics; money was not even mentioned.[1] A 1985 nationally representative random sample by *Family Circle* magazine found only one money-related issue in the running for married couples' most-argued topic. Of the ten areas represented, "major household purchases" was eighth in rank behind problems with children, relatives, leisure time, politics, household jobs, affection, and time devoted to work.[2]

But *after* the final decree, the role of money looms menacingly, banging ex-spouses together and apart over a period of many antagonistic years. When couples no longer have the household to argue about; when the custody has been arranged; when the furniture has been divided and the court date duly recorded in history, haggling over and enforcing financial decisions has just begun.

The very fact that our society allows economics to continue to bind a divorced couple—and encourages it through legal precedent—ought to be enough deterrent to avoid a "messy" divorce. Even the most loving wife can

218

become a tiger in divorce court, given a vindictive attitude and the right lawyer.

After entertainer Johnny Carson split from his third wife, Ellen Goodman wrote a column about Joanna's request for $220,000 a month in temporary support. Goodman appropriately asks if our horror at this astronomical sum is wrongly based: "If the Carsons were still married we would regard her as no more than the overindulged wife of an overindulged performer. It is only on divorce that the wife of a rich man is reclassified as a greedy harpie who is trying to 'take him to the cleaners.' "[3]

In divorce, it is, logically, every spouse for him- or herself. It is only because Joanna Carson's financial needs became a matter of public record that we can even criticize her claims for $37,000 a month on jewelry and furs and $5,000 a month for clothing. Notes Goodman: "The request for $2.6 million a year surely makes Joanna Carson a candidate for the hit parade of top ten spenders. Who can resist the temptation to award her the title of money-grubbing divorcée of the year?"

And yet, who wins in such a battle? Johnny got plenty of sympathy and outrageous legal bills; Joanna got reasonably settled alimony and a publicity black eye. Though few divorces are so openly argued, every couple undergoes hostility in dividing possessions, dissolving joint assets, and deciding what, if any, further support should be granted. The process of dismantling a household, especially if the resources have been commingled, is sure to dampen any shred of civility or fondness that remains between you and your "ex."

A NOSEDIVE FOR WOMEN'S STANDARD OF LIVING

Men and women both suffer from divorce, but they do so differently. You'll recall that sociologist Lenore Weitzman, Ph.D. of Harvard University, studied the impact of California's "no-fault" divorce laws, which have been adopted in some form in fifteen states. Her shocking findings bear repeating: *Women's standard of living drops a whopping 73 percent after divorce*, while men's climbs a striking 42 percent. Weitzman's *The Divorce Revolution* reveals that "the major economic result of the divorce law revolution is the systematic impoverishment of divorced women and their children."[4] This comes about through the following means:

—The courts' "minimal and unrealistic standards of self-sufficiency," which assume that the two-thirds of women who never supported themselves while married should suddenly undertake that responsibility. They have to. Five out of six divorced women receive no alimony at all, and those who do averaged only $350 for two years (in 1984 dollars).

Weitzman interviewed a slew of divorce judges and concluded that "work is rehabilitation" for the divorced mother in judicial eyes.

—Liquidation of the family home. Of course, at the end of her workday the divorced mother must now return to cramped quarters, even if she needs lots of room for her children: "Arrangements that delay the sale of the home so that minor children do not have to move are viewed with disfavor by the courts because they 'tie up the father's money.' " Weitzman writes.

"Judges rarely grant a wife's request for a forced sale of the family business so that she can obtain her share of the equity, because they see an overriding interest in preserving the husband's business intact. However, when a *husband* requests an immediate sale of the family home so he can cash out his share of the equity while the wife seeks to delay the sale to ensure housing for the children, the judges tend to see the overriding interest as, again, the husband's need for his share of the equity. In the first case they tell the wife that it is reasonable to make her wait for her share of the equity, but in the second case they say it is unreasonable to make a husband wait for his share."[5]

—Raising the children alone and in poverty. Though the concepts of "joint" and fathers' custody have been given a lot of press, in reality the vast majority of single-parent families are headed by women. Eighty-one percent of mothers heading single-parent households are separated or divorced. Weitzman emphasizes: "When a couple with children divorces, it is probable that the man will become single but the woman will become a single parent. And poverty, for many women, begins with single parenthood."[6] Further, "The National Advisory Council on Economic Opportunity estimates that if current trends continue, the poverty population of the United States will be composed solely of women and children by the year 2000."[7]

—Unreliable child support. Weitzman reports that judges and attorneys show an "obvious reluctance 'to bother' with enforcement of court-ordered support."[8] She also doubts the ability of the 1984 child support enforcement law to improve the situation. Certainly before the law, the number of fathers contributing to the support of their children was pitiful. A Census Bureau study cited by *Newsweek* magazine in a 1983 cover story on American divorce reports that "judges order fathers to make support payments in just 60 percent of the divorce cases. Only one-half of those told to pay make full payments. It's an easy dodge."[9]

—Negating women's contribution. Women typically add much more to their marriage's worth than is easily divided on paper. Working to put a husband through graduate school is rarely counted, for example. Political scientist Herbert Jacob of Northwestern University, quoted in *Good Housekeeping* magazine, July 1987, says; "The major asset of most marriages is the income stream—the earning power of the chief wage-earner—and that's not touched by divorce law."[10] Though one precedent awarded a wife part of the value of her husband's medical license, the impact of that decision overall has been minimal.

And what of the wife who enjoyed creating a cozy home, who preferred being there when her children were young? If she's smart, she'll rush to trade school: "The courts rarely reward her for the job she has done," notes Dr. Weitzman. "Rather, the new assumptions imply that her motherhood years were wasted and worthless for she too is measured against the all-important new criterion of earning capacity.

"The treatment that housewives and mothers receive under the new laws conveys a clear message to the young woman who is planning her future. They tell her that divorce may send her into poverty if she invests in her family ahead of—or even alongside of—her career."[11]

So much for the misfortunes of older women left stranded on their sinking familial ship without a life raft. Younger women, the beneficiaries of the feminist movement, may smugly think they're immune from panic about lack of a career. Trained as they were with enlightenment, they spent languorous years completing graduate school and climbing onto the career ladder. They reeked of self-confidence and success and could certainly support themselves whether married or not.

But do they truly want to? Susan Crain Bakos, writing in *This Wasn't Supposed to Happen*, thinks the glistening new image of the typical career woman as portrayed triumphantly in the film *9 to 5* is a crock: "Suddenly we all saw her as a bright, witty, inventive woman coping imaginatively with paperwork overload, lack of respect, sexual harassment, office technology. Still, we hadn't begun to admit there were many more secretaries than management women—that there were in fact many more women holding all manner of low-salary, low-opportunity jobs than women who fit our new glamour model of working woman: she who resides in the executive suite."[12]

U.S. Census figures show that more than half of married women in the United States hold outside jobs—and yet "the vast majority of women with children under twelve years of age admit frankly that they would much rather stay home," asserts Ann Landers in a *Family Circle* magazine article.[13] Still, financial pressures force moms out into the work world, to jobs we once hailed as "fulfilling." And what do they get for it? "In an unexpected and ironical way, the liberated, educated, gainfully employed career woman has made herself more 'divorcable,' " Landers continues. "Men these days feel less guilty about leaving a wife who can support herself—or worse yet, heaven forbid, who makes more money than he does."[14]

Once the divorce arrives, all the lifestyle benefits of being a "DINK" (dual income, no kids) or "DIK" (dual income, kids) evaporate. Suddenly you're left to fend for yourself—and your children, who, Lenore Weitzman notes, usually receive less child support than required to pay for their necessities. And while you're probably better off than the woman who has no job skills, your standard of living still drops drastically, since two wage-earners certainly live more comfortably than one.

You might say, "So what, I'd rather live in a shoe box in peace than in a palace with that scoundrel." "I'd rather shop at the Salvation Army than have to put up with his cheating/obsession/neglect/stubborness." "Money isn't that important—sanity is. I started out poor and I can stand it again; at least I'll only be accountable to myself."

These are valid points, but your sanity and peace of mind can be completely destroyed if you find yourself in pressured or depressed financial circumstances. It's one thing to pontificate about how surroundings don't matter to you and how you can blithely scrounge a gourmet dinner out of trash bins, but it's another to have to actually do it night after night. You may think, "I can get a loan from my parents." But then imagine asking for the money and your changed relationship afterwards. Imagine worrying about parts of your life you may have taken for granted: going to movies or concerts, buying furniture or appliances, paying off car repairs. Imagine having to deny your child summer camp, or even having to go (crawling?) to his daddy for the money.

A drop in economic status not only affects the physical environment you inhabit, but also many intangibles, such as the class of people with whom you rub shoulders and the way you feel about yourself in social situations. It hits you every time you pull your car into your driveway; it permeates every menu you plan for dinner parties.

After a divorce you either feel more desperate or more dependent: more desperate if you must now rely on only yourself to try to maintain the standard of living you had or desire; more dependent if you must look to your ex-spouse for support, which by virtue of not being married anymore, you now feel less entitled to. You can give yourself a pep talk: "I earned this money for all the crap I took while I was with him." But every month, when you cash that alimony check, you're still thinking that somehow, if only you were a self-sufficient—worthwhile—person, you could make it on your own and show that so-and-so that he's not Mr. Important in your life after all.

In divorce, piles of money form the great battleground.

If you don't want to let go of your marriage, you squabble about money. It happened to Jennifer Reiter, thirty-seven, married to Jacob Reiter, a forty-one-year-old Hollywood studio musician. Jacob insisted that he'd tried to keep his marriage together; he was stunned when his wife of eleven years announced she was leaving. He begged her to stay and took her on a romantic two-week vacation to demonstrate his devotion. But Jennifer pointed to his workaholic nature, his disinterest in their four children, and his authoritarian, overbearing stance in their relationship. For six months, Jacob tried the exercises the marriage counselor suggested. But while he expressed single-minded sincerity, secretly he thought Jennifer was overreacting to a perfectly decent situation.

Dissatisfied, Jennifer moved to her family's vacation home in a mountain community about an hour away. Jacob reluctantly helped Jennifer lug the furniture onto the U-Haul. He let her take several items he thought he deserved, such as some expensive stereo speakers and a set of crystal they had received from his family for their wedding. Jennifer's attorney was particular about spelling out her part of the settlement—she would get the R.V., the more expensive of the two cars, and half of the present value of their home. She would have custody of the children; Jacob could visit them weekends and other days by arrangement. Jacob wanted to be as accommodating as possible and didn't contest her demands, though he thought them unfair.

But he wanted to avoid upsetting her further. Every day without fail, Jennifer would return to Jacob's house, ostensibly to pick up an item she wanted or that a child had forgotten. Then she would let loose with a shouting tirade, punctuated with fits of tears, decrying Jacob's mistreatment and dredging up examples of his insensitivity, selfishness, and oppression.

Jacob genuinely felt bad. From her hysteria it was obvious that Jennifer was emotionally damaged. Incidents he had forgotten or dismissed were cited as reasons for her fear, self-loathing, or resentment. His conscience would not let him deny her the monetary compensation she desired. He knew that his earning capacity was high; though she came from a wealthy family, hers was insecure. He pledged her generous alimony and child support and continued accepting her outpourings day after day for several months, in person or by telephone.

Then he met Lisa Cotner. She was thirty-three, lithe, and full of sunshine. The founder of a thriving party entertainment business that she ran out of her home, Lisa's time was her own, since her twenty employees could run the business without constant supervision. She was referred to Jacob because she needed a replacement for a musician who canceled at the last moment; they got to talking and soon were meeting for morning hikes and hamburgers at all-night stands.

Suddenly, Jacob wasn't available as much as he had been, and Jennifer began to suspect there was someone new in his life. Amidst her daily tirades she would grill Jacob on finding someone new to make miserable, someone with whom to play the charade and ultimately reveal his wicked inner character. While he continued to soothe and sympathize with Jennifer, it became easier and easier for Jacob to tune out her rantings. He could lapse into a daydream about his latest escapade with Lisa, or fantasize about new adventures they'd share. When Lisa hit it off with his children, Jacob was even more enchanted.

After four months of courtship, Jacob was spending several nights a week with Lisa. It was blissful, peaceful, romantic. Lisa was understanding when Jacob told her about Jennifer's daily bouts. She was sweet and fun-loving in direct contrast to the venomous posture now taken consistently by his estranged wife.

Seemingly quite suddenly, Jacob got a call from Jennifer's lawyer demanding more compensation for Jennifer's "expenses." Jennifer felt entitled not only to alimony and child support but tuition so that she could be professionally trained. She wanted money for the daily care of the children and reimbursement for the psychotherapy she was receiving three hours weekly. It was Jacob's fault, Jennifer charged, that she had been intimidated out of pursuing the career she had desired, and it was due to Jacob that her mental health had been impaired. The additional expense was to be three hundred dollars weekly for therapy, two hundred weekly for child care, and six thousand dollars per year for the next four years for her schooling.

Jacob was floored. He'd tried so hard to give Jennifer

all that she'd asked for; how dare she discard their property settlement and ask for such an exorbitant increase? It was outrageous, absurd! She decided that she needed three hours of therapy a week—should Jacob simply nod his head, say, "Yes, you're extremely crazy," and take out his checkbook? She decided that all of a sudden she wanted to go back to school—should Jacob simply say, "Yes, your previous choice not to finish college is my responsibility," and order tickets for the next university football game?

For the first time in weeks he brought as much passion to their regular confrontations as Jennifer did. They screamed and argued back and forth for two hours, until Jacob was hoarse. Jennifer's combativeness got to Jacob, and he carried it over to his relationship with Lisa. Not wanting to interfere in Jacob's affairs, Lisa suggested, "Maybe you need a little time to be alone right now."

Jennifer's was a good ploy. When she sensed that Jacob was getting too withdrawn from her and attached to Lisa, Jennifer used the ammunition at hand to get what she really wanted: Jacob's attention. She'd moved out and conducted her tirades with one unconscious but overriding purpose—for Jacob to take her seriously and capitulate to her. She wanted him to respect her, to see that she had important, worthwhile needs. She maintained her own home to prove to him that she was self-sufficient, that she didn't depend on him as much as they both seemed to think. When he missed the kids enough and could start to respect her, Jennifer's unwritten script read, Jacob would beg to have her and the children back on new terms.

Jennifer hadn't counted on Lisa's entry into the picture. She already had uncontested custody of the kids, so in order to maintain her grip on Jacob and stop the progress of their divorce, she embraced her one sure weapon, money. Maybe if Jacob understood that it was only her need to please him that made her repress her feelings and therefore require therapy . . . Maybe if Jacob could see that it was only her devotion to him and his career that made her place their family and his progress above her own education . . . Maybe if he saw how hollow life was without the inquisitive and delightful presence of his children . . . If he could just know how much he meant to her; how he was her whole life—not only would he want her back, but he would treasure their family and her selfless gifts.

Rather than expose herself to possible rejection by telling Jacob these things directly, Jennifer demanded more money. Now their meetings centered around her justifications for the additional cash; they talked about the kids' futures and their past decisions. Jacob tried to convince her that she didn't need to see a shrink so often. He tried to show her how an advanced degree at this point in her life was senseless and would not enhance her ability to make a living.

In the end, because she could not send—and he would not listen to—her true message, Jennifer extracted as much money as she could from Jacob. And she dragged the "negotiations" out as long as possible—two years from the time of their original agreement. Money was not only the battleground of their emotions, it was the tool that kept Jacob and Jennifer from really talking, from really addressing their problems and perhaps working them out. If Jennifer hadn't used separation and divorce as threats, her moving out and pleas for money would not have been distractions from the real issues—and ultimately would not have caused the exact opposite of the outcome she really sought.

MEN, MONEY, AND DIVORCE

While Jennifer Reiter suffered because of the way she used money to manipulate her husband, ultimately it was her husband who lost the most financially. When he finally chalked up his costs for the divorce, he had spent more than $300,000. The couple's home, purchased several years earlier for $80,000, had jumped to an assessed value of $275,000, and just to stay there Jacob had to take out a loan for $110,000. This substantially depleted the amount of money he had to live on month-to-month and diminished his overall standard of living.

That may be okay for a man anticipating swinging bachelorhood and becoming a "wild and crazy guy." Single men can get away with living in a slightly ragged apartment with sagging furniture and only two wine glasses. They're expected to subsist on fast food and

Twinkies, as long as their cars move swiftly and their hair is clean.

But what happens when he wants to once again get married and head a family? When he needs a complete income for his present wife and either one or more step-kids or new babies of their own? The likelihood is that he will remarry—U.S. Census Bureau figures say 83 percent of divorced men walk down the aisle a second time. It doesn't even matter how old he is. Norman Sheresky and Marya Mannes in *Uncoupling* note succinctly: "The older man has a second, third, or even fourth chance for an intimate union while the older woman, with few exceptions, is offered none."[15]

You must've heard the stories about a second wife's hardship while her husband supports the "ex" and a house full of children in another city. The new bride is in her mid-thirties and hoping to have a baby because her biological clock is winding down. But she doesn't see how she can do it, she complains bitterly, because they can't afford for her to quit her job. In the meantime, they can't even take a vacation because they can't afford it; but even if they could, her hubby's got the kids for the summer. Of course her life is made miserable because of the constant phone calls from the "ex" for money for the children. Yes, they're good kids, but when will he be allowed to have a life of his own with her?

Glynnis Walker surveyed two hundred second wives, average age thirty-two, for her book *Second Wife, Second Best*. She warns second brides: "You will probably have to go out to work, not to make ends meet for your family, but to help your husband make ends meet for his. Among the wives who participated in the survey, there were some who worked virtually just to pay their husbands' alimony and child support from their previous marriages. Others saw a large chuck of their salaries go to support ex-wives who did not work. Seventy-four percent of the second wives in the survey worked, while 60 percent of their husbands' ex-wives did not."[16]

What does this pressure mean for your postdivorce future, men? In one sense, it means living to pay off the past. Thirty percent of the second wives Walker surveyed "wanted children but felt they could not afford them while their husbands were still paying for children from their previous marriages."[17]

If a man can't feel secure about the assets he has to start a new married life, at least he always has his business, right? Not in the case of divorce. *Inc.* magazine (March 1986) subtitled its article on "Divorce, Entrepreneurial Style" with the line, "to plan for it may ruin your marriage; not to plan for it may destroy your company." When the courts decide to view a man's business as community property, the outcomes can be devastating: "If the case becomes such a pitched battle that word of the divorce leaks out into the industry grapevine or the newspapers, the company may begin to appear unstable to customers, lenders, and investors."

In many cases, wives suspect their husbands of earning far more than they purport to and go to great lengths to discover any hidden assets. Often they need to—crafty businessmen, anticipating divorce, often feel forced into the inconvenience of " 'damage control'—a euphemism for hiding money from one's spouse," the article explains.[18]

Even if your company survives financially intact, your ability to run it—and therefore to generate or sustain efficiency and profits—is likely to be impaired. *Inc.* quotes attorney Paul D. Pearson, who advises his entrepreneurial clients to "consider themselves emotionally disabled for the duration of the divorce proceedings." Pearson warns that no matter what your level of competence before, a divorce will bring "distraction and a reduced capacity to concentrate. Having to shut the door once a day and cry shouldn't be considered uncommon."[19]

What if you're not self-employed? Those statistics suggesting that men average a 42 percent higher standard of living postdivorce look pretty inviting. But when I interviewed Lenore Weitzman, who authored the study producing that finding, she cautioned: "The economic benefits for men are artificial." In *The Divorce Revolution* she describes a study by economists Saul Hoffman and John Holmes, who followed changes in income for divorced and married people over seven years: "The dollar incomes of both divorced men and divorced women declined, while the income of married couples rose. Divorced men lost 19 percent in income while divorced women lost 29 percent. In contrast, married men and women experienced a 22 percent rise in income."[20]

It is only when each family member's needs are taken into account that men appear to do much better than women upon divorce, due to the fact that mothers must bear the responsibility for children on greatly reduced budgets. Their plight is certainly lamentable—but that does not negate the fact that men suffer a decrease in absolute dollars of income after divorce.

The divorce itself is a costly process, with lawyer's fees, moving expenses, and often therapy for everyone in the family. Of course, no one should feel bound in a dangerous or unbearable marriage simply because he or she lacks the wherewithal to escape. On the other hand, you should think what the loss of liquid cash—and the obligation to provide payments to someone you probably hope to avoid seeing ever again—will do to your earning capacity, *joie de vivre*, and world view. With these crucial elements dented, you may not be any happier divorced than married.

NOTES

1. Diegmueller, Karen. "Breaking the Ties That Bind." *Insight*, October 1986, p. 8–13.
2. Rubenstein, Carin. "What's Become of the American Family." *Family Circle*, October 5, 1985, pp. 24–26, p. 28.
3. Goodman, Ellen. "He-e-e-e-re's a Real Alimony Dialogue." *Los Angeles Times*, October 26, 1983, p. 5.
4. Weitzman Lenore. *The Divorce Revolution.* New York: Free Press, 1985, xvi.
5. Ibid., p. 397.
6. Ibid., p. 350.
7. Ibid., p. 350.
8. Ibid., p. 369.
9. "Divorce American Style." *Newsweek*, January 10, 1983, p. 42–48.
10. Hunt, Morton. "What the New Divorce Laws Are Doing to Women." *Good Housekeeping*, July 1987, p. 64, pp. 160–163.
11. Weitzman, p. 373.

12. Bakos, Susan Crain. *This Wasn't Supposed to Happen.* New York: Continuum Publishing, 1985, p. 111.
13. Landers, Ann. "What's Happening to Today's Marriages." *Family Circle*, November 16, 1982, p. 62.
14. Ibid., p. 52.
15. Mannes, Marya, and Sheresky, Norman. *Uncoupling, the Art of Coming Apart: A Guide to Sane Divorce.* New York: Viking Press, 1972, p. 35.
16. Walker, Glynnis. *Second Wife, Second Best.* New York: Doubleday, 1984, p. 10.
17. Ibid., p. 38.
18. Wojahn, Ellen. "Divorce, Entrepreneurial Style." *Inc.*, March 1986, p. 62.
19. Ibid., p.62.
20. Weitzman, p. 337.

CHAPTER 15

Hurting the Ones You Love

When you're on the edge of your marriage, it's easy to become wrapped up in the pros and cons of separation. You think: Will I be able to find somebody else? Will I be lonely on my own? Can I manage on a fraction of my usual bankroll? How will I cope with living by myself? How will I explain this to my family and the children?

There's one question that you *don't* ask yourself: "Am I causing a disastrous emotional turning point in their lives?" The thought—and the guilt—lurks in the back of your mind, but you don't want to face it. When *you're* miserable, you can't be expected to speculate about somebody else's pain, can you?

Of course, the answer is that you can—and *should*.

CASE #1: OVERHEARD AT A HEALTH CLUB

A vivacious young grandmother confessed her lingering sadness to her chums on the exerccycle at the gym. This forty-nine-year-old dynamo, married at age twenty, bore the first of her three children at twenty-two, completed a doctorate in developmental psychology at twenty-six, and four years later earned a respectable position on the faculty of a major university in the Chicago area.

After she described her activities with enthusiasm to a newcomer seated on the next bike, her cycling mate remarked, "You seem to have it made."

"Pretty much," she agreed. "My only grief is with my son. He just got divorced and not only is he moody and withdrawn, but I never get to see my two-year-old granddaughter." Her friend sympathized and she continued, "I was always so fond of the woman Jeffrey married. She's got her own catering business that she runs out of her home so she can be on call for the baby. She's articulate and beautiful, and little Amanda is just the most adorable child you could ever meet. But Jeffrey got involved with someone else, a temporary affair, and my daughter-in-law threw him out. Jeffrey tried to make it up to her, but she wouldn't hear of it and now there's such friction I wouldn't dare try to see Amanda on the sly. Which means I don't see her at all."

Grandparents' groups have won the right to ask for judicial hearings to earn them visitation privileges in forty-two states, but the professor in the nautilus room isn't interested in court resolution. She doesn't want to alienate her son or become involved in legal hassles; she's hoping that with time, the hostility will cool down and she can gently ask Jeffrey to arrange some regular contact. In the meantime, she's often consumed with sadness about the situation, and frustrated that there's little she can do.

CASE #2: AT THE BANQUET OF A PROFESSIONAL ORGANIZATION

Charlene Morgan, twenty-seven, was in the audience at a speech I gave on men and women's roles. Afterward she took me aside, introduced herself, and asked me for advice regarding her closest girlfriend, Stacy.

"She's making a mess out of her life," Charlene explained. "She's got the greatest husband, but she's willing to risk her marriage for sexual thrills. She met a hunk in an elevator and now she's having this torrid affair. She's asked me to cover for her—I refuse and beg her to quit playing with fire. But she still keeps playing around and then calls me to brag about it. I've known her since we were kids in elementary school together, and I feel helpless. Somebody's got to shake some sense into her."

After Charlene tearfully insisted that Stacy get counseling, the twenty-seven-year-old legal secretary finally relented and met with me professionally. She was nice looking, with long, dark hair and an engagingly flighty manner, but she was no drop-dead knockout. She described in giggly detail how she met and was breathlessly pursued by her boyfriend, an "incredibly handsome" health club owner. She proudly enumerated her ploys for deceiving her husband; she reveled in reliving each moment of her passionate trysts in deserted offices.

After her monologue, Stacy admitted: "I know I'm ruining my marriage, but I'm just having too much fun to stop. I know I'm just a big kid. But I don't see why I should give up life's pleasures. Not everybody is cut out to be responsible."

We went through all the possible consequences of her actions, which she blithely acknowledged. "But I don't care. I don't want to change and I don't want to drop my new relationship."

Naturally her husband was crushed when he found out. He pleaded with her to join him for marriage counseling, but Stacy didn't want to "waste" even one afternoon.

Stacy never returned to see me, and after weeks of anguish, her husband gave up. She weaseled half a million dollars from his real estate development business. She bought a Mercedes. Then she pitched out the hunk and took up with a rock musician.

"I won't be her friend anymore," Charlene told me with disgust three months later. "She knows I hate her behavior. Whenever I talk to her we get back to what an immature, selfish bitch she is. I've been yelling at her so much that we've started just to avoid each other. Still, it kills me to just throw away a friendship I've had for more than twenty years. But it seems I have no choice."

CASE #3: AT SUNDAY SCHOOL

Lori was five years old when her mother took her and her older brother and sister to Los Angeles from London, England, four years ago. Her daddy, ostensibly a respected religious leader, had become violent in arguments with her mommy—and so the kids were whisked off to live with their mother near Uncle Matt, pastor of a Congregational church near Los Angeles.

They had packed and hurried to the airport. "What's going on, Mommy? Where are we going?"

"To visit Uncle Matt. Now hush, Lori. We've got to rush to make the airplane."

Only it wasn't really a visit, and Lori knew it. Daddy was staying home. Mommy took too many suitcases. A long flight; a new country. Uncle Matt was serious, whispering to Mommy, trying to smile, but his smiles were so short-lived.

There were so many strangers at Sunday School. Lots of people and so many names. They all came up and said "How pretty!" and asked how old "we" are and where "we" got such a pretty dress. Lori was scared, so she decided not to answer any of them. Or ask for anything either. Lori just stopped talking.

She'd nod or shake her head in response, but other than that she'd look petrified and grab her Mommy's skirt to hide behind. Or she'd wrinkle her brow, stare at the floor, and shake her head "no." "No, I won't answer. I won't be here. I won't let this happen."

Lori didn't talk for six months. Mommy took her to a psychologist who had her play with doll houses and draw pictures and who told Mommy that the trauma was from the move and the divorce and that with time, she should be all right. Mommy learned not to try to force her to talk; Lori soon noticed that her weekday teacher and all the people at Sunday School were leaving her alone as well, and she was glad for that.

For six months she did not say anything, not one word. She was excruciatingly shy. She cried every night. It made her Mommy cry too, but no, they could not go back home, not ever. Gradually Lori realized that she was going to live in Los Angeles. And one day, when she was asked if she wanted some ice cream, as people always did ask her, she said, "Yes." Her mommy was so excited, she cried some more.

These three cases are typical of "secondary divorce." Just as the smoldering tobacco in cigarettes produces deleterious effects on people near the smoker who are not directly inhaling, a divorce brings harmful consequences to those on its perimeter. The negative results radiate outward, first to those closest to you who may be hit as squarely with your breakup as yourself, and then to others more distant but still profoundly moved. These are "ruinous ripples" of liquid poison—bad feelings that disturb children, in-laws, and friends.

FORMATIVE PAIN

While much of the effect of divorce on children has been well-documented and publicized, new information on its far-reaching trauma is emerging daily. And there's lots of data to mine—1.5 million children under the age of eighteen are affected each year by their parents' divorces. One out of every five children lived in a single-parent home in 1984. One-third of all children never see one of their parents after the divorce.

It seems shocking, and yet a nationally representative *Family Circle* magazine poll found that Americans are increasingly tolerant of aberrations of the two-parent family ideal: 83 percent accept a single working father with custody of children as "normal," while 81 percent don't mind a single working mother heading her brood.[1]

Judith Wallerstein and Joan Berlin Kelly conducted an in-depth longitudinal study of sixty divorced parents and their children, creating a rare opportunity to really probe its effects (*Surviving the Breakup*, 1980, plus many follow-up articles). According to their findings, divorce is actually a lengthy process with many stages. After following their subjects for five years, the authors concluded: "The multiple changes in the individual lives of the adults and the children and in their relationships with each other, which were set into motion by the decision to divorce, exceeded our expectations in their drama, their complexity, and their widening effects."[2]

Wallerstein and Kelly say the stages include an initially traumatic period of high stress, a transition period of at least two to three years with relationships changing and repositioning, and lastly the process of creating a new "blended" family through remarriage or stabilizing life in a single-parent household. Effects continued ten years postdivorce, for both parents—who regretted their divorces and harbored pain and bitterness—and children who, as adolescents and adults, showed inability to form romantic attachments.

Susan Arnsberg Diamond, in *Helping Children of Di-*

vorce: A Handbook for Parents and Teachers,[3] describes nine emotional reactions of children to the divorce of their parents. As you read them, consider that these disturbing symptoms are supposedly *normal* byproducts of your divorce on your children:

1. Sadness and depression, fatigue, daydreams, bursting into tears, withdrawing from friends, difficulty concentrating, and occasionally, plunging into schoolwork as a means of withdrawing;

2. Denial;

3. Embarrassment, which may last for years and brings loss of self-esteem;

4. Intense anger;

5. Guilt because of a conflict in loyalty;

6. Concern about being cared for, even if the family is affluent;

7. Regression, lack of normal development, or return to dependency;

8. A necessitated maturity foisted upon them by circumstances that often separates the child from his peers;

9. Somatic symptoms, typically stomachaches or headaches.

Summarizes Gordon Livingston of the Columbia, Maryland, Medical Plan: "The disillusionment that comes with the knowledge that your parents do not love each other anymore and are not going to stay together . . . is not only a tremendous blow to a child's conception of the world as an orderly place, but it shakes his fundamental faith in everything."[4]

Is the emotional strain of your marriage so bad that you would knowingly inflict these problems on your innocent children? Or isn't your effort better spent healing your marriage to make it more rewarding to you and certainly more safe and healthful for your child?

"Does anyone really know which is worse for children: to be brought up in a home where parents are always quarreling, are even at each other's throats, or to be brought up in a home by a single parent (usually a mother) often in an emotionally shaky state, harassed by money worries, and probably having to be at a job and thus far away from home for the better part of the day?" asks Joseph Epstein in *Divorced in America*. "Either way, no one will dispute, children get short shrift. What is also indisputable is that a solid home with both parents getting along is best of all. If one is genuinely concerned 'for the sake of the children,' then this is what one ought to do one's damnedest to provide."[5]

The two-parent home is better for your children's development. Write Wallerstein and Kelly: "There is, in fact, no supporting evidence in this five-year study for the commonly made argument that divorce is overall better for children than an unhappy marriage."[6]

It should be noted that this particular study didn't find that living in an *unhappy* home was any better than divorce (remember that they were studying families who divorced, not those who argued but ultimately stayed together). But the researchers *did* find that children maintain a steadfastly high emotional need for both parents, even through remarriages and moves, many years after the divorce. Unfortunately, only *one-fifth* of children from divorced homes maintain a good relationship with both parents, according to 1983 Senate testimony by Nicholas Zill of Child Trends, Inc. At the same time, just "fifty-seven percent had a close relationship with their mothers; only one-third did with their fathers."[7]

In addition, Wallerstein and Kelly conclude that *children develop better when their parents stay married*: "Unfortunately, it appears clear that the divorced family is, in many ways, less adaptive economically, socially, and psychologically to the raising of children than the two-parent family."[8]

What is the upshot of all this? That when your marriage is shaky, you should stay together and try to solve your marital problems. Don't just rationalize that the kids will be better off out of your unstable environment, that they're being hurt more by your marital woes than if you just got the whole thing over with. Wallerstein and Kelly's authoritative work doesn't back you up.

CHILDREN SUFFER IN THE LONG RUN

Of course, it's true that kids are flexible and can, with the right environment, attention, and encouragement, bounce back. Wallerstein and Kelly found that children who were very young when their parents split often showed frightening immediate symptoms but five years later seemed to adapt. But if the kids were older at the time of the breakup, the harm from that one event was less obvious in the short term but over time turned out to be severe and lasting.

As reported in the *Insight* magazine cover story of October 1986, University of Nebraska sociologist Alan Booth found that " 'children of divorce are much more active, much more likely to have experienced sexual relations' than are students from intact families or whose mother or father had died.''9 Edward Teyber and Charles D. Hoffman, in *Psychology Today*, April 1987, concur, noting that while ''boys at every age suffer more from divorce than do girls, adolescent girls, raised with little fatherly contact, are more likely than girls with an available father to become sexually promiscuous.''10

And sociologist Hunhild Hagestad of the College of Human Development at Pennsylvania State University found that parental divorce is even tough on young adults: ''There's an enormous sense of loss. Many of [those interviewed] did say their world was falling apart.''11

College students suffered in other ways as well, often dropping out of school due to reduced financial resources and worrying about the well-being of their parents. This theme even compelled movie audiences: the film *Nothing In Common* (1986) starring Tom Hanks and Jackie Gleason, focused on the stress of a hedonistic advertising exec upon learning of his parents' divorce. The event becomes a catalyst first for parent-child role reversal and ultimately for redefining each family member's sense of identity.

Other research by Norval D. Glenn and Kathryn Kramer of the University of Texas at Austin pooled data from eight national surveys, comparing adults from families that were intact, had experienced divorce, or in which one or both parents died: "We found that the adult children of divorce compared unfavorably with the other groups on almost all of the measures of well-being covered by the study," Dr. Glenn writes in *Psychology Today*, June 1985.[12] He also found that "the negative effects (of parental divorce) persist undiminished throughout the lifespan," and concludes ominously: "One must seriously entertain the disturbing hypothesis that the increased numbers of children of divorce will lead to a slow but steady erosion of the population's overall level of well-being."[13]

Pretty heavy stuff. But intuitively, despite the efforts of single parents to legitimize their lifestyle, both parents and children know that divorce just isn't the way it's supposed to be.

When writer Delia Ephron became a stepparent of a three- and six-year-old, she discovered the devastation divorce brings to children—and the sense of humor necessary to cope with it. She calls the new conglomeration of my-kids-your-kids that sociologists label the "blended family" "Funny Sauce, a sauce that was never meant to be mixed."[14]

And yet, the impact of divorce on family and friends doesn't seem to sink in—we don't look at these tragedies as deterrents to divorcing. While divorce statistics seem to have peaked, advice-givers still ask "what do *you* feel?" as the source of all wisdom. *We've got to stop allowing selfish concerns to be the only criteria for the appropriateness of divorce.*

Even looking at it selfishly, by ignoring the impact of your divorce on others you create more problems than you escape by leaving your marriage—especially if you have children, which in Los Angeles, not known for its emphasis on family, includes 60 percent of those filing for dissolution. For every wrenching disagreement you have with your spouse now, you'll have several more after the divorce. The questions are unavoidable: Which school to send the kids to? Can I have our daughter for Easter week? What church should she belong to? How much will you pay toward our son's college tuition?

So you can look forward to years of dilemmas relating

to your "ex" about the children. At the same time you must contend with the aftereffects of divorce on your kids themselves. Many of these traumas surface when your children are teenagers, as reported by Michael and Jessica Jackson in *Your Father's Not Coming Home Anymore*: "Many kids used dope as an escape from depressing scenes at home. When stoned or drunk, one can forget about problems for a while."[15]

They interviewed several teenagers, asking Ellen, sixteen: " 'Do you think you'll ever get married?' "

" 'No, I don't want to get married,' " she replied. " 'I never want to make that commitment. I don't want to have any kids. I'm afraid that I'll end up too much like my mother.' "

What kind of image do *you* think your children will have of *you*?

RUINOUS RIPPLES

Let me just make a few points regarding the costs of your divorce on people other than just your nuclear family.

Your parents are thrown into an awkward and painful position. They know they must support you, their own son or daughter—and yet it was you who brought them the son- or daughter-in-law they have come to love. Now they're expected not just to see less of their grandchildren, but to sever all cordial relations with the "ex."

It's likely that the person now relegated to the title of "ex" called them "Mom" or "Dad." You probably made every effort during your time together to make your spouse feel that he really belonged to your family—and they tried equally hard to keep him from feeling like a "by marriage" tag-along. One woman gave her daughter-in-law a ring that had been in the family for generations; another daughter-in-law "inherited" a keepsake set of glassware. Now, whenever they use these they have either a guilty or wistful pang, and the in-laws are filled with sadness.

Even when this pain cuts deeply, most parents won't discuss it. Instead, they suffer in silence as part of their obligatory support for you. They know you're undergoing a lot of trauma—what right do they have to burden you with the pain *they're* feeling? Few divorcing children even give their parents' suffering a moment's thought.

Many parents are additionally hurt because your divorce is felt, quietly and internally of course, to be a disgrace for the family. With divorce everywhere—and perhaps with they themselves divorced—they can't just come out and tell you these kinds of feelings. But few older adults escaped early inculcation about the permanence of marriage and the shame that divorce brings. In their eyes, the son or daughter they worked hard to make a success has just failed. They can brag in the beauty parlor about your graduate degree, your lovely children, and your beautiful home. They can only look away when someone mentions your divorce.

Your siblings suffer too. If they're married, they may have grown accustomed to your company in a foursome as a regular part of their social life. They may have become too close to your ex-spouse and now feel that friendship torn away by something out of their control. Perhaps you, as an older brother or sister, have always been a model for your siblings, and now their long-held admiration must be dashed. They may become less secure about the stability of their own marriages if they see yours crumbling.

Again, they can't very well jump in and instruct you to fix your marriage before letting it go. They can't easily tell you about all the ways their own lives are being changed and how your actions are affecting them. Especially if you're close and assume that your brother or sister *could* communicate with you, they're likely to believe their duty to support and console you comes ahead of any personal advice they'd give. They figure that when you're determined to leave, or when your spouse has rejected you, you need strength—not someone telling you to put in the colossal energy required to turn things around.

And as discussed in an earlier chapter, *your friends* have a real stake in your marriage. Their social lives are dependent on the stability of their alliances—and you've just disturbed that equilibrium. Your divorce calls into question the security of their marriages, as it does for your siblings. And it demoralizes them, especially if they're single, because they see one more example show-ing that the chances for a truly happy marriage are slim.

Friends and family both will be forced to "choose sides" even if they swear that they're impartial and will forever be close to both of you. But they now can't have you both over at the same time—one of you gets an in-vitation and the other is left out. Even if you announce that your divorce is cordial and that you don't mind being in the same room with your "ex," which is, frankly, nearly impossible to achieve, the two of you won't be invited to the same party because the *other* guests will feel awkward and uncomfortable. And any new lover may be received with hesitation and certainly with compari-sons to the "ex" they all knew so well. You'll have to contend with all of it—the feelings of your hosts, the uneasiness of your present date, and the speculation in your own mind about how to most diplomatically handle every move.

Your divorce has an impact on *society at large* as well as the people with whom you have contact. Seems pretty far removed, I know—you can't make a personal decision based on some abstract conglomerate of unknown masses. Still, you're deluding yourself if you deny that everything you do has important consequences to far more people and forces than just yourself.

By divorcing, you detract from the stability of the overall society, adding to the rootlessness and lack of continuity or connection many people feel. You're dete-riorating the values of society, affecting everyone who sees the statistics on the runaway divorce rate. Observers such as children in school, and anyone planning whether or not to marry—learn from these numbers that society is devaluing the institution of marriage, which in turn inevitably decreases its value for *them*. It plants the no-tion that "divorce is all right because everybody's doing it." Or for a prospective bride or groom, "I can get married to so-and-so, whom I'm not really sure about, because if it doesn't work out, there's always divorce."

In other words, your divorce gives permission to others to break up their marriages—anonymous as they are in the divorced multitudes. Ann Landers wrote that "di-vorce is contagious" because the germ of that disease is so easily transmitted from one mind—and one heart—to another.

NOTES

1. Rubenstein, Carin. "What's Become of the American Family." *Family Circle*, October 15, 1985 p. 25.
2. Kelly, Joan Berlin, and Wallerstein, Judith. *Surviving the Breakup*. New York: Basic Books, 1980.
3. Diamond, Susan Arnsberg. *Helping Children of Divorce: A Handbook for Parents and Teachers*. New York: Shocken Books, 1985.
4. Francke, Linda Bird. *Growing Up Divorced*. New York: Simon and Schuster, 1983, p. 51.
5. Epstein, Joseph. *Divorced in America*. New York: E.P. Dutton, 1974, p. 179.
6. Kelly and Wallerstein, p. 306.
7. Diegmueller, Karen. "Breaking the Ties that Bind." *Insight*, October 3, 1986, p. 14.
8. Kelly and Wallerstein, p. 308.
9. Diegmueller, p. 16.
10. Hoffman, Charles D., and Teyber, Edward. "Missing Fathers." *Psychology Today*, April 1987, p. 38.
11. Diegmueller, p. 16.
12. Glenn, Norval D., and Kramer, Kathryn. "Children of Divorce." *Psychology Today*, June 1985, p. 69.
13. Ibid., p. 69.
14. Ephron, Delia. *Funny Sauce*, New York: Viking. 1986.
15. Jackson, Jessica and Michael. *Your Father's Not Coming Home Anymore*. New York: Richard Marek, 1981, p. 15.
16. Ibid., p. 16.

CHAPTER 16

Missing the Boat: The Benefits of Staying Married

By now you understand why you shouldn't get divorced, but that's not good enough—you need positive reasons to hold your marriage together. You can't just "stick it out" with nothing romantic, no spark, no warmth. Your marriage should be something to cherish, something you want to preserve not only because of logical arguments, but because it sustains you.

Several years ago I interviewed Ben and Minnie Rabinowitz, married seventy-one years at the time and looking forward to many more anniversaries. Born in Odessa, Russia, where they met at ages fifteen and eighteen, the couple emigrated to the United States in 1913, where they were married "in a nice hall with a hundred guests and a big dinner—and it only cost us one hundred twenty-five dollars," recalled Mrs. Rabinowitz. "We came straight from our wedding and moved into the back room of our store—that was our honeymoon. Those days I was ashamed, we were so poor."

They remain an oddity because of the longevity not only of their marriage, but of the friendship and closeness they radiate. "The secret to staying happy is love and respect," Minnie Rabinowitz said with authority. "I took good care of my husband. If all the people in the younger generation took care of their husbands like I do, there'd be no divorce."

That's one of the benefits of being married—having

someone to *take care of you*, rather than simply coexisting side by side in mutually respected but distant worlds. That's not to say you cannot assert your individual personalities, but rather that the concern you show for your mate's feelings comes back to you tenfold. The habits of gentility and respect then carry over to your broader dealings and bring you success in the larger world. "We argue lots of the time, but we never fight," was the way Minnie Rabinowitz phrased it. And their friends confirmed that they were beloved and respected in business as well as their personal life.

There must be something compelling about marriage for 95 percent of the population to seek it, and for the entire population to admire it. Paul Ciotti, in an article in the *Los Angeles Times* magazine on June 14, 1987, wrote of the frustrating development of unfulfilling, unserious relationships, which he calls "Lite Romance—all the relationship but half the baggage." Clearly, this does not go down well, especially for the desperate women Ciotti interviewed: "Q: How do you meet men? A: I pray to St. Jude. Q: What's he got to do with it? A: You know, St. Jude—the patron saint of hopeless and impossible causes."[1]

Do you have to tell someone like that about the benefits of marriage?

Or the others: The one who trips attractive men on the jogging track at the health club. The one who goes to church functions in order to meet guys—the Catholic, Lutheran, Presbyterian, Episcopal, and Baptist churches in her neighborhood. The one who reads her *Family Circle* magazines in the law library.

What about the *men* who claim their life's mate is equally elusive: The one who lied on his computer dating form because he didn't think anyone would choose a man five-foot-seven. The one who took a class in *dim sum* though he only eats Big Macs. The one who joined a coed aerobics class so he could slip in ten minutes before the end.

These people all want to be married. And you're contemplating giving it up.

Before you do, ruminate a little on what you have. Consider the following benefits of marriage—a good marriage to be sure, but who's to say yours can't be good with enough commitment?

ONLY MARRIAGE BRINGS TRUE ROMANCE

What a lie that romance is exotic trysts in dark and secretive places. True romance is the kind that develops only over time. Igor and Vera Stravinsky. Hume Cronyn and Jessica Tandy. Irving and Sylvia Wallace. And do read the movingly romantic letters of John Adams, written to the wife he loved for nearly seventy years, Abigail.

You cannot compare the depth of a relationship that has lasted for two years to one that has been nurtured for twenty. Even those tinged with conflict are more romantic because the phases of encountering and resolving problems bring the partners ever closer and add enhancing nuances to a core of dedication.

And what is romance but *interest*? Someone who teases your thoughts even when concentration should be on other topics. Someone who offers conversation and companionship that is on a deeper level, with a greater basis, than any other relationship possible.

And how do you know that this person will maintain your interest? Why can't you become so bored that your marriage is simply another description rather than an intimate dynamic? The answer is that you *know* this person; you know, from experience over the years, that she doesn't remain static—that she likes certain adventures, that she doesn't want to become bored with *you*.

W. H. Auden noted that "any marriage, happy or unhappy, is infinitely more interesting and significant than any romance, however passionate."[2] Romance distracts you from the central issues of opinion and personality by its sheer chemistry and novelty; marriage allows the essence of your partner to shine. Over time, people inevitably change; they inescapably add to their personalities. Sometimes what they add is not so appealing; usually it's terrific.

Which brings me to the next point.

MARRIAGE IS GOOD FOR YOUR CHARACTER

If you start to swerve from your more lofty goals; if you develop an obnoxious habit; if you become involved with something that is more deleterious than different—your husband or wife can tell you so. A single person has only his own intuition and perhaps some well-meaning family and friends to use as guidance in shaping his personality over time.

But friends and family can give conflicting advice, and few people are close enough to you every day—with knowledge of your depressions, your triumphs, and your physical desires—to have enough of a picture of you to advise wisely. Your spouse sees how you act with your parents (your parents have only a parental view) and then how you change when you're around your friends. Your spouse knows your moods and how they change from morning to bedtime. Your spouse watches you make plans and mull over concerns and understands the processes in your mind. Only a husband or wife has such a unique and personal vantage point from which to be a mirror and reflect to you who you are, what you've become, and hopefully where you want to go.

That is only one way wedded partners enjoy the opportunity to give to each other. An essential part of human nature is the desire both to give and to give thanks. Marriage offers a convenient and available setting to fulfill these basic needs.

"Giving" means such simple daily activities as ironing a shirt for your mate in the morning, says Tricia Lester, thirty-eight, a member of one of my workshops who has been connubially delighted for six years.

"My husband and I had both been married before, and the day after our honeymoon he got up to go to work," she told me in an interview later. "He hovered near his closet and I just couldn't figure out what was going on. In the meantime, I was rushing around, trying to get ready for my own workday, but I perceived him getting more and more irritated.

"Finally I asked him what the problem was, and he exploded. 'I thought you really cared for me, but you don't even want to do little things. Why won't you even iron my shirts?' he ranted. That set me off. 'What makes you think I'm going to stop my life to inspect your wardrobe and iron your shirts when I'm not doing any ironing of my own?' I yelled. 'Why can't you be a big boy and iron your *own* shirts?' ''

After much haranguing, Tricia finally learned her husband's unexpressed code for caring. When his wife cared for his clothes, he was reassured that she cared for *him*; if she insisted that he plan out in advance what to wear and iron his own shirts, he felt neglected. Once she understood this, Tricia gladly seized this small opportunity to show her husband how much she loved him. (And instead of ironing his shirts herself, she simply dropped them off at the local Fluff-and-Fold.)

So giving means expending time and effort with no immediate or directly corresponding reward. The best relationships are built on this kind of uneven delivery of effort. Dr. Joyce Brothers, in *What Every Woman Ought to Know About Love and Marriage*, reminds her readers: "At almost any time during your marriage, you are going to be giving more than your husband. 'A successful marriage is never really the fifty-fifty proposition that it is talked up to be,' says Betty Ford, wife of former President Gerald R. Ford. 'We settled for a seventy-five-twenty-five deal. Sometimes the seventy-five would come from my side. Sometimes from Jerry's.' ''[3]

Sounds like the Fords have a relationship that works. Yet hardly anyone recognizes the pleasure and *fulfillment* that comes from being the giver.

Just as few people recognize their fundamental need to say thanks. Religious individuals have a context in which to be grateful for majestic and mysterious as well as mundane parts of life, and prayer offers them a regular outlet for their appreciation. Similarly, married couples can give *each other* thanks for visible manifestations of love and for the sweet aspects of home life that are clearly present every day. Not only does expressing gratitude make you feel good because your thanks brings someone else pleasure—which it does—but it also allows you to accept the joy in your life without feeling that somehow you don't do enough to deserve it. In other words, by showing appreciation, you don't have to feel guilty for having so much or enjoying what you have.

Marriage is also good for your character because *it*

elevates your life and gives it a higher purpose. The other day I overheard two forty-ish men who were waiting in line for concert tickets discussing their relationships. The first one said, ''Jane and I've been living together for three years, and we really love each other.'' The second one replied, ''Yeah, but I've been with Lois for three years, and not only do I love her, but I have a marriage and a twelve-month-old daughter to show for it.'' Marriage gives you something to show for your time on earth—a family base that has permanent consequence and significance.

How does this affect your character? When you think of yourself as a married man with a daughter, you conduct yourself differently than if your self-image is as a single person, or a bachelor who happens to live with someone. You can say you have a ''commitment,'' and really mean it, but if there weren't some fundamental difference between the depth and quality of the commitment you have cohabiting and the one you'd feel if you were married, you'd simply *get* married.

Married people *are* different from single people. They take better care of their health and therefore live longer. Even in the face of serious disease, married people have a better prognosis. A 1988 study by James Goodwin of the Medical College of Wisconsin, reported in the *Journal of the American Medical Association*, found highest survival rates for cancer among the married of every age. (The divorced, as opposed to the never married or widowed, had the poorest survival rates.)[4] Married people plan for the long term rather than simply the short haul. This means they show signs of permanence—a home with a yard, an insurance policy, a bank account with enough for an emergency. They tend to stay longer in their jobs, or take chances on businesses that may require substantial investment of energy but that could leave an indelible mark on their communities. Not that single people can't or don't do these things—but there's much more compelling a married person to put down roots and make a home.

And their children know it. People living out social experiments seem to be the ones with the mixed-up offspring, the adolescents with drug problems and rainbow-colored hair. Parents with solid, old-fashioned values seem to be the ones whose children lead stable, healthy, and productive lives—and who in turn want to pass those values on to their own children.

It's telling that the weird variations of family life that were fairly recently exalted and tried have not lasted. How often nowadays do you read articles that young women can't find the right free-sex commune—versus their laments that men won't make a commitment? If the communes were so great, a hitchhike to the country would be the widely desired end, instead of a two-step down the church aisle.

MARRIAGE MEETS OUR NEED FOR ATTACHMENT

Some primordial part of our soul requires that we bond deeply with another person. Robert Weiss, in his book *Marital Separation*, writes that this need begins in childhood and in adolescence is transferred to a potential sexual and life partner. Once this link is formed (after two years of marriage) your basic identity becomes fused into your relationship to the object of your attachment.[5]

Why is this beneficial? Because it provides a grounding from which we can venture out. Judith Bardwick, in *In Transition*, writes: "I think the most crucial implication of the legality of marriage is that one theoretically enters this contractual relationship for a time which extends into the future. Marriage creates a specific identity and commitment forever. In spite of the divorce rate, the legal permanence of marriage increases the psychological sense that marriage is a primary existential anchor."[6]

Erich Fromm, in *The Art of Loving*, writes that the "deepest need in man is the need to overcome his separateness."[7] While close family ties can provide a context, only a complete physical, spiritual, and emotional live-in relationship with a peer can really overcome the feeling of being alone.

MARRIAGE IS A SAFE HAVEN

Once that basic anchor is in place, we have the freedom to take risks to revamp our ideas and interests without fear that our identity can be ripped out from beneath us. Quoting Judith Bardwick once again: "While it has become chic to emphasize the ways in which commitment, especially in permanent relationships, diminishes choice, narrows experience, and therefore truncates growth, one can argue quite the opposite. People may be far better able to grow when they are in a mutually committed relationship because, feeling secure, they are better able to take risks. The more one trusts the relationship, the more one will protect it and, simultaneously, the more one will feel free to change within it."[8]

Not only does marriage provide a committed base to change *within*, but also a "safe haven" of security from which to tackle the world at large. The frustrations of commanding an office full of employees, the fear accompanying a job interview, the anxiety of advancing an innovative plan in the company of higher-ups can all be accepted with the knowledge that your built-in "shrink" awaits you at home for support and encouragement. A husband or wife gives you the proverbial "second head" that is certainly more useful than one when polishing a written article, deciding which career option to pursue, or making a personnel choice. You can view each turning point from two perspectives and ask a "devil's advocate" to help you recognize pitfalls of decisions before they turn into blunders.

And being married lets you embrace the challenges of career, friendships, and family more fully. With your own love life solidly determined, you don't have to bother with the time-soaking process of finding a lover or mate. My colleague Suzanne Walker, thirty-four, is a beautiful single woman employed as the West Coast publicity director of a major publisher. "Dating is such a drag," she says candidly. "It takes so much energy to find a guy who's worth going out with—or so you think. Once you get together, nine times out of ten there's something wrong with him. You find this out in the first half hour of your date, and then the whole rest of the time you're wondering why you have to waste an entire evening on this dud." She shrugs. "But that's the game—and even when you do find somebody worthwhile, he may not find *you* all that fantastic. Even if everything clicks and you're in ecstasy, the relationship usually only lasts for a few months, and then you're back facing the hoards of nerds and egomaniacs all over again."

Married people don't have to contend with any of that, and so have more time and energy to invest in activities that lead to real advancement. In addition, when married people approach people of the opposite gender, they don't have to play "does-he-or-doesn't-he?" games, wondering if a certain brawny vice president is available, and if so, how to catch his eye. The business lunch is all business. The aerobics class at the gym leaves you worked out, not worked up. You can approach women or men with the same sense of friendship, not determined by hormones or chemistry. This is not to say that you can't admire attractive men or women, but simply that with your love life in committed order, you can appreciate beauty without thinking that you really should follow up on it.

Single people I've talked to frequently approach the world with a sense of uncomfortable tension, which usually exists unconsciously. They're always on the lookout for a potential spouse, and so must always appear their most physically presentable, even in casual situations. (Who knows who you might be standing next to in line for a movie?) They worry that their words to new acquaintances won't be witty enough. They assume they're constantly being judged on their bodies, their accomplishments, and their demeanor.

Juliette Ringer, a hair dresser, is in the habit of telling men she meets that she is a sociologist writing a book on the world of cosmetologists. Her salon co-worker at the next station, married for eight years, laughs when she hears this—once you're out of the marriage market, you can relax and be yourself.

You can think this is irrelevant to you. Yes, you're contemplating divorce, but you won't be single for long. You've found someone far better than your first spouse and will be remarried in a matter of months. All you want to do is let your current husband or wife down easy. Okay, so it's never easy, but still, the new lover is so superior—you'll have your "safe haven" in a snap.

In one sense, yes. You'll have someone to provide sympathy and understanding—an important role, to be sure. But a second marriage can never have the same grounding that a first marriage has. Shared history gives you something in common from which to respond, something you cannot build up until you've spent the same amount of time with your new mate as you've invested in your current spouse.

And much as you want to deny it, the experience of divorce forces you to withhold just a little bit. You're always cognizant in a corner of your consciousness of your first marriage, even if your second mate is perfect. You can't help recalling that you were "head over heels" in love with your first mate in the beginning too. Then he changed, or you changed, and well, there are no guarantees that it couldn't happen again.

No guarantees. In a second marriage you still hope for the best but you know, in a way no one in a first marriage can, that there are no guarantees. You walk on eggshells a little more, tiptoeing so that the relationship you hope is not fragile won't have to withstand the slightest crush. In a sense this is good. It keeps you attendant to the needs of your partner; it makes you polite and courteous. But it also curbs your naturalness, your casualness, and prevents you from giving yourself wholeheartedly.

Marriage is a safe haven, made all the safer by the fact that it has weathered storms and still remains to shelter you.

STRENGTH COMES THROUGH CRISIS

Facing problems in your marriage can be good for you. Not that we should create problems to improve our characters, but surviving them together does strengthen both you and the bond you have with your partner. Separating and then reconciling is one such crisis—when you come together again, you are twice as strong as before.

Ask the couples interviewed for a February 1986 *Redbook* magazine story, "Will You Marry Me—Again?" Chronicled are the meetings, weddings, separations, divorces—and reunitings—of several couples, among them Abby Dalton and Jack Smith ("three years off for bad behavior") and Patti and Gavin MacLeod ("forgiveness is the key word"). They say their rekindled love is even more precious: "There's a cherishing of one another that's so much better than before," says a woman remarried for ten years.[9]

You don't have to go through divorce and remarriage

to have that feeling. Reconciling after a period of distance or disillusionment can bring the same result. Surmounting a marital crisis is an "annealing" process. Like steel that must be heated red hot, almost to the melting point, and then cooled repeatedly to become strong, your relationship and your character are transformed into stronger, more durable entities as a result of your ordeal.

For one thing, you learn from upsets how to avoid such calamities in the future—and how to heal the smaller ones that are sure to arise. Only within the context of marriage—with its commitment *not to give up* when anger prevails or boredom intervenes—can you work through difficult times with a mutual goal. You know you're on the same team, and that a win for one of you brings glory to you both.

And the *process* of conquering problems is in itself gratifying. Solving a dilemma brings excitement, vitality, and satisfaction within the context of the most intimate relationship possible. The emotional risks are greater, yes—but without those vulnerabilities, the heights of ecstasy spouses can achieve would not be possible.

THE ONLY TRUE COMMITMENT

Commitment—all the articles about "How we stayed happily married for a trillion years" and "Ten ways to make sure your marriage lasts" mention it. Commitment *is* marriage, and vice versa. You can't really say that marriage "involves" commitment, or that you're "committed" to your live-in without marriage. By separating the two, we allow room for "commitment-phobia," the fear of becoming inexorably attached to the point where such connection is impossible.

Notes writer Maxine Schnall in *Savvy* magazine, May, 1981: "We need to reduce the fear of commitment by dispelling the notion that commitment is synonymous with the loss of identity. We must reassure ourselves and each other that it is possible to be both autonomous and deeply committed to another . . . And finally, our popular literature and mass media must convey the message that a deep commitment to one person and the experiences of a life lived together, far from being antithetical to personal fulfillment, are often prerequisites for it."[10]

THE ULTIMATE SETTING FOR FULFILLING LIFE'S PURPOSE

"Marriage lets us refine out the essential from the trivial, from the paltry. It keeps us from squandering ourselves on petty things. It lets us use ourselves on things that matter, things that make a life." In this way, Lawrence Shames, in the March 1981 issue of *Savvy* magazine, capsulized why we marry—*to do something that matters*.

Perhaps the most worthwhile purpose of life itself is the creation and nurturing of a family through its complete cycle of development: Generating love out of friendship or lust. Executing the intention of permanence. Using our bodies sexually in the way they most naturally and lovingly fit together. Giving birth. Nourishing a child in body and mind.

We're coming to realize that. The crowd-pleasing movies of 1987 and 1988 bowed respectfully to marriage and family. Michael Douglas deeply regretted the weekend fling with Glenn Close in *Fatal Attraction* (1987) that threatened his marriage, his daughter, and even his life. Tom Selleck, Steve Guttenberg, and Ted Danson in *Three Men and a Baby* discovered they'd trade the swinging singles life for the responsibilities—and rewards—of fatherhood. Kevin Bacon and Elizabeth McGovern proved that maturity and family provide the greatest fulfillment in *She's Having a Baby*. And Cher, surrounded by loving relatives in *Moonstruck*, joyfully toasted her upcoming marriage with the now-celebrated line: "A la Famiglia!"

The markers of marriage involve youth, mid-life, and old age. They cross every activity boundary. Nurturing a family through two or three generations offers an invigorating sense of understanding and an intense spiritual connection. In fact, raising a family involves an act of creation that is as close to Godlike as humans can come. There is no higher purpose than giving yourself over to these profound tasks.

At times this may not be easy. But the greatest reward comes from riding out stressful times, confident that with your devotion and effort, your relationship will right itself. Notes Judith Bardwick: "A goal of happiness . . . [is] based on the immature perception that to wish and do are the same, to want is to get . . ."[11] She continues: " 'Happiness' is a fantasy image which denies the constraints imposed by living."[12] For her, a successful marriage is accomplishing concrete tasks, not experiencing fleeting feeling states.

Of course, marriage should and does provide positive feelings; in fact, marriage is the proper context for the most powerful emotions imaginable. And most married people state their pleasure clearly. The National Opinion Research Center in 1988 reported that almost two-thirds of married couples say they are "very happy," and only three percent say they are "not too happy," with nearly a third claiming to be "pretty happy."

Even the humdrum days extend bountiful rewards, not just from the little pleasures and comforts, but from the basic and embedded knowledge that by being married you are part of a grand and magnificent scheme. You are contributing to the harmony of the world and are acting in harmony with man's most serene and decent instincts. You are choosing a path that has proven itself across nearly every culture existent throughout the eons of time. And you are part of a wondrous continuity linking yourself with your ancestors. A happy family is the most natural means to nobility of purpose and personal peace.

NOTES

1. Ciotti, Paul. "Lite Romance." *Los Angeles Times* magazine, June 14, 1987, p. 12.
2. Auden, W.H. quoted in Epstein, Joseph. *Divorced in America.* New York: E. P. Dutton Co., 1974, p. 28.
3. Brothers, Joyce. *What Every Woman Ought to Know About Love and Marriage.* New York: Simon and Schuster, 1984, p. 137.
4. Benderly, Beryl Lieff. "For Cancer, Try Marriage." *Psychology Today*, October, 1988. p. 14.
5. Weiss, Robert. *Marital Separation.* New York: Basic Book, 1975.

6. Bardwick, Judith. *In Transition*. New York: Holt, Rinehart and Winston, 1977, p. 103.
7. Fromm, Erich. *The Art of Loving*. New York: Bantam, 1963.
8. Bardwick, p. 127.
9. Byron, Ellen. "Will You Marry Me—Again?" *Redbook*, February 1986, p. 146.
10. Schnall, Maxine. "Commitment Phobia." *Savvy*, May 1981, p. 41.
11. Bardwick, 120.
12. Ibid., p. 120.